Closed Borders

Closed Borders

The Contemporary Assault on Freedom of Movement

Alan Dowty

A Twentieth Century Fund Report

Yale University Press
New Haven and London

Published with the assistance of the
A. Whitney Griswold Publication Fund.

Designed by Sujata Guha
and set in Garamond No. 3 Roman by
Brevis Press, Bethany, Connecticut.
Printed in the United States of America by
Vail-Ballou Press, Binghamton, N.Y.

Library of Congress Cataloging-in-Publication Data

Dowty, Alan, 1940–
    Closed borders.

    (A Twentieth Century Fund report)
    Includes index.
    1. Emigration and immigration—Government
policy.
I. Title.   II. Series.
JV6091.D68   1987   325   86–23399
ISBN 0–300–03824–0 (alk. paper)

---

*The paper in this book meets the guidelines for permanence
and durability of the Committee on Production Guidelines
for Book Longevity of the Council on Library Resources.*

---

10   9   8   7   6   5   4   3   2   1

To my father

whose lifelong concern over man's inhumanity to man
is the real origin of this book

Contents

Foreword

There was a time when the movement of people around the world was regarded as a temporary phenomenon, the aftermath of either natural disasters or war. But we now recognize that people on the move from one or another country are a permanent feature of the global landscape. Some are political refugees; some are economic victims seeking a better or more productive life than their homelands can provide; and a fortunate few, who are not victims at all, are young people who have been extensively educated either at home or abroad and who then opt to settle, at least for a time, where the opportunities seem brightest.

Despite these continual flows, the present movement of people around the world would be larger still if it were not for the restrictions on emigration imposed by some countries. If people were free to vote with their feet, it is probable that today's millions would be joined by millions more. At the same time, though, a substantial number of those in the ranks of current refugees are people who have been forced by the governments of their homelands to emigrate. These two developments, the refusal of countries to allow people to emigrate and the forcible expulsion of people, have never been more pervasive than they are at present. Given the tendency to restrict legal immigration in many countries, including the United States, and reinforced efforts to curb illegal immigration, it is obvious that we will experience mounting difficulties concerning the movement and non-movement of people over the next decade and probably longer.

When Alan Dowty, a professor of government and international studies at the University of Notre Dame, proposed a study of the pressures impelling some states to seal their borders and others to force citizens to leave, the staff and Trustees of the Twentieth Century Fund welcomed the opportunity. The Fund, which has been interested in immigration policy, thought it worthwhile to support a study of why some nations have sought to keep some of their people from leaving and others have attempted to rid themselves of not just a few dissidents but large numbers of their citizens. A touchy and controversial subject, the United Nations has tried to deal with it but, not surprisingly, with less than constructive results.

It is never easy, of course, for people to leave their roots. In the past, people usually emigrated only when their governments were so hostile or demanding or economic conditions were so unpromising that they felt they had no choice. Even then, many returned to visit or to retire. Nowadays, people who want to leave are forbidden to do so in, for example, the Soviet Union, which also retaliates harshly against the most active dissidents. And in Asia and Africa, people have been banished from their homelands, unceremoniously dumped across borders or set on stormy seas to fend for themselves.

There is something basically uncivilized about such actions, as Dowty, in tracing the history of emigration and expulsion, makes clear. He explains why governments in this allegedly enlightened age resort to such ugly methods, and how successful they have been. It is his belief that freedom of movement is an essential right, one that merits the support of all people. And he calls on the United States to change its current immigration and refugee policies, which make it difficult for us to defend the principle of freedom of movement worldwide.

We are grateful to Alan Dowty for presenting so clear a case for open borders and for backing his recommendations with examples and statistics that are hard to dispute. I think his book deserves to be read by all those who care about human rights and freedom.

M. J. Rossant, *Director*
THE TWENTIETH CENTURY FUND
October 1986

Acknowledgments

My first acknowledgment ought to go to the Syrian cabinet minister, quoted in chapter 1, whose frank statement of his government's nondiscriminatory opposition to all emigration inspired this entire project. But for obvious reasons he shall remain unnamed.

The first person I want to thank explicitly is Theodore Draper, who put me in touch with the Twentieth Century Fund and whose support at critical moments was essential in both inception and implementation. Nobody, to my mind, more clearly represents the finest in the gentleman scholar tradition.

The support of five other people in public or academic life was instrumental in acceptance of the project, and should be recorded: John Brademas, President of New York University (and my former congressman); Congressman Lee Hamilton of Indiana, chairman of the subcommittee on the Middle East in the House Foreign Affairs Committee; the Reverend Theodore M. Hesburgh, President, University of Notre Dame; Seymour Martin Lipset, Stanford University; and Avner Yaniv, University of Haifa.

At the Twentieth Century Fund, Carlos Sandoval took an interest in the original idea and was largely responsible for shepherding it through to acceptance as a Fund project. As Program Officer, Carlos also oversaw the critical first stage of the research and writing. He was ably succeeded in this role by Cameron Munter and, in the final stages, Scott McConnell. My thanks also go to M. J. Rossant, Director of the Twentieth Century Fund, who can still find considerable room for improvement whenever an author naively thinks he has peaked; to Beverly Goldberg, Assistant Director, whose supervision of the editing process combines just the right amounts of quality professionalism and tender, loving care; and to Wendy Mercer, Controller, who managed to make the project budget look more rational than it had any right to look.

It is always a bit disconcerting to see what a top-flight professional editor can do to one's treasured prose, but it can also be instructive. In this case, it was a learning experience of the first order. Michael Massing, editor on behalf of the Twentieth Century Fund, was the instructor. I am also grateful to Nancy Woodington, the capable editor at Yale University Press who put the manuscript in its final form.

Some of those who extended help on the content of the study deserve special mention. Hurst Hannum, Executive Director of The Procedural Aspects of International Law Institute, completed his own study of legal aspects of the right to leave and return (cited often in the following pages) while this project was under way, and most generously shared his conclusions and counsel with me at all stages. Sidney Liskofsky, Program Director of the Jacob Blaustein Institute for the Advancement of Human Rights, brought me in touch with related activities in a variety of contexts and made valuable suggestions on contacts and material—as well as furnishing me with U.N. material that the United Nations Library itself could not locate. Aristide Zolberg, of the New School for Social Research, is engaged in a large-scale study of international migration policies that should revolutionize the field; I am indebted to him for setting me straight at the outset on certain historical aspects of the topic and for providing extremely useful guidance and counsel at every step.

In a special category are José D. Inglés of the Philippines and C. L. C. Mubanga-Chipoya of Zambia. Judge Inglés, who wrote the 1963 U.N. study of the right to leave, was an encouraging correspondent, and Mr. Mubanga-Chipoya, who is currently writing the second such study, took time from a busy schedule to discuss the progress of his work. Edward H. Lawson, formerly of the U.N. Human Rights Division, provided an especially valuable commentary on the parts of this book dealing with U.N. activities.

Others at the United Nations who were especially helpful were Jay Long, of the Secretary-General's Office; Kurt Herndl, Hans van Aggelen, and Alfred-Maurice de Zayas, from the United Nations Center for Human Rights; and Hania Zlotnik, Ellen Brennan, and Joseph Chamie of the U.N. Population Division.

I regret that I cannot record the same benevolent attitude toward outside researchers at the United Nations Library, in New York. I spent many long hours there and found the staff efficient and helpful in locating requested material. Midway in my work, however, the library imposed new restrictions on access that stand, it seems to me, in complete opposition to everything a research library should represent and that would deter even the most legitimate scholars. In fact the new policy—requiring a two-to-three week "security clearance" and justification of the need to use U.N. sources—seemed designed to keep people out. One can only hope for the quick restoration of procedures more consonant with "the open forum of mankind."

A number of other people helped with advice, material, and ideas, among them Gretchen S. Brainerd, Intergovernmental Committee for Migration; Orest Deychak, U.S. Commission on Security and Cooperation in Europe; J. d'Oliveira e Sousa, United Nations Conference on Trade and Technology; Patricia Weiss Fagen, Refugee Policy Group; Meg Henry, International Commission of Jurists; Allan Kagedan, American Jewish Committee; Ed Klein, Chalidze Publications/Khronika Press; Paul Martin, Center for the Study of Human Rights, Columbia University; Paul W. Meek, International

Parliamentary Group for Human Rights in the Soviet Union; Mark J. Miller, Center for Migration Studies; Harris O. Schoenberg, B'nai B'rith International; Varda Shiffer, Amnesty International; Gene Sosin, Radio Free Europe/Radio Liberty; Charles Sternberg, International Rescue Committee; Leonard Sussman, Freedom House; and Laurie Wiseberg, Human Rights Internet.

A number of people in academic life were kind enough to comment on parts of the manuscript or otherwise provide guidance in their areas of expertise. I would like to thank, in particular, George Brinkley, Michael Francis, Martin Gilbert, George Gins-burgs, Zvi Gitelman, William Glaser, Neil Harding, Sidney Heit-man, Peter Juviler, Walter Laqueur, Gilburt Loescher, Peter Reddaway, Robert Sharlet, Astri Suhrke, Cynthia Watson, Myron Weiner, Frederick Whelan, and Robert C. Williams.

Then there are those who submitted to interviews on issues that were often, from their viewpoint, rather sensitive. In fact, under the ground rules I cannot even name the representatives of Bulgaria, Hungary, Pakistan, Romania, and Yugoslavia who agreed to speak to me. And despite repeated efforts, I was unable to secure more than a comment over the telephone from any representative of the Union of Soviet Socialist Republics. The others interviewed and their relevant positions or affiliations were:

Morris Abram, former member of the Subcommission on Prevention of Discrimination and Protection of Minorities, United Nations

Ada S. Adler, Office of United States Coordinator of Refugee Affairs

Ludmilla Alexeiva, U.S. representative of the Soviet Helsinki Watch Group

Felipe R. Alvarez, First Secretary, Cuban Interests Section, Washington

Igor Belousovitch, Bureau of Intelligence and Research, U.S. Department of State

Omer Y. Birido, Ambassador of Sudan to the United Nations

Enrique M. Brú Bautista, International Labour Office

Abraham Brumberg, Sovietologist and former editor, *Problems of Communism*

John Carey, member of the Subcommission on Prevention of Discrimination and Protection of Minorities, United Nations

Roger Conner, Executive Director, Federation for American Immigration Reform

Wesley A. Fisher, Secretary, International Research and Exchanges Board

William Glaser, New School for Social Research

Jerry Goodman, Executive Director, National Conference on Soviet Jewry

Girma Haile-Giorgis, Ethiopian Mission to the United Nations

John Hertzberg, U.S. Mission to the United Nations

Grace Ibingira, Consultant, United Nations Fund for Population Activities

R. K. Jenny, Intergovernmental Committee for Migration

Leon M. Johnson, Jr., Director, Office of Asylum Affairs, U.S. Department of State

Max Kampelman, U.S. representative at the Helsinki Review Conference, Madrid

Mfute E. C. Kazembe, Zambia Mission to the United Nations

William Korey, Director of International Policy Research, B'nai B'rith International

Rustum Lalkaka, Deputy Director, United Nations Interim Fund for Science and Technology for Development

Edward H. Lawson, United Nations Human Rights Division

Luke Lee, Office of the U.S. Coordinator for Refugee Affairs

Ilya Levkov, Soviet emigré

Pavel Litvinov, Soviet emigré

R. Lohrmann, Intergovernmental Committee for Migration

Omotunde A. J. Mahoney, Gambia Mission to the United Nations

Dan Manyika, Zimbabwe Embassy to the United States

Douglas Martin, Director of Information, International Baha'i Community

Gary Messina, U.S. Immigration and Naturalization Service

Haider Refq, Chargé d'Affaires, Afghanistan Embassy to the United States

Igor Reichlin, Soviet emigré

Miguel Ruiz, Mexican Mission to the United Nations

Robert Sewade, Embassy of Benin to the United States

Arkady Shevchenko, former Soviet diplomat

Dale Frederick Swartz, Coordinator, National Immigration, Refugee, and Citizenship Forum

Fernando Torres-Torija, Office of the Secretary-General, United Nations

Nicholas Van Praag, Public Information Officer, United Nations High Commissioner for Refugees

Roger P. Winter, Director, U.S. Committee for Refugees

Elias Jaime, Mozambique Mission to the United Nations

Finally, the personal notes that often reflect debts greater than those incurred by mere intellectual larceny. Avis and Ralph Miller, through their kind hospitality, made possible an extended stay in Washington during which many of the above interviews were conducted. Likewise, I am grateful to Betty Lubitz for the use of her apartment in Brooklyn, without which an extended stay in New York would have been impossible (and I would never have discovered the pleasures of jogging in Prospect Park). The fact that this book is dedicated to my father speaks for itself; I would like to add a warm note to my stepmother, Mary Elizabeth Dowty, for her never-failing interest, support, and love.

My family deserves more than an acknowledgment; Gail is a full partner in life's enterprises, and Rachel and Rafi did far more than just stay out of the way (in fact, they didn't stay out of the way at all). As for other members of the Window Co-op, Sandra Winicur was there at every stage, from commenting on the proposal to fielding transatlantic messages to editors, but perhaps her most valuable contributions were her ever-reliable unvarnished reactions to the matter at hand—which are twice as perceptive as anyone else's and three times as unvarnished. Dan, Zev, and Paula Winicur were also sterling second-time survivors and mainstays of a support system that all writers should have.

I would also like to acknowledge the support of the Leonard Davis Institute for International Relations at the Hebrew University in Jerusalem for help in the final editing.

1

The Right of
Personal Self-Determination

*If I am accused of stealing the towers of Notre Dame, I can
only flee the country.*

—Anatole France

The Subhanis are a family of Iranian Baha'is. They are thus a target
for violent persecution by the fundamentalist Islamic regime that
rules that country. Attempts to suppress Baha'ism are hardly novel
in Iran, having occurred off and on since the religion was founded
in the mid-nineteenth century. Since 1979, however, the ruling mul-
lahs have added a new twist, forbidding Baha'is to leave the country
to practice their faith elsewhere. Nonetheless, Firuz, one of the Subhanis' two sons, managed to escape in 1981 when a sympathetic
official honored his student passport, a document legally denied
Baha'is. His father, Hossain, and his younger brother Aziz also
managed to escape that year by paying a Baluchi tribesman to smug-
gle them into Pakistan. And a cousin walked twenty-four days in
winter through mountainous Kurdistan in order to reach foreign
soil. Sadly, Firuz's mother, Mona, physically unable to engage in

1

such strenuous undertakings, remains trapped in Iran, separated from her family.[1]

Yusuf, a young craftsman in Damascus, also cannot leave his country. To the occasional foreign tourist he is able to meet discreetly, he says: "We just want to leave. We are ready to leave with nothing but the clothes on our backs. Please help us." Yusuf is Jewish, but government spokesmen assert that—in contrast to Iran's practices—no communal discrimination is involved. As a cabinet minister put it, "The restrictions on Jews are not special; no Syrian citizen can leave the country unless he can justify the trip."[2] While Jews may find it more difficult to "justify" their trips, the minister is basically correct. The government's restrictive attitude toward departure applies to all Syrians.

Jews in the Soviet Union may suffer discrimination, but in one respect they are regarded as specially privileged: they have a better-than-average chance of obtaining an exit visa. (As a popular witticism has it, "A Jewish wife is not a luxury but a form of transport.") This is small comfort to Vitaly, a middle-aged Jewish butcher. For more than ten years he has been separated from his wife and children, who were allowed to emigrate. Vitaly's application to leave has been denied repeatedly on the novel ground that as a "meat technologist" he possesses "knowledge of state secrets."[3] Vitaly's situation is typical. Whether they work in meat or in molecules, Soviet Jews insist that their desire to leave has nothing to do with the Soviet state or system. As one of them puts it, "We are not, and do not intend to become, critics or opponents of the Soviet Government. We are not dissidents. . . . We don't want their power. We don't want their wealth. We just want to buy a ticket to go to our country."[4]

1. Personal interview, January 29, 1986. In this and the following two personal accounts, names have been changed to protect those involved.

2. Author's interviews of local resident and governmental minister during visit to Damascus, June, 1977.

3. Personal interview, Moscow, August, 1979, and subsequent correspondence.

4. Quoted in Martin Gilbert, *The Jews of Hope* (London: Macmillan, 1984), p. 91.

Mona, Yusuf, and Vitaly represent a new class of victims of contemporary political persecution. Throughout the world, members of minority groups are prevented from leaving their country of residence. In addition, in some two dozen countries not only minorities but everyone is denied the right to emigrate.

It may have seemed that there was little room for innovation in man's inhumanity to man. Our ancestors long ago perfected most of the injustices and brutalities that human creativity could devise. But in one respect modern states have managed to shackle individuals in a way that tyrants of old might have envied: never before have states so effectively controlled the right of their citizens to leave or stay. The plight of the refugee has never been easy, but today many are denied even the right to become refugees. The only way they can escape, paradoxically, is to be expelled.

At the same time that many of the world's peoples cannot freely leave the countries in which they live, millions of others have been directly or indirectly forced from their homelands. Many countries resort to both practices at once. Forced emigrants—the modern term is refugees—have been a tangible index of social and political turmoil throughout the ages, from the Jewish exiles in Babylon to the religious refugees of medieval Europe to the Afghans, Ethiopians, and Indochinese of today.

The plight of those denied the right to emigrate has fewer historical precedents. There is no widely accepted term to describe such people; the modern label "refusenik" comes closest, but it is not inclusive enough. To be sure, freedom of movement was limited in the past by such institutions as slavery and serfdom, but at least two aspects of the twentieth-century situation are new. First is the widespread notion that a state's integrity and well-being require that its entire population (apart, perhaps, from unwanted minorities) be sealed within its borders. The closest historical parallel was the mercantilist era of the seventeenth and eighteenth centuries, when many European states outlawed emigration in order to maximize population growth. For the mercantilists, however, emigration was not taken as a threat to political control, national identity, or ideological sway. They simply wanted as many bodies at their disposal as possible. It was only after the First World War that new statist conceptions began to portray departure from one's country as a shameful and even treasonous act.

Second, modern regimes can more effectively control their borders than in the past, and are thus able to enforce a ban on emigration. Historically, efforts to restrict exit seldom succeeded. States could easily create refugees, but they found it much more difficult to prevent people from leaving if they wished. In the seventeenth and eighteenth centuries, for example, most European states tried unsuccessfully to prevent emigration to America; had they had the resources to erect Berlin walls or other modern barriers, the history of America might be quite different.

Freedom of movement here implies both the right to leave one's country and the right to remain in it (as well as to return after leaving). In the simplest terms, individuals should be able to choose whether or not to remain in their own land. The only major United Nations study of this question, published in 1963, suggested that the right to leave and return was nothing less than a right of "personal self-determination."[5] Although this term has not gained wide currency, it captures the fundamental significance of the concepts under discussion here. Personal self-determination connotes the right to accept or reject the political jurisdiction in which one happens to live—in other words, the right to remain party to one's current social contract or to seek another.

The choice of societal membership, or, more properly, national

5. José D. Inglés, *Study of Discrimination in Respect of the Right of Everyone to Leave Any Country, Including His Own, and to Return to His Country,* United Nations, Economic and Social Council, Commission on Human Rights, Subcommission on Prevention of Discrimination and Protection of Minorities (E/CN.4/Sub.2/229/Rev. 1, 1963) (New York, 1963), p. 9. Apart from Inglés, the other major study of the topic is Hurst Hannum, *The Right to Leave and Return in International Law and Practice* (Washington: The Procedural Aspects of International Law Institute, 1985).

citizenship, is the most basic social and political choice we can make. Most of us choose by default, remaining bound to the culture and nation into which we were born. Yet we also feel that we *ought* to be able to choose otherwise, should personal inclinations and available alternatives so move us. Surely a society may regulate the entrance of newcomers, but do we also want to cede it the right to decide that those of us already here must stay, or must leave?

It has been observed that the right to leave "is no doubt not the most important of possible human rights as measured either by the number of people who intensely desire to exercise it or by the suffering that accompanies its infringement."[6] Consider the many millions subjected to torture, political suppression, religious or racial persecution, and other expressions of inhumanity. Why not focus on such brutal injustices as these?

Even on the basis of numbers alone the right to remain or return ranks as one of the major problems of our times. The number of refugees in the world is estimated to be as high as sixteen million. It is more difficult to assess the number affected by curbs on emigration, since many countries systematically discourage their citizens from even applying to leave. When was the last time an Albanian dared ask for an exit permit? The actual number of would-be refugees and potential voluntary emigrants is unknowable until the doors are open, but it is certainly larger than the number of explicit refusals would indicate.

But even if few chose to exercise the right to leave, its significance would be critical. The importance of a public issue is not necessarily proportionate to the number of people directly involved. Were that the case, discussion of capital punishment, for example, would be fleeting. Nor would so much attention be focused on such isolated human rights cases as those of Andrei Sakharov and Nelson

---

6. Frederick G. Whelan, "Citizenship and the Right to Leave," *American Political Science Review* 75 (September 1981): 636. Whelan adds, however, that neither does it seem to be a "trivial matter."

Mandela. The threat to even a single individual can sometimes touch all of us.

At first glance, a policy of preventing people from leaving seems to present the opposite problem from a policy of expelling them. It would seem unlikely that a state blocking emigration would also expel large numbers, or that mass expulsions would be accompanied by tight restrictions on exit. Yet that is exactly what occurs in many countries. In recent years, for example, few doctors or other professionals in Kabul have been able to obtain an exit visa from the Afghan government; at the same time, villagers in areas of anti-government military activity have been forced to flee the country. Similar double-sided situations have occurred in Ethiopia, Vietnam, Cuba, Burma, Iraq, Angola, Mozambique, and Rwanda, among others. The position of these governments is, in essence: "If we want you, you *must* remain; if we don't want you, you *must* leave." The decision hinges on the individual's usefulness to the state; personal interests and predilections count for little. Both the right to leave and the right to remain are swept aside by the claims of the state. In such cases, governments are motivated by an urge to mold the character and composition of a population in the presumed interests of the society as a whole. When state power expands to the point of controlling the demographic makeup of society, restrictions on movement become particularly intense.

We live in such a period. Seldom have restrictions on freedom of international movement been so pervasive, and never before have they been so effective. Across thousands of miles of sealed frontiers, nations have eliminated nearly all unauthorized departures. The Soviet Union has converted its border areas into virtual war zones; as a result, very few people have been able to make it clandestinely across Soviet frontiers, despite their enormous length. As physical controls are perfected, the manipulation of population flows among nations has become a common feature of international relations. The result is a new serfdom in which entire populations serve as pawns, some tied to an allegiance they abjure, others forced into an exile they did not seek.

This book is a study of the new serfdom. Beginning with past efforts to control international movement, it traces the emergence of coercive migration policies developed in this century. I attempt to explore why governments resort to such measures and to describe the effects the measures have had. For example, do exit restrictions have a sound economic basis, or do they primarily reflect an impulse for political and ideological control? Third-World nations often cite the "brain drain"—the flow of skilled manpower from countries that most need it to those that already abundantly possess it—as justification for exit restrictions. Are emigration controls an effective way to deal with such a problem? How serious a problem in fact is the brain drain?

I also evaluate efforts that have been made to combat controls on movement. Have such efforts been successful? How might barriers to free movement be lowered further? And what are the implications of all of this for the United States? As I show, efforts to promote free movement abroad can begin in our own backyard, through badly needed changes in U.S. immigration and refugee policies.

Above all, this study examines the principle of free movement as it defines the individual's relation to the state. The right to stay or leave is commonly posed as a conflict between the individual and the society. Rarely has that assumption been examined in any detail. I have attempted to do so here, and have come to some conclusions that may surprise.

First, however, just what are the claims of the individual and of the state?

The Claims of the State

Few maintain that the right of movement is absolute. Just as domestic movement is limited by laws relating to property and privacy, so international movement is subject to certain limitations. First of all, the right of emigration does not imply a corresponding right of immigration; the state does not have to let anyone in. The individual's right to leave is therefore limited in practice by the availability of a destination.

Second, since the right to leave puts the individual beyond the reach of authority, states assume a right to make sure that departure is not for the purpose of evading the law or such other obligations as military service or debts. The Eichmanns, Mengeles, and other Nazi war criminals who managed to flee to South America after World War II were not exercising a basic human right.

Surely, the state has a legitimate interest in restricting travel on the grounds of public health, legal incapacity (minors, mental incompetents), and public emergency. A state may act to prevent the spread of disease by forbidding its citizens to enter affected areas. It may also block the exit of citizens likely to become a public charge elsewhere and require repatriation at its expense. And, during wartime, travel abroad may conflict with the state's need to defend itself.

Other claims regarding national security or interests are more difficult to assess. Many countries, including the United States, assert the right to forbid the departure of any persons whose activities might, in the words of official policy, "cause serious damage" to national security. The potential for abuse in such a vague standard is obvious, and appeals to "national security" ought to be scrutinized with particular care. For instance, more and more governments are invoking national security to deny exit to those who might utter unpleasant opinions abroad.

More broadly, many states in the world today justify restrictive emigration policies on the grounds of protecting the greater social good. From this perspective, gaining an exit visa, far from being a natural right of the individual, is an act of grace on the part of authorities.

The argument is an ancient one. Plato, in his *Laws,* urged restrictions on foreign travel that, in some cases, are very similar to those in effect today. Only older citizens of proven loyalty should be let out, and then only as members of government-supervised delegations. Thus Plato sought to protect his ideal society from the subversive influence of alien thoughts and practices, a preoccupation not unknown to modern regimes. Similarly, the laws of Sparta, drawn up by Lycurgus in the ninth century B.C., completely prohibited travel abroad in order to spare the city "the infection of foreign bad habits."[7]

This fear of contamination obviously applies primarily to temporary travel. But states commonly make much more far-reaching claims. One is their responsibility for molding national character. In this view, the state is a common project of its citizens rather than a voluntary contract. The citizen has irrevocable duties, reflecting both the imperative of loyalty to the collectivity and the debt owed society for the benefits it has provided him.[8] Thus Eastern European regimes argue that the generous support provided by the socialist state—especially free education through the highest levels—obligates recipients to repay the particular society by remaining productive members of it.

But such governments go even further, arguing that controls on movement are in the best interest of the individuals themselves, whatever their own opinion of the matter. In this view, citizens are easily misled by the illusion that the grass is greener on the other side of the border. Once they are cut off from the homeland that has nurtured them, once they are cast into a harsh, alien environment, most emigrants wake up to the futility of their restlessness. But the state, in its superior wisdom, spares its citizens the agonies of disappointment and rootlessness by eliminating the option of movement altogether. The media of contemporary closed societies are

7. Plato's *Laws* and Plutarch's *Lycurgus* are both quoted by Whelan, p. 643.

8. For development of this conception, see A. James Gregor, *Contemporary Radical Ideologies: Totalitarian Thought in the Twentieth Century* (New York: Random House, 1968), pp. 346–47. For a fuller discussion, see chapter 3.

filled with admonitory tales of disillusioned emigrants seeking to return to the womb.

To many contemporary governments, there exists no ground for asserting an abstract right to leave. These states do not recognize the existence of any "natural" rights, only those granted by collective authority. With collective authority as the point of reference, individual nonconformity has to be judged against the interests of society, with the burden of proof on the nonconformer.[9] Exit from the society clearly qualifies as the ultimate case of nonconformity.

Related to this is the doctrine of perpetual allegiance, according to which an individual cannot unilaterally renounce his obligations to the land of his birth. This doctrine was at the heart of the dispute between Britain and the United States in the War of 1812, when Britain impressed British-born seamen from American ships, despite their American citizenship, on the ground that they were still British citizens. Not until 1870 did Britain explicitly recognize the right of British subjects to renounce their nationality.[10]

But it is modern ideologies that have perfected the idea that the interests of the state, assumed to represent society as a whole, should take priority over individual whim and caprice. According to the collectivist ethic, the burden is on individuals to demonstrate why they should be allowed to leave, rather than the state to show why they should not. This line of reasoning simply concludes that the happiness of the whole is better served if individuals are compelled to remain a part of it.

In recent years, many states have fastened on the problem of brain drain. For instance, an estimated 10 percent of all doctors from India work in the United States or Britain.[11] Jamaica maintains that 60 percent of its professionals left for the United States between

9. Ibid., pp. 32–33, 36.

10. Whelan, p. 645.

11. Gregory Henderson, *The Emigration of Highly Skilled Manpower from the Developing Countries*, UNITAR Research Reports no. 3 (New York: UNITAR, 1970): 130.

1977 and 1980. Haiti has probably lost an even greater proportion. Brain drain claims are not limited to the Third World; East Germany cited the loss of professionals to the West to explain why it built the Berlin Wall. Overall, the brain drain is among the most common explanations that governments advance to justify restraints on the movement of their citizens.

This, then, is the case for the state. What are the claims of the individual?

The Claims of the Individual

Since personal self-determination may lead to a change of national allegiance, it potentially puts the interests of the individual and those of the state into sharper and more insoluble conflict than any other right. In the tension between individual and society, what question can be more fundamental than that of the individual's very membership in society?

The conflict is not new. The Biblical story of Exodus records an early clash between a state interest and the right to leave. Faced with demands to permit the emigration of the Israelites, Pharaoh responded, "Who is the Lord that I should heed him and let Israel go? I do not know the Lord, nor will I let Israel go." It took ten plagues—a strategy unavailable to modern refuseniks—to force the Egyptians to open their borders, and even then Pharaoh and his courtiers immediately reversed themselves, regretting the loss to the state: "What is this we have done, releasing Israel from our service?" (Exodus 5:2, 14:5). [12]

In ancient Greece, the Delphic priests regarded the right of unrestricted movement as one of the four freedoms distinguishing liberty from slavery. Ceremonies held to free slaves ritualistically proclaimed that the slave could now "run away to whomsoever he

12. God's command to Pharaoh—"Let my people go"—has become the rallying cry for those working for Soviet Jewish emigration today.

may wish." And the major restraint that Sparta placed on its half-free Helots was depriving them of the right to move elsewhere.[13]

In that era, the definition of liberty was tied to the idea of movement. One Greek term for freedom, *eleutheria,* derives from a phrase meaning "to go where one wills." Freedom of movement also figures strongly in the way liberty has been defined by political philosophers. Thomas Hobbes, for one, wrote, "Liberty, that we may define it, is nothing else but an absence of the lets and hindrances of motion. . . . every man hath more or less liberty, as he hath more or less space in which he employs himself. . . . the more ways a man may move himself, the more liberty he hath."[14]

At bottom, freedom of movement means nothing less than the freedom to choose the society in which one wants to live. As a result, modern democratic theory accords it a very high priority. Freedom of movement is regarded as a natural right, meaning that it takes precedence over all prerogatives asserted by the state. The contemporary political philosopher Maurice Cranston goes even further, calling it "the first and most fundamental of man's liberties."[15]

From the times of Pharaoh until today, then, the right of free movement appears as a universal aspiration. It is significant that primitive tribes, which are closest to the "state of nature," rarely impose restraints on movement. Recent studies show that the right to leave or remain is respected from the Nambikuara of central Brazil to the Nuer and Bushmen of Africa.[16] In these societies, as in more modern ones, the right to move has traditionally served as a vital

13. W. L. Westermann, "Between Slavery and Freedom," *American Historical Review* 50 (January 1945): 216–18.

14. Thomas Hobbes, *De Cive,* ed. Sterling P. Lamprecht (New York: Appleton-Century-Crofts, 1949), pp. 109–10.

15. Cranston, *What Are Human Rights?* (New York: Taplinger, 1973), p. 31.

16. The Nambikuara were studied by Claude Lévi-Strauss, the Nuer by E. E. Evans-Pritchard, and the Bushmen by Lorna Marshall. For full descriptions of these studies and others, see Albert O. Hirschman, "Exit, Voice, and the State," *World Politics* 31 (Winter 1978): 92–95.

outlet for dissatisfaction. In all, the irrepressibility of movement seems a powerful argument against state efforts to suppress it.

Efforts to limit exit can also be challenged on grounds of reason and common sense. For example, should military service remain an obligation for someone who, in seeking to leave a country, no longer claims its protection? How does refusing to allow emigration because of financial obligations differ from the universally condemned practice of imprisoning people for debts they owe?[17] Many obligations could clearly be handled by agreements among the nations involved.

The denial of exit on national security grounds can easily be abused. "Knowledge of state secrets" has been invoked to reject applications from people in the most innocuous occupations, from agriculture to meteorology; in many cases, any technical expertise the individual may possess is too outdated for security considerations to be even remotely relevant. (In one popular anecdote, the rejected applicant points out that his "secret" knowledge lags decades behind technical expertise elsewhere, prompting the official to respond, "Aha! *That* is the secret!") In the view of most jurists, national security should be invoked only when the individual has actually committed a criminal offense against security. Such a standard would invalidate most claims made today in the name of state security.

Restricting exit on the grounds of potential political opposition seems even more dubious. It is perfectly true that opponents in exile have often organized against their home governments: Cubans in Florida, the Ayatollah Khomeini before 1979, the Bolshevik exiles in Europe before 1917. Similar apprehensions today move Nicaragua to discourage the foreign travel of anti-Sandinista figures, South Africa to forbid the exit of prominent black leaders, and Iran to quarantine the Baha'i "virus" within its own borders.

But in almost all nations, legal codes guarantee the right of

17. Hersch Lauterpacht, *International Law and Human Rights* (London: Steven and Sons, 1950), p. 349. Hannum, pp. 24–51 and 153–62, analyzes the very limited nature of permissible exceptions to the right to leave under contemporary international law.

free speech; so do such international documents as the Universal Declaration of Human Rights. What is in principle guaranteed to citizens within their own borders can hardly serve as a pretext to keep them from leaving.

Most suspect of all is the notion that the good of the whole requires restrictions on the few. Maurice Cranston has persuasively argued that this is essentially the same argument once offered on behalf of slavery—that the miserable condition of slaves is justified by the benefits they provide to society as a whole.[18]

Of course, the right to leave does not imply the corresponding right to enter a particular country. Whatever the arguments over the authority of the state to block emigration, there is little dispute over its right to limit *immigration*. The two issues are not symmetrical: departure ends an individual's claims against a society, while entry sets such claims in motion. Control of entry is essential to the idea of sovereignty, for without it a society has no control over its basic character. Even in countries where the right of exit is taken for granted, few contest the right, or even duty, of the state to regulate the influx of newcomers.[19]

The state's responsibility for the character of society does not, however, endow it with the right to expel. No major political theory or ideology currently claims that the state has a right to expel nationals who have not committed a specific offense. Even in the case of aliens, most jurists hold that a state has no right of expulsion until another country has offered refuge. The idea of a person permanently deprived of a home may make for interesting fiction, as in the case of the protagonist in Edward Everett Hale's *Man without a Country* who, disowned by his nation, was shunted among naval vessels for fifty-five years. But it has no known historical counterpart. In recent years, some nations have committed themselves to prevent

18. Cranston, pp. 35–36.
19. See the discussions in Michael Walzer, *Spheres of Justice: A Defense of Pluralism and Equality* (New York: Basic, 1983), p. 40; Cranston, p. 33.

the creation of stateless persons—a sign of progress, even if such commitments have wavered in practice (see chapter 4).

A few states maintain exile as a legal punishment directed at individuals guilty of a crime and carried out by established judicial procedures. Even where provided for in law, however, formal exile is infrequently carried out today. On the other hand, expulsions— which are typically not authorized by law and which are directed at individuals or groups guilty of no specific crime—remain common, as a result of political convulsions in Latin America or harsh campaigns against ethnic groups in Africa and Asia.

Few states attempt to justify such expulsions. Likewise, when it comes to restrictions on emigration, governments are loath openly to propound them as a matter of law or clear policy. In few areas is it easier to conceal restrictive policies behind a screen of procedural obstacles and invisible pressures. Even those states that have impeded international movement wholesale shy away from asserting a formal right to do so. This reflects a healthy embarrassment on the part of offenders. Roger Nett, an advocate of unrestricted international movement, argues that "those who build walls or other barriers to keep people within their boundaries have little disposition to try to make doing so credible to outsiders—building walls is a peculiarly lonely job and an admission of the inadequacy of a system."[20]

The right to leave thus gets at the very essence of government by consent—a concept that has achieved near-universal acceptance in principle, even among states that rarely abide by it. Since government by consent holds that citizenship is a voluntary act, the right to leave a country implicitly serves to ratify the contract between individual and society. If a person who has the right to leave chooses to stay, he has signaled his voluntary acceptance of the social contract. From this follow his obligations to society. But if he does not have the option of leaving, then society's hold on him is based only on coercion.

20. Roger Nett, "The Civil Right We Are Not Ready For: The Right of Free Movement of People on the Face of the Earth," *Ethics* 81 (1971): 224.

The analogy of a prison is perhaps not too extreme. Hersch Lauterpacht, a leading expert on international law, put it this way: "A State which denies to its citizens the right to emigrate reduces itself to the level of a prison. A State which, in so far as this lies within its power, refuses to its citizens in time of peace the right to renounce their allegiance, transforms into a relation of subjection what must be in essence a voluntary partnership."[21]

While the right of personal self-determination may directly affect only a small minority, it can have important implications for society as a whole. Just erecting barriers can generate a strong urge to break them down. As the 1963 U.N. study noted, denial of the right to leave can have a spiraling psychological effect. Individuals otherwise content to remain at home may develop a "morbid fear of being hemmed in—a sort of collective claustrophobia," translating into an obsession with escape.[22] This, in turn, can reinforce the regime's fear of free emigration and its conviction that stronger controls are needed, creating a vicious circle that ends with the imposition of extreme measures. The case of East Germany and the Berlin Wall is a good example (see chapter 4).

Freedom of movement is also vital to the fulfillment of other basic human rights and needs, including marriage and family life, an adequate standard of living, education, gainful employment, and the practice of religion. Unrestricted movement is a precondition for the enjoyment of many other human rights. Conversely, regimes intent on limiting freedoms often strike first at foreign travel. South Africa's apartheid regime, for example, could probably not survive without its complex system of restrictions on internal and foreign travel.

The right to leave is most important when other rights are denied. In that case, it becomes the ultimate defense of human dignity. In the words of Anatole France, "If I am accused of stealing

21. Lauterpacht, *An International Bill of the Rights of Man* (New York: Columbia Unviersity Press, 1945), p. 130.

22. Inglés, p. 17.

the towers of Notre Dame, I can only flee the country."[23] From the exodus of the ancient Israelites from Egypt, to the Pilgrims of colonial America, to the Hungarian refugees of 1956, human history is, in many respects, the history of escape.

Denial of the right to flee can therefore be seen as a more basic insult to human dignity than anything save loss of life itself, for it eliminates the means to escape all other forms of persecution and injustice. And only in modern times has the possibility of flight been so effectively foreclosed.

The right to leave is thus the *ultimum refugium libertatis*—the last refuge of liberty. As Senator Henry Jackson once put it, "the freedom to leave a country is the traditional final lifeline for victims of racial, religious, and political persecution."[24]

The Implications of Open Borders

As the discussion above indicates, governments perceive very definite costs in respecting the right of personal self-determination. Open borders can mean the loss of engineers, doctors, and chemists. It can result in diminished control over economic planning. It can cause a blow to national self-esteem and carry the seeds of contamination from abroad. On a long-term basis, emigration can upset delicate demographic balances, and, in extreme cases, cause depopulation.

Less obvious, but potentially more important, are the benefits that open borders could provide. Cultural diffusion is the mainspring of human progress, and movement has been a key force in promoting the interaction of ideas and cultures. The most prominent writer of universal history in our age, William H. McNeill, concludes that "inter-civilizational exchange and stimulus provided a major—perhaps *the* major—stimulus to change within civilized communities

23. Quoted by Hannah Arendt, *The Origins of Totalitarianism* (New York: Meridian, 1958), p. 295.

24. *Congressional Record,* 95th Congress, 1st Session, July 2, 1977, p. S3289.

ever since the plurality of civilized cultures became knowable to suitably located and strategically situated individuals."[25]

Emigration can also help reduce tension in society by relieving economic pressures and providing an outlet for frustration and discontent. Societies are not dependent on their own resources alone if they function, through open borders, as part of a larger system.

In addition, the existence of an option forces a government to pay more attention to sources of discontent. A regime concerned about emigration will tend to be more responsive to the welfare and wishes of its citizens. By the same token, if a government simply forecloses emigration, it loses an important index of social discontent. In the language of modern social theory, an organization needs an open exit in order to receive feedback about its performance.[26]

For all the encroachments of the new serfdom, then, the vision of an open world continues to exert a strong attraction. The ideal of free movement would allow people to flow in response to pressures and opportunities, as goods in a free market flow in response to supply and demand. Classical free-market economics held that national territory should be "indifferent"; unrestricted immigration and emigration were important correlates of free trade.[27] Mismatches of resources and people would be righted by the "invisible hand" of international migratory movements. Political and social tensions would presumably be defused by the same process.

I have already noted some reservations about unrestricted entry into countries. Apart from its political impracticality, such a suggestion raises the prospect of massive disruption in a world marked by

25. William H. McNeill, "Human Migration: A Historical Overview," in *Human Migration: Patterns and Policies,* ed. William H. McNeill and Ruth Adams (Bloomington: Indiana University Press, 1978), p. 12. McNeill describes his own influential study, *The Rise of the West: A History of the Human Community,* as "a paean to the world historical significance of elite migration" (ibid.).

26. See the discussion in Albert O. Hirschman, "'Exit, Voice, and Loyalty': Further Reflections and a Survey of Recent Contributions," *Social Science Information* 8 (February 1974): 16.

27. Walzer, p. 37.

vast cultural and economic differences, areas of crushing overpopulation, and greatly varying political systems.

Having made this qualification, however, is achieving an open world still a valid ideal? Do we want a world in which no one is prevented from leaving his country, or is forced to do so? There are some far-reaching implications. For one thing, such a world implies a fairly loose conception of citizenship, of the idea that membership in a social community means lasting ties. The claims of nationalism would also be weakened, since an individual's choice of allegiance would become a matter of personal discretion.

Clearly, though, a world of free movement would promote less parochial, more universalized habits of thought and loyalty.[28] As Pope John XXIII said in affirming the right to emigrate: "The fact that one is a citizen of a particular State should not prevent anybody from being a member of the human family as a whole, nor from having citizenship in the world community."[29]

This may be utopian. As an ideal, however, the right to leave or to remain has lost none of its validity, even in an age of fierce nationalism. Freedom of movement is not only an end in itself but also an important means to achieve such other widely espoused goals as greater economic justice, a better distribution of resources, and the spread of shared values.

Because it is a last line of defense in the realization of other rights, the right of personal self-determination could well be considered the capstone of human rights. The right to change one's nationality may be, as Nett expresses it, "fundamental to the structure of human opportunity."[30] The ideal may not be completely achievable, but it is not a bad one to keep in mind.

28. Whelan, pp. 636, 651, discusses these implications more fully.
29. Encyclical *Pacem in Terris*.
30. Nett, p. 218.

2

The Old Serfdom

No nation can have too many inhabitants.
—*Prussian Minister Johannes von Justi, 1760*

Migration in Human History

Human history is the history of movement. Modern man originated in Africa, but by 20,000 B.C. he had penetrated every major land mass apart from Antarctica. By the time humans began keeping records, they had reached even such remote spots as Easter Island, some 1200 miles from any other strip of land. No other animal species has achieved a wider distribution.[1]

Past migrations help account for who we are. Almost all existing nationalities have roots in migratory mass movements. For Aztecs, Jews, Hungarians, Anglo-Saxons, and Thais, to name a few, collective memory begins with migration from an ancestral homeland. Islam dates its start from the hegira or migration of Muhammad and his followers from Mecca to Medina. Modern England is a product of incursions not only from Anglo-Saxons but also from Celts, the Norse, and Norman French. A crossroads nation like Egypt is an amalgam of dozens of peoples come to intrude and conquer over the millennia.

1. Kingsley Davis, "The Migrations of Human Populations," *Scientific American* 231 (September 1974): 93.

Consider the world's map only a thousand years ago. There were no Germans in Berlin, no Russians in Moscow, and few Turks in what is now Turkey. Spain was mostly Moslem, the southern Ukraine was inhabited by Turkish tribes, and most Bulgarians lived in Central Asia. There were no Thais in Bangkok or Malays in Singapore, and most of present-day Vietnam was occupied by the ancestors of today's Cambodians. In Africa, Bantu-speaking peoples, who now occupy most of sub-Saharan Africa, were still confined to the center and the east coast of the continent. Most strikingly, of course, the New World was inhabited only by native American Indians.

In the intervening period, migrations have transformed every continent. The eastward movement of millions of Russians converted much of Asia, culturally, into an extension of Europe. At the same time, the Han Chinese continued their inexorable southward expansion, forcing such peoples as the Thais and Vietnamese to relocate further south. Bantu speakers in Africa crossed the Limpopo in the eleventh century and, by the sixteenth, had reached the Transkei, on Africa's southern coast; meanwhile, Moslem immigrants in the area of the western Sudan stimulated the emergence of several states there. In pre-Columbian America, conquerors carried Aztec and Andean civilization over vast areas.

What explains the universality of human movement? Historians stress the stimulus of technological inequality among different groups, which encourages the expansion of more advanced peoples into the domains of those unable to resist. To this must be added the impressive human capacity for adaptation to new environments, leading, as noted, to an impressive distribution across widely varying climes and conditions.

Furthermore, the dominant historical interpretation sees this encounter between peoples of different levels as "the principal drive wheel of historic change."[2] Meeting strange and often threatening

2. William H. McNeill, *The Great Frontier: Freedom and Hierarchy in Modern Times* (Princeton: Princeton University Press, 1983), p. 10.

people sparks invention and imitation. Migration is the mechanism for cross-fertilization, the means by which ideas, techniques, and culture have been diffused and new advances stimulated.

The most dynamic civilizations arose where human traffic was the heaviest. The ancient Near East, the Indian subcontinent, China, the areas of Islamic conquest, the Americas in the age of European expansion—all were exposed to waves of migrants who induced ferment and renewal. Conversely, those areas most insulated against alien intrusion became backwaters of history: Ethiopia, Yemen, Tibet, and Nepal, rain forest dwellers from Brazil to New Guinea, and even—in a relative sense—American Appalachia.

Most movement took place in the face of enormous difficulties. Until modern times, anyone on the move faced an uncertain, often hostile reception wherever he alighted. Just getting there was a daunting task; until the last century, even the most efficient means of transport, by land or sea, moved the traveler no more than a hundred miles a day. Much movement was on foot. The common phrase puts it accurately: American pioneers *trudged* westward.

Few migrants had reliable information or communication to guide them. Knowledge about other peoples and places was sparse and unsystematic. Fear of the unknown was a profound deterrent. European mariners, for instance, refused for centuries to venture beyond Cape Bojador, on the West African coast, unshakably convinced that no one could survive beyond that point. Others were drawn by improbable visions of paradise, as with the millions inveigled to America by unscrupulous shipping agents promising instant riches. Nonetheless, whatever the uncertainties and hardships, people in every age moved. According to recent studies, even traditional agricultural societies, made up of stolid peasants supposedly rooted to the soil, seem to have been highly mobile.

Governments in earlier centuries rarely interfered with the right to move, at least in the modern sense of such interference. In the Biblical story of Exodus, Pharaoh tried to prevent the Jews from leaving Egypt. And Sparta forbade the half-free Helots from departing. But the rationale underlying such restrictions was very different from the contemporary notion of "state interest." In recent centuries, the concept of national sovereignty has endowed the state with the right to control all movement within its precisely defined borders. In ancient times, however, only slaves, like Pharaoh's Jews, were subject to confinement. All others could go where they chose. Thus, in Greek city-states, freemen could and did travel widely, leaving their cities permanently if they wished. In Plato's *Crito,* Socrates notes that "we further proclaim to any Athenian by the liberty which we allow him, that if he does not like us when he has become of age and has seen the ways of the city, and made our acquaintance, he may go where he pleases and take his goods with him."[3]

Beyond Greece, the ancient Mediterranean world as a whole was shaped by the constant movement and mingling of the many peoples who lived there. Africa also has a strong tradition of free movement; numerous studies have indicated that "fissiparous politics"—the secession or movement of dissident groups—was a common phenomenon in traditional African societies. In the Middle East, the concept of *Dar-al-Islam* (the House of Islam), as distinct from the non-Islamic world, reinforced earlier traditions of free movement by stressing the essential unity of Islamic civilization and the artificiality of geographic divisions within it.

Even in China, where strong government and family ties discouraged movement, internal mobility and voluntary individual migration was common. China's southward expansion was accomplished through both voluntary and government-sponsored emigration. This constant movement helps explain the emergence of a homogeneous Chinese people over such a large territory.[4]

3. Plato, *Crito,* trans. B. Jowett (Roslyn, N.Y.: Walter J. Black, 1942), p. 75.

4. James Lee, "Migration and Expansion in Chinese History," in McNeill and Adams, pp. 20–47.

Classic European Serfdom

One of the major historical exceptions to freedom of movement was medieval serfdom in Europe. It originated in the late Roman Empire, during the third and fourth centuries A.D., and survived in some places into the nineteenth century. In theory, serfdom was distinct from slavery in that the master owned the services of the serf, rather than his person. To most serfs, though, this was a distinction without a difference. Serfs, like slaves, were forbidden to leave their place of employment; they were thus subject to whatever conditions their lords imposed on them. Having lost the option of leaving, they also lost the most effective means of improving their condition.

Initially, the Roman Empire was not hostile to movement. At one point Rome itself harbored a population that was almost 90 percent foreign-born. But, in the third and fourth centuries A.D., as the Empire became increasingly subject to barbarian incursions and internal anarchy, it compelled peasants to remain on the land. Under Constantine (A.D. 309–37) and his successors, free subjects were gradually bound to their places of work. An imperial decree of the late fourth century noted that "a law passed by our ancestors detains the *coloni* [peasants tied to the soil] by a kind of eternal right so that they are not permitted to depart from those places whose fruits nurture them nor to desert those places which they have once undertaken to cultivate."[5] In practice, two classes of *coloni* emerged: the free *coloni,* who were considered free except for the prohibition of departure, and the *adscripti,* who were essentially full serfs. The latter group may have originated as conquered peoples forced into servitude.

By medieval times, such distinctions had blurred. A large part of Europe's population was bound in place, deprived in perpetuity of the right to leave, and traded as so much chattel by the lords and petty sovereigns of the time. In this feudal order, there was little

5. W. L. Westermann, "Between Slavery and Freedom," *American Historical Review* 50 (January 1945): 220–23; J. S. Critchley, *Feudalism* (London: George Allen and Unwin, 1978), pp. 132–33.

room for human migration; apart from the occasional requirements of warfare or politics, movement was considered inimical to order. The typical serf, being an agricultural laborer, was tied to the soil. Moreover, laborers, craftsmen, and artisans could be tied to particular workshops or to the service of a particular lord.

But for all its oppressiveness, the medieval system did have some loopholes. Medieval serfdom was primarily an *economic* relationship; in theory, and sometimes in fact, serfs could buy their freedom. Moreover, serfdom was a *personal* tie, involving obligations to a particular lord, rather than to the community at large. Once released from this relationship, serfs were free to go wherever they could gain admittance (which could certainly be a problem). Towns, for instance, provided relative freedom and better chances for employment, and serfs who escaped there from their manors were seldom apprehended. By the twelfth century, a person who resided within a town for a year and a day usually became a free man. Furthermore, medieval serfdom was *specific*; it did not involve an entire population, only one stratum of it. Many members of society—nobles, townsmen, free peasants—were not locked in place.

Serfdom was later extended to eastern Europe, as part of the struggle between the nobility and centralizing monarchies. In the late 1500s, the Russian Tsar granted the landed aristocracy control over the peasantry in order to lessen opposition to the crown as well as to secure a more stable tax base. Finally, the one day a year on which peasants had been allowed to leave—St. George's Day—was eliminated. By 1649, when the period of limitation on the recovery of fugitives was abolished, serfdom was fully in place. Significantly, in Russia, unlike Western Europe, the state played a central role in the establishment and maintenance of serfdom.

The realities of a new commercial and industrial order led to serfdom's demise. Wage labor and a mobile workforce replaced the fixed feudal system. The growth of towns provided expanded opportunities of escape. In England serfdom withered away during the sixteenth century, and in France it had almost disappeared by the time of the Revolution. Serfdom was abolished in the Hapsburg Empire by 1848, and in Russia, where it had begun later, in 1861.

Mercantilism: Hoarding Bodies

The decline of European serfdom did not give rise to free, unfettered movement. Feudalism was replaced by absolutism; centralized sovereign states now claimed exclusive control over their own territories and over all movement across their borders. The decisive relationship was no longer between lord and serf, but between sovereign and subject. Control of international movement now shifted to governments.

Monarchical power, which had gathered force in the twelfth and thirteenth centuries, expanded greatly in the fifteenth century— the age of Joan of Arc in France, Ferdinand and Isabella in Spain, the first of the Tudor kings in England. Monarchies became entrenched after the Peace of Westphalia, in 1648, which ended a period of religious wars and firmly established the principle of territorial sovereignty against the competing claims of the church and feudal lords. This was the age of Louis XIV and of his son, who was taught that "as all perfection and all strength are united in God, so all the power of individuals is united in the person of the prince."[6]

The monarch's efforts to promote the power and interests of the state implied tight regulation of its economy and foreign trade. Jean Baptiste Colbert, controller general of finance under Louis XIV, perfected a system of controls that Adam Smith would later disparagingly call *mercantilism*. Mercantilism marked the emergence of the modern notion of national economic interest and centralized economic planning.

The mercantilists, who took control throughout western Europe, believed that wealth was measured in gold and silver; to accumulate these metals, a nation should sell as much abroad and buy

6. Jacques Benigne Bossuet, "Politics Drawn from the Very Words of Scripture," in *Readings in European History,* vol. 2, ed. James Harvey Robinson (Boston: Ginn, 1906), pp. 275–76.

as little as possible. This meant building up domestic industries while making it hard for other nations to build up theirs.

Demographically, mercantilism adhered to one simple tenet: people are wealth. As Prussian Minister Johannes von Justi proclaimed, "No nation can have too many inhabitants."[7] The centralized monarchies of Europe thus embarked on campaigns to increase not only their store of gold and silver, but also the number of bodies at their command. This, in turn, would lower the prevailing wage rate, making exports more competitive. Mercantilists believed that a large, impoverished working class would be of great benefit to the nation as a whole.

Skilled artisans were also a valuable asset, one that monarchs sought to keep out of the hands of others. In 1534 the king of England prohibited the foreign travel of those who knew how to mix certain metals and to make tools of them.[8] Classical mercantilism systematized these restrictions; Adam Smith, in *The Wealth of Nations,* noted that an "artificer may be obliged to give security at the discretion of the court, that he shall not go beyond the seas, and may be committed to prison until he give such security." Smith observed "how contrary such regulations are to the boasted liberty of the subject, of which we affect to be so very jealous."[9]

In an age of recurrent dynastic wars, population was also valued as a foundation of military power. Greater numbers meant not only more soldiers but also more revenues to support costly mercenary armies.

Population, meanwhile, was a scarce resource. The Thirty Years' War (1618–48) and other bloody struggles had decimated Europe. Population growth was slow. The embryonic manufacturing

7. Quoted in Marcus Lee Hansen, *The Great Atlantic Migration, 1607–1860* (Cambridge: Harvard University Press, 1940), p. 19.

8. William Searle Holdsworth, *A History of English Law,* 3d ed., vol. 4 (London: Methuen, 1945), pp. 335–36.

9. Adam Smith, *An Inquiry into the Nature and Causes of the Wealth of Nations* (New York: Modern Library, 1937), pp. 624, 625.

enterprises of the period, which were labor intensive, suffered chronic shortages of manpower. Finally, the opening up of overseas colonies introduced a competing pull on population. By the sixteenth and seventeenth centuries, the entire world was fused into a single migratory network; for the first time, international movement became truly global in scale. Intercontinental movement was not yet convenient or universal, but it was feasible. This posed yet another dilemma for Europe's crowned heads: should manpower be diverted to colonization overseas, or hoarded at home for application to industry and army?

In response to this dilemma, governments sought to increase numbers in a variety of ways. First, they encouraged more births. Colbert granted tax exemptions for early marriages and provided a sizable bounty for large families. He also tried to restrict the number of priests and nuns, whom he regarded as nonproductive resources. Governments also actively sought immigrants. Spain exempted newcomers from certain taxes, and other nations offered such incentives as easy naturalization and even dowries for immigrants' daughters.[10] Catherine the Great enticed large numbers of Germans to settle along the Volga and elsewhere in Russia. England and Holland, among other countries, competed to attract refugees from countries foolish enough to let religious differences overcome economic self-interest. Except for a few outstanding cases, neither ethnic nor religious animosities were allowed to stand in the way of increasing national numbers. The spirit of the time is conveyed by Ottoman Sultan Bajazet, who, in welcoming Jews expelled from Spain, reputedly exclaimed, "What! Call ye this Ferdinand 'wise'—he who depopulates his own dominions in order to enrich mine?"[11]

Finally, states prohibited their own populations from emigrating. In some cases, the stress was on retaining skilled workers. In

10. Aristide Zolberg, "International Migration Policies in a Changing World System," in McNeill and Adams, p. 247. This entire chapter is heavily indebted to Zolberg's pioneering work on the history of migration policies.

11. Cecil Roth, *History of the Jews* (New York: Shocken, 1961), p. 252.

1669, for example, Louis XIV ordered all navigators, shipbuilders, pilots, sailors, and fishermen to remain in France or to return if they had left. By 1700 most Swiss cantons had prohibited emigration without permission; so did Frederick William of Prussia, in a 1686 edict. Various ploys were used to discourage departure. In 1701 Bern levied a 10 percent property tax on all emigrants. Bavaria forbade the departure of anyone under the age of sixteen, thereby inhibiting the movement of families. Later German ordinances prohibited the transfer of property, forcing would-be emigrants to leave penniless.[12]

Remnants of serfdom also limited movement. In some places, serfdom had given way to village communes, which assumed the right to keep members from leaving. And local religious authorities, fearing declines in their congregations, invoked Biblical injunctions against those who would forsake home and family for adventure elsewhere.

The end of serfdom, therefore, did not mean the end of restricted movement. While peasants could now move more freely within national borders, they were usually forbidden to cross those borders. In some respects, the restrictions of mercantilism were even more inclusive than those of serfdom, since they applied to the entire population rather than to one segment of it. Mercantilism in the service of absolutism—the combination of national economic calculation with the habits of authoritarian rule—produced a strikingly modern system of emigration control.

But mercantilism was not nationalistic in the modern sense. Governments welcomed immigrants of various backgrounds and persuasions. They opposed emigration not out of ethnic or ideological motives, but out of a concrete state interest in building population. Mercantilism did, however, anticipate latter-day emigration policies in two respects—their tendency to regard individuals as state re-

12. John Duncan Brite, "The Attitude of European States toward Emigration to the American Colonies and the United States, 1607–1820" (Ph.D. diss., University of Chicago, 1937), pp. 195–200; Marc Raeff, *The Well-Ordered Police State* (New Haven and London: Yale University Press, 1983), p. 72.

sources, and their corresponding willingness to restrict the movement of those individuals.

While the mercantilists were on the rise in Europe, Asian dynasties, too, were adopting highly restrictive policies on all foreign travel. In China, during the early Ming Dynasty (1368–1644), a remarkable series of Chinese maritime expeditions, which had reached as far as the southern African coast, was abruptly cut off by the Great Withdrawal of the early fifteenth century. Instigated by palace intrigues, this withdrawal reflected traditional Chinese attitudes of self-sufficiency and indifference to the outside barbarian world. Severe punishments were decreed for anyone going abroad, and within a century all seafaring was abolished. Even building seafaring junks was made a capital offense. The closing off of China culminated symbolically in the restoration of the Great Wall during this same period.

Sanctions intensified under the Manchus (1644–1912). Any Chinese found abroad was subject to beheading (should he be so foolish as to return). The law apparently was not always enforced, and officials could be bribed to overlook it, but the provision certainly did discourage travel. Even when overseas Chinese were persecuted and massacred, as in the Philippines in 1603 and the East Indies in 1740, the Chinese government refused to intercede, instead denouncing the "vile" and "unworthy" persons who had deserted their homeland. The official prohibition of emigration was not revoked until 1860.

In Japan, the period of great turbulence leading up to the establishment of the Tokugawa Shogunate in 1603 was marked by fairly free travel. Japanese settlers had moved to the Philippines, Siam, and Cochin China, and Japanese vessels had penetrated the Indian Ocean. Under the new regime, however, the fear of foreign influence became an obsession. All missionaries were expelled in 1614, and ten years later the remaining Spanish were forced to follow them; conversely, Japanese Christians were forbidden to leave. At about the same time, the Japanese, like the Chinese, outlawed shipbuilding and seafaring. Following the suppression of a Japanese Christian rebellion in 1637, the entire country was closed off to the outside world, except for a Dutch trading post on a tiny island in Nagasaki harbor. In 1640 it became a capital crime for Japanese to leave the country or, having left it, to return.

This prohibition remained in force until the midnineteenth century, when Commodore Matthew Perry's famous mission led to a new opening. Shortly before the fall of the Tokugawa Shogunate in 1865, emigration was legalized. The Meiji Restoration of 1868, which brought to power a modernizing government, permitted some travel, but the state policy remained highly restrictive.

The Other Side of the Coin: Mass Expulsions

If population is wealth, then forcing large numbers of productive citizens to leave seems highly irrational. As Sultan Bajazet's comment about King Ferdinand indicates, mass expulsions of religious or ethnic minorities would seem to show bigotry overcoming a state's best interests. But for the governments of countries like Spain and France in the fifteenth to seventeenth centuries, such actions served a definite purpose: molding the character of their populations in order to build homogeneous nation-states. As King Philip II of Spain put it, he would rather be king in a desert than a king of heretics. Thus, for two and a half centuries, Europe generated refugees while generally forbidding emigration.

This is not to say that sheer prejudice and unreasoning hatred had nothing to do with the matter. Neither commodity was scarce in this turbulent period. But the major refugee flows resulted primarily from policies aimed at national integration and the consolidation of monarchical power. When internal cohesion seemed more important than numbers, regimes simply expelled those who refused to adapt to the emerging national ethos.

The main instrument of integration was religion. While the Hapsburg Empire, for instance, mixed dozens of nationalities, religious divisions were considered an invitation to war. Expulsions under every regime were thus directed principally at religious minorities: Jews and Moors in Spain, Protestants in France and the Spanish Netherlands, dissenters and separatists in England, Catholics in some Protestant German states.

During the early period of centralizing monarchies in Western Europe, Jews were expelled from England (1290), France (1306), and Naples (1288).

In the late fifteenth and early sixteenth centuries, Jews were forced to leave Spain, Portugal, and most of the smaller German states. By the end of this period, Jews had been expelled from most of Western and Central Europe.

The most interesting case, by virtue of its "modern" character, was the expulsion of the Jews from Spain in 1492.[13] This expulsion coincided with the emergence of a strong monarchy that not only controlled the entire territory of Spain but also was committed to a vigorous program of national integration. Jews comprised between 10 and 20 percent of the population and played an important role in the economy. For almost a century, Spanish monarchs had tried to assimilate them into Christian Spanish society by promoting conversion. Many Jews had in fact converted, but this did not solve the problem, since the converted Jews—labeled *Marranos,* or swine— were still not fully accepted by Spanish society. Over the protests of the church, converts were excluded from positions of privilege as a means of preserving *limpieza di sangre* (purity of blood). (In adding the criterion of race to that of religion, the Spanish anticipated more modern styles of persecution.)

To prove their worthiness, some converts even joined the ranks of the persecutors. Nonetheless, many converts were suspected of

13. Aristide Zolberg, "State-Formation and Its Victims: Refugee Movements in Early Modern Europe," in *Beyond Progress and Development: Proceedings of the Symposium on Macro Political and Societal Change,* ed. N. J. Berting, W. Blockmans, and U. Rosenthal (Rotterdam: Faculty of Social Sciences, Erasmus University, 1983). The following analysis of the Spanish expulsions is based primarily on Zolberg's case study in this article.

being insincere. Distinguishing true converts from fake ones was a principal reason for the introduction of the Inquisition into Spain.

Perhaps the greatest obstacle to the conversion process was the continued presence in Spain of unconverted Jews. They kept alive a culture that, to the church and crown, interfered with the assimilation of converts. And when some Jews fled to the "enemy camp" in Islamic North Africa, their flight raised further questions about the loyalty of those who remained. A series of anti-Jewish measures followed, culminating in a final decree ordering all Jews to convert or leave. Some 120,000 to 150,000 did leave, making them Europe's largest group of refugees to that date.

The Moors in Spain faced a somewhat different situation. They occupied a low economic position and lived in a few concentrated rural areas. Needed by the local nobility to work the land, the Moors were at first regarded as less potentially dangerous. But, as in the Jewish case, political considerations triumphed in the end. The Moors' ties to the Islamic enemy made them a security threat in Spanish eyes. In 1566 Philip II, still determined not to rule heretics, ordered the Moors to speak Castilian rather than Arabic, adopt European dress, and drop the alien custom of hot baths. The Moors revolted, and Philip responded with savage repression. He proceeded to scatter the Moors across the entire country, but this served only to transform a regional problem into a national one. Finally, in 1609, all Moors were ordered expelled.

In Northern Europe, the greatest forced migration took place in the Spanish Netherlands, where in the late 1500s an estimated 175,000 Protestants were expelled or provoked to flee in fear. Philip II, the same monarch who so distinguished himself in Spain, had been awarded the Low Countries (present-day Belgium and the Netherlands) when the Hapsburg dominions were divided between him and his uncle in 1555–56. By 1566, the same year he issued his notorious hot-bath edict, Philip had managed to goad the Protestant Dutch into open revolt. A Spanish army sent to suppress the uprising established a "Council of Blood," which boasted of executing some 18,000 heretics. The Spanish were unable to vanquish the seven northern provinces, and in 1609 these achieved independence as the Netherlands. In the southern provinces, however, Spanish policies forced out waves of refugees from the 1560s through the 1580s, with smaller numbers thereafter. Most fled to the Netherlands, others to England and Germany. The result was to make Belgium, as it came to be called, an almost purely Catholic state.

France, too, had to deal with a large and economically important Protestant minority, the Huguenots. During the sixteenth century, as much as half the French nobility—plus many local magnates and a significant segment of the population—had been swept up in the Protestant fervor. Such numbers, together with their tight organization, made the Huguenots a threat to the crown; it also made them hard to suppress. This was especially so because of the convoluted politics of the time, when the king needed the Huguenots to help him consolidate his rule and to fight Spain. King Henry IV (1589–1610) had, as Henry of Navarre, been a Huguenot himself, converting to Catholicism only in order to secure the throne (an act memorialized by his phrase "Paris is worth a Mass"). In 1598 he issued the Edict of Nantes, granting the Huguenots freedom of worship, full civil rights, and such benefits as control of some two hundred fortified towns.

This outburst of tolerance represented a reluctant accommodation to reality, not a sudden flowering of liberal thought. In the century that followed, French kings gradually rescinded many of the privileges that had been granted to the Huguenots. Under the prodding of the imperious Cardinal Richelieu, Louis XIII took control of the fortified towns in 1629. However, neither Richelieu nor Louis XIV (1643–1715) favored the "Spanish solution" to the problem of heresy. The Huguenots were too valuable a resource to be forced out. Instead, the government both encouraged conversion and discouraged the practice of Protestantism, going so far as to foment occasional "pogroms" as state policy.

The Catholic clergy continued to remind Louis that Protestantism in France was a threat to his dignity and authority, and in 1685 the king revoked the Edict of Nantes, prohibited Protestant worship, and had Protestant children baptized as Catholics. And, in an effort to ensure uniformity without losing bodies, the French expelled Huguenot ministers while prohibiting the departure of lay individuals (thus repeating the historical pattern in which population groups are simultaneously forced to leave and to stay). France, which in 1682 had forbidden the emigration of Huguenot seamen and artisans, now declared that any Huguenot caught trying to escape, or helping someone else to escape, would be sentenced to the galleys for life. In 1698, sea pilots were forbidden to depart from French ports without permission, and other tight controls on shipping were enacted. Nevertheless, some 200,000–300,000 Huguenots—over 20 percent of the total—fled, many of them to the New World.[14] As it happens, it was to these fugitives that the term *refugee* was first applied.

The English government of the same period readily exempted Catholics and dissenters from their general policy of discouraging emigration. It also did not stand in the way of Irish or Scots who wanted to leave, whether they were religious dissenters or not. The results were evident in the population of the early English colonies, which consisted primarily of the various nonconformists from the British Isles.

When problems within the colonies developed, however, the English reacted as Spain's Philip II might have. In 1755 they expelled 15,000 French settlers from Acadia (Nova Scotia), an act that was immortalized in Longfellow's *Evangeline*:

Waste are those pleasant farms, and the farmers forever departed!
Scattered like dust and leaves, when the mighty blasts of October

14. Myriam Yardeni, *Le Refuge protestant* (Paris: Presses Universitaires de France, 1985), pp. 32, 49.

> Seize them, and whirl them aloft, and sprinkle them far o'er the
> ocean.
> Naught but tradition remains of the beautiful village of Grand-
> Pré.

Russia, too, was the scene of forced migration. Rulers had long since perfected the techniques of mass expulsion within the vast reaches of Russia itself, a method which, in the words of a modern observer, "gives people the worst of both worlds: emigration from their homeland together with the same oppressive regime as before."[15] As early as 1031, Grand Duke Yaroslav I relocated an entire group of Poles from Galicia to elsewhere in Russia. Sometimes groups were scattered over a wide area, as Ivan III did to the German merchant class of Novgorod in 1478 (an act echoed by Soviet treatment of Volga Germans during World War II). Later, during a period of restive nationalism in the late nineteenth century, political opponents and minorities fled abroad in large numbers, despite official prohibitions on emigration. And, as late as 1891, Jews were expelled from Moscow.

The Great Regression: African Slavery

In all, from the fifteenth through the eighteenth century, about one million people in Europe became refugees as a result of expulsion policies. Another two to three million Europeans moved to the New World. Overshadowing both of these movements, however, was the shipment of millions of West Africans to enslavement in the Americas—the largest involuntary migration movement in history. Coming as classic serfdom was beginning to disappear, the rebirth of slavery in the Western world represented a massive regression for the right of personal self-determination.

The slave trade was initiated by the Islamic world. By one estimate, Islamic states enslaved about 17 million Africans between

15. Leszek Kolakowski, "In Praise of Exile," *Times Literary Supplement,* October 11, 1985, p. 1133.

650 and 1920. [16] In 1442 a Portuguese ship dispatched by Prince Henry the Navigator returned some Moorish captives to their homeland and received as payment ten African slaves. This prompted the Portuguese to develop their own slave trade along the African coast, and a small flow of slaves began trickling into Portugal and Spain.

In Europe, however, the market for slaves was limited. It was the opening of the New World that produced a sustained demand for bodies. The settling of frontier areas has, throughout history, required steady supplies of manpower to till land, exploit natural resources, and build roads and houses. Furthermore, it is hard to keep a labor force settled on a frontier; the ease of movement and the attraction of virgin land draws settlers ever onward, as with Daniel Boone in search of "elbow room." Thus, the same frontiers that fostered independence and equality also usually required some form of compulsory labor. [17] In Russia, for example, the development of serfdom was partly a response to the pressures produced by the country's eastward expansion toward the Pacific. And, in the Americas, the use of indentured servants soon gave way to the cheaper, more efficient use of black slaves. In 1502—only ten years after Columbus—black slaves were sent from Spain to Haiti. Within a few years King Charles V of Spain authorized a Flemish courtier to carry 4000 slaves annually to Haiti, Cuba, Jamaica, and Puerto Rico. A Dutch ship brought slaves to Jamestown in 1619, only twelve years after its founding; blacks thus preceded the Pilgrims to America.

Africans were preferable to native Americans as slaves in a number of ways. The latter had a disconcerting tendency to succumb to the white man's diseases. And, while native Americans could

16. Ralph A. Austin, "From the Atlantic to the Indian Ocean: European Abolition, the African Slave Trade, and Asian Economic Structures," in *The Abolition of the Atlantic Slave Trade: Origins and Effects in Europe, Africa, and the Americas,* ed. David Eltis and James Walvin (Madison: University of Wisconsin Press, 1981), p. 136.

17. For an arresting discussion of this pattern, see McNeill, *The Great Frontier.*

often move from the white man's reach, Africans, disoriented by their strange environment, were reduced to pathetic dependence. Racial differences further made control easier; all blacks, it could be assumed, were slaves. In all, between eight and ten million Africans were brought to the New World during the three centuries of the slave trade—four to five times the number of European colonists arriving in the same period.[18]

The impact of this emigration on Africa was clearly enormous. Since only about half survived the infamous "middle passage" across the Atlantic, the number transported was probably twice the number that actually arrived. To this must be added the lives lost in getting the slaves to the ships. Dr. David Livingstone, the nineteenth-century missionary, claimed that at least ten lives were lost for each slave that reached the coast. Whatever the figures, by the time the slave trade ended in the nineteenth century, it had caused wholesale depopulation and disruption throughout West Africa.

Combating the Pull of America

For the first two centuries after Columbus, the number of Europeans who emigrated to America was quite small. That reflected, in part, the ambivalence that Europe's colonial powers felt toward their New World possessions. On the one hand, overseas possessions added to a nation's power and resources; on the other, they drained population from the home country and created economic competition. Some mercantilists concluded that colonies were worthwhile only if they complemented the economy of the mother country rather than duplicating it. Thus, for England, the West Indies were a good idea, but New England was a mistake. Benjamin Franklin struggled

18. Philip Curtin, *The Atlantic Slave Trade: A Census* (Madison: University of Wisconsin Press, 1969), estimates the number of Africans brought to the New World by 1820 at 7.8 million. Brinley Thomas, "Migration: Economic Aspects," in *International Encyclopedia of the Social Sciences,* vol. 10, ed. David Sills (New York: Macmillan, 1968), p. 293, puts the figure at over 10 million for the 1619–1776 period.

against this thinking after Britain's victory in 1760 over the French in Quebec; as an American agent in London, Franklin had to argue against those who coveted the tiny though sugar-rich island of Guadeloupe but were happy to let the French keep the vast reaches of Canada.

Spain at first viewed colonialism as a commercial or missionary enterprise; as a result, the idea of permanent settlement took a while to develop. Apart from brief periods of liberalization, movement to Spanish colonies was tightly restricted. Throughout the sixteenth century, officials, merchants, and soldiers usually served overseas for a limited time and then returned home. In fact, Spanish law often required them to return after a specified period.

At the same time, only Spanish citizens were permitted to enter Spanish colonies, and then only with a license. In order to get a license, even for a limited period, applicants had to furnish a sufficient reason, provide proof of their morals, and, as a 1522 order required, establish that they were "neither Jews nor Moors, nor children of such, nor persons newly reconciled, nor sons or grandsons of any that have been punished, condemned, or burnt as heretics, or for heretical crimes." Anyone leaving without a license would forfeit his property, be forced to return to Spain at his own expense, and be excommunicated. In 1607, the death penalty was decreed for any ship's officer carrying illegal passengers to the Indies. [19]

In such circumstances, it is not surprising that the European population of Spain's New World possessions grew slowly. By the middle of the sixteenth century, there were still only about 7500 Spaniards in Mexico and 6000 in Peru. Throughout the century, only 1000 to 1500 migrated from Spain each year, many of them

---

19. Julius Isaac, *Economics of Migration* (London: K. Paul, Trench, Trubner, 1947), p. 16; Wilhelm Roscher, *The Spanish Colonial System* (New York: H. Holt, 1904), pp. 17–18; Edward Gaylord Bourne, *Spain in America, 1450–1580* (New York and London: Harper and Brothers, 1904), pp. 243–47; Bernard Moses, *The Establishment of Spanish Rule in America* (New York: G. P. Putnam's Sons, 1898), p. 56.

temporarily. So low were the numbers that in 1529 King Charles V made leaving the Indies a capital offense.[20]

The French pursued similar policies. Only French Catholics were allowed access to the colonies; at the same time, most French Catholics were forbidden to leave France. This severely retarded the growth of New France. Only about 10,000 French immigrants entered Canada before the British took it over in the late eighteenth century. At one point French colonial authorities became so desperate that, like the Spanish in the Indies, they decreed the death penalty for anyone caught trying to leave the colony.[21]

The British, meanwhile, found a convenient way to resolve the conflicting demands of population at home and in the colonies: they simply shipped dissenters overseas. Oliver Cromwell, for example, sent shiploads of Irish papists to the West Indies, thus removing troublesome domestic elements and populating the colonies at the same time. Other colonies were, as noted, established more voluntarily by religious nonconformists ranging from separatists and Irish Catholics to Quakers and Mennonites. By 1780, the British Isles had furnished about 750,000 emigrants to North America—the only mass colonial emigration prior to the nineteenth century. Furthermore, the English colonies became a haven for minorities and refugees from other lands, including German Protestants, French Huguenots, Spanish and Portuguese Jews, and various minor sects. As a result, by the mid-eighteenth century, the New World had twenty British colonists for every French one, which helps to explain Britain's success in expelling the French from North America.

Countries that lacked colonies faced less of a dilemma. Intent on conserving population, they opposed all departures for the New World. The problem became critical when the British colonies were opened up to settlement in the early eighteenth century. In the Swiss canton of Zurich, for example, a 1734 decree required permission

20. Roscher, p. 17; Bourne, pp. 248–51.
21. Hansen, p. 7.

for emigration, forbade the sale of emigrants' property, and outlawed promotional activity. As even these measures proved ineffective, emigration was banned outright in 1735. The canton of Bern had already prohibited emigration in 1717 on grounds that it was a threat to religious faith. The prohibition was apparently not fully effective, however, as increasingly harsh penalties were imposed in 1742, 1749, and 1753.[22] The first mass emigration from the Rhineland, in 1709, impelled a number of German states—the Palatinate, Hesse-Darmstadt, Württemberg, and Nassau—to close off their exits. Similar restrictions were announced in 1732 by Karl Albrecht of Bavaria and Frederick William I of Prussia, and in 1764 and 1766 by Maximilian Joseph of Bavaria.

It was in this period that national passports were introduced to control movement. Documents requesting safe passage for the bearer had been used as early as the Roman Empire, but the passport did not appear in Europe in the modern sense, as a document for border control, until the sixteenth and seventeenth centuries. By the end of the eighteenth century, it was obligatory everywhere in Europe except England.

For three centuries, then, the governments of Europe tried to prevent, or at least contain, the movement of Europeans to the New World. Given the difficulty of transatlantic travel, they had some success. But not much. Once the British welcomed immigrants to their colonies, the main obstacle was escaping the jurisdiction of one's own government; emigrants could then embark for America from ports in other countries.

Despite passports and other, more desperate measures, governments of the time simply lacked the physical and bureaucratic means to seal their borders effectively. France's Draconian penalties did not prevent Huguenots from fleeing. The sheer repetition of decrees and edicts in Switzerland and the German states attests to the futility of

22. Information on Swiss and German policies in this section is taken from Brite, pp. 201–20.

their efforts to contain emigration. In fact, probably a majority of the settlers who colonized the United States were "illegal" emigrants. As a Württemberg report of 1713 stated, "No remonstrance helps to check such people from departure who are once infatuated by the better circumstances of the American islands."[23] This porous control was the saving grace of a system that, unconcerned with individual rights and motivations, regarded human movement solely as a matter of state concern.

The Liberal Interlude

Throughout the age of absolutism, the monarch's authority to control emigration was virtually limitless. The early figures of international law—Grotius, Pufendorf, Wolff, Burlamaqui—regarded the right to emigrate as subject to the discretion of the state.[24] English common law recognized the right of the king to prevent an individual from departing if there was suspicion "that you design to go privately into foreign parts and intend to prosecute there many things prejudicial to us." By the end of the seventeenth century, however, the sovereign's power came under challenge from theorists who, appealing to natural rights and the social contract, placed new stress on the prerogatives of the individual. John Locke laid the foundation by insisting that the very nature of the social contract implies the right to withdraw from it: "Tis plain then . . . by the Law of right Reason, that a Child is born a Subject of no Country, or Government. He is under his Fathers Tuition and Authority, till he come to the Age of Discretion; and then he is a Free-man, at liberty what Government he will put himself under; what Body Politick he will unite himself to."[25] This is a classic statement of the right of personal self-determination. Like Socrates, however,

23. Ibid., p. 223.

24. See discussion in Frederick G. Whelan, "Citizenship and the Right to Leave," *American Political Science Review* 75 (September 1981): 648–49.

25. From the *Second Treatise*; quoted and analyzed by Whelan, pp. 647–48.

Locke felt that this choice could be exercised only once; after the individual had bound himself to a state, he could not revoke his allegiance to it.

Enlightenment thinkers enlarged the territory Locke had staked out. The first dramatic expression came in the Declaration of the Rights of Man, during the French Revolution. The revolutionary regime regarded the passport system and other attempts at control as vestiges of the old order. The French Constitution of 1791 guaranteed "the freedom of everyone to go, to stay, or to leave, without being halted or arrested unless in accordance with procedures established by the Constitution."

Before long, however, heavy emigration and the desertion of soldiers caused the National Assembly to renege on this guarantee. A series of measures in 1792–95 reinstituted passports and limited travel abroad, all in the name of national security—a justification with a modern ring to it. Nonetheless, the language of the French declaration and constitution helped shape later statements asserting the right to leave.

Free movement gained further support from the emerging school of laissez-faire economics. Directly challenging mercantilism, Adam Smith and his followers preached the virtues of free trade and a free labor market, objecting to anything that obstructed "the free circulation of labor from one employment to another."[26] As for international movement, the implication was that governments had no business interfering.

Adam Smith also helped change thinking about the role of colonies. Colonies, he argued, were valuable not just as suppliers of goods unavailable in Britain, but also as equal trading partners. Furthermore, the more population colonies acquired, the more valuable they would become. A British pauper who emigrated to the New World could become a buyer of British goods. No longer was there any economic justification for hoarding a country's population as if it were a precious metal.

26. Smith, p. 135.

By this time, the success of Britain's "open-door" colonial policy in North America, and of a similar Dutch policy in colonial South Africa, had demonstrated the wisdom of removing barriers to population movement. The American Revolution conversely showed that stocking a colony with dissenters and foreigners was not exactly an ideal way of assuring its loyalty. It might be preferable, in the future, to allow staunch citizens to take the lead in colonial emigration.

Meanwhile, the need to increase population at home was slackening. During the eighteenth century, the population of Europe had grown from about 118 million to 187 million. Apart from France, which had been devastated by the Revolution and the Napoleonic Wars, European states began to worry more about overpopulation than underpopulation. In 1798, Thomas Malthus published his gloomy treatise on the perils of population growth. Throughout the nineteenth century, population pressures played a major role in stimulating emigration. One student of the period has even detected a direct correlation between rises in birth rates and rates of emigration twenty years later, when the products of the current "baby boom" began to crowd the labor market.[27]

All these forces combined to push nineteenth-century Europe and the Americas close to the ideal of free international movement. As we have seen, such an ideal was approximated in premodern periods and in non-Western regions; for the modern Western world, however, this was a unique era, coming between the old serfdom and the new. For a few decades, movement within the Western world was governed largely by individual choice, making for a liberal interlude in an otherwise bleak continuum.

In Britain, the change was dramatic. As late as 1803, the government had enacted a Passenger Act designed to curb emigration. But, by the end of the Napoleonic Wars in 1815 there was a

27. Frank Thistlethwaite, "Migration from Europe Overseas in the Nineteenth and Twentieth Centuries," *Rapports,* vol. 5 (International Committee of Historical Sciences, Uppsala, 1960), p. 51.

new mood. Unemployment, social unrest, and a growing welfare burden brought home the costs of a proliferating population. Some worried that the country would not be able to feed its increasing numbers; others were wary of the rapid proliferation of the Irish Catholics. With the unseating of mercantilist orthodoxies, there was renewed enthusiasm for populating the Empire.

In the years that followed, the British government not only allowed emigrants to leave freely; it even assisted their departure. From 1815 to 1826 there were six different experiments in which the government organized, financed, or otherwise supported emigration to British colonies. The Colonial Land and Emigration Department, from 1847 to 1869, sponsored the travel of 339,000 emigrants to Australia and elsewhere.[28]

Attitudes toward national citizenship also changed. Britain had long subscribed to the doctrine of perpetual allegiance, which held that a British subject could not unilaterally renounce his duties to the crown. To enforce this principle, British officers had stopped American ships on the high seas to impress British-born seamen, despite their claims of American citizenship. The new American government took such exception to this that in 1812 it went to war with Britain. By the second half of the nineteenth century, however, the doctrine was at last abandoned. In 1870, Parliament voted that any citizen should be free to transfer his loyalty to another state.

One exception was skilled workers, especially those headed for the United States. For a time, prospective emigrants had to prove that they were not manufacturers or artificers (artisans) who might reveal important secrets to the competition. This requirement, like most others, was widely evaded, either through the use of forged certificates or through transit to the United States via Canada or France.

Following Britain's lead, other European countries gradually

28. H. J. M. Johnston, *British Emigration Policy: "Shoveling Out Paupers"* (Oxford: Clarendon, 1972); Isaac, p. 51.

dropped restrictions on movement. Switzerland did so in its 1798 and 1848 constitutions; Belgium, upon gaining independence in 1831; and Austria in 1832. By the late 1800s, it was possible to leave almost any European or American country and freely enter any other. The right to leave was becoming a cornerstone of modern democratic thought.

France, which considered itself underpopulated, retained some restrictions. Article 17 of the Civil Code deprived Frenchmen abroad of their citizenship if they failed to return. Additional restrictions were imposed during the Restoration (1815–30) and the reign of Napoleon III (1852–70). France also welcomed foreign workers, mainly Belgians and Italians, making it some time after midcentury the first European nation in modern times to attract more people than it sent out.[29]

The liberalization of this right did not necessarily extend to the vast areas of the globe under European rule. Colonial administrations typically limited movement in the interests of the imperial power. Where exit was allowed, it was often limited to destinations within the same colonial empire: Africans could move from one Portuguese colony to another, Indians to other British-controlled lands. Such movement was frequently manipulated to solve the ever-present labor shortages attending colonial expansion. As slavery disappeared, a new system of contract labor was developed to meet manpower needs. The British sent Indians to work in Malaya, Burma, Ceylon, Fiji, South Africa, and the Caribbean. Between 1835 and 1920, in one of the most massive—and most unpublicized—movements in history, some 27.7 million Indians left India for other British dominions.[30]

In its worst manifestations, contract labor inhibited free movement almost as much as serfdom had. While the contract was in theory voluntary, it was often concluded under conditions where

29. Zolberg, "International Migration Policies," pp. 262–63.

30. D. K. Fieldhouse, *Colonialism, 1870–1945* (New York: St. Martin's, 1981), pp. 69–78; McNeill, *The Great Frontier,* p. 50.

economic desperation left laborers with few options. Once transported, the laborer was effectively tied to the place of employment for the length of the contract, after which return home could be mandatory. The same was true of other systems with elements of compulsory labor, including peonage in parts of Latin America, sharecropping in the American South, and the exploitative labor system of South Africa—all of which survived into the twentieth century.

America: Love It or Leave It

The nations of the New World were settled by people exercising their right to leave. Not surprisingly, then, North and South Americans developed into perhaps the most outspoken champions of unrestricted movement. The nations of Latin America, once freed from the suffocating grasp of Spain, sought to attract as many new settlers as possible. So did the United States and Canada. The nature of the frontier, in particular, placed a premium on unfettered movement and helped make the United States perhaps the most internally mobile society ever.

Restrictions on movement constituted one of the critical issues dividing the American colonists from George III. The Declaration of Independence accused the king of obstructing immigration to the colonies in order to limit their population. Thomas Jefferson, in proposing instructions to Virginia's delegates to the 1774 Continental Congress, wanted to remind King George "that our ancestors, before their emigration to America, were the free inhabitants of the British dominions in Europe and possessed a right which nature has given to all men of departing from the country in which chance, not choice, has placed them, of going in quest of new habitations, and of there establishing new societies under such laws and regulations as, to them, shall seem most likely to promote public happiness."[31]

31. Quoted by Whelan, p. 650.

The right to leave was central to Jefferson's overall indictment of the Crown. If the colonists had needed permission to leave England, this implied an allegiance they could not break unilaterally. If, on the other hand, migrants were exercising a natural right, then they were also free to reassess their relationship with the British sovereign.

After gaining independence, the United States in practice respected the right of movement. Curiously, though, despite the dispute with the British, not to mention the country's long tradition of mobility, American law was at first quite ambivalent on the subject of international movement. Building on English common law, which seemingly allowed the government to prohibit departures, leading American legal authorities argued as late as 1851 that *in theory,* at least, no one could leave the country without permission.[32]

Furthermore, despite American hostility to the British claim of "once British, always British," scholars also disputed a citizen's right to relinquish his American citizenship. In 1799, an American judge, seeking to resolve the contradiction, dubiously argued that "in countries so crowded with inhabitants that the means of subsistence are difficult to be obtained, it is reason and policy to permit emigration. But our policy is different; for our country is but sparsely settled, and we have no inhabitants to spare."[33] Presidents Madison and Monroe—both supposedly strong disciples of Thomas Jefferson—asserted that Americans could not voluntarily expatriate themselves, and in 1830 two Supreme Court decisions backed them up.

Only after the Civil War was the issue resolved. Again, it was the British who stirred matters up, this time by arresting some naturalized Irish-Americans in Ireland and dealing with them as

32. From the commentaries by Story and Kent, as noted by Stig Jagerskiold, "The Freedom of Movement," in *The International Bill of Rights,* ed. Louis Henkin (New York: Columbia University Press, 1981), p. 169.

33. I-mien Tsiang, *The Question of Expatriation in America Prior to 1907* (Baltimore: The Johns Hopkins University Press, 1942), pp. 32–33; see also pp. 38, 62, 69–70, 113.

British citizens. This affront to American dignity goaded Congress to pass an act in 1868 declaring that "the right of expatriation is a natural and inherent right of all people, indispensable to the enjoyment of the rights of life, liberty, and the pursuit of happiness."

While this would seem to imply that U.S. citizens, too, possessed the right of expatriation, the U.S. government was not yet ready to concede it. The State Department still had the right to exercise discretion in such cases. Through the end of the nineteenth century, it recognized the loss of U.S. citizenship only when a person had undergone statutory naturalization abroad. Finally, in 1907, Congress passed into law explicit guidelines that recognized the right to surrender U.S. citizenship and detailed the procedures for doing so. This at last brought the law into line with reality, and put the United States firmly on the side of free movement and personal self-determination.

The Great Atlantic Migration

In the century following 1815, about 55 million Europeans went abroad, mostly to the New World. The population of the "new" regions of the globe (the Americas and Oceana), which made up 3 percent of the world's population in 1750, accounted for 16 percent in 1930.[34] Since the "cost" of emigration is a matter of current concern, it is important to consider the impact of this massive movement on the countries of origin. Did the outflow help relieve population pressures? Did it threaten to depopulate these countries? How did the movement affect social structures, national development, and living standards?

Curiously enough, emigration did little to slow population growth. It did, however, enable countries to avoid having to lower their birth rates. The countries with the highest rates of emigration took the longest to reduce their birth rates. Despite massive emigration, Europe's population as a whole grew from 194 million in

34. Davis, p. 99.

1840 to 463 million in 1930—double the growth rate of the world as a whole.[35]

The one exception was Ireland, which was severely depopulated by emigration. In 1841, just before the Great Famine, the country had 6,529,000 inhabitants; by 1881, this had dropped to 3,870,000—the result primarily of emigration triggered by economic distress and political unrest. Ireland therefore provides a good test case for the argument that massive population loss causes a nation grave ills.

Surprisingly, the large-scale emigration, far from causing a crisis, apparently benefited those left behind. The exodus of surplus workers caused wages to rise. The sale and consolidation of small farms helped place agriculture on a more efficient footing, easing the transition from tillage to pasturage. The economy was buoyed by remittances from America, which totaled $250 million from 1850 to 1900. The "Yanks" who returned to Ireland, though small in number, made a sizable contribution in capital and know-how. Historians now conclude that, at the end of the century, the standard of living was higher than it would have been had no emigration taken place.[36]

In Europe as a whole, emigration contributed to social stability. Emigration helps explain how Europe managed to survive a period of such wrenching social and economic change with so few internal convulsions.[37] America served as a safety valve. The exit of many activists and potential revolutionaries probably facilitated the political accommodation of those left behind. In Italy, for example, the rate

35. Ibid., pp. 98–99.

36. Arnold Schrier, *Ireland and the American Emigration, 1850–1900* (Minneapolis: University of Minnesota Press, 1958), pp. 149–53; Isaac, p. 143.

37. See, for example, Richard C. Haskett, et al., "Problems and Prospects in the History of American Immigration," in *A Report on World Population Migrations as Related to the United States of America* (Washington, D.C.: The George Washington University, 1956), p. 49.

of emigration during the decade previous to World War I is clearly correlated to a decline in votes for Socialist parties.[38]

Moreover, concern over mass emigration spurred governments to make needed reforms. In Sweden, for example, "the granting of home loans on easy terms, the development of a frontier in Lappland, the establishment of old age insurance, a state mortgage bank, universal suffrage, and the adoption of religious freedom came as a conscious effort to make the homeland more attractive to those who might otherwise desire to leave."[39]

Another consequence of easy movement in the nineteenth century was a drop in the number of refugees. While the revolutions of 1848–49 produced a flow of political refugees, mainly from the German states and Hungary, the major flows occurred in politically less developed areas, where the right to leave or remain had not taken root. In the late nineteenth and early twentieth centuries, large numbers of Jews and other persecuted minorities were forced from Russia and, to a lesser extent, from Romania and the Slavic areas of the Austro-Hungarian Empire. In the Ottoman Empire, growing Turkish nationalism was directed at the Armenian minority in particular, culminating in massive expulsion and genocide during World War I (see chapter 3). Despite these exceptions, the deliberate displacement of entire population groups was not common. The more freedom individuals had to choose their home, the less pressure governments felt to resort to coercion.

Meanwhile, by the end of the century, the patterns of the "Great Migration" were changing. Movement within Europe itself became more common than overseas migration, and some states,

38. John S. MacDonald, "Agricultural Organization, Migration and Labour Militancy in Rural Italy," *Economic Historic Review* 2d ser. 16 (1963–64): 61–75, cited by Albert O. Hirschman, "Exit, Voice, and the State," *World Politics* 31 (Winter 1978): 102.

39. Franklin D. Scott, *Emigration and Immigration* (New York: Macmillan, 1963), p. 56.

especially France and Germany, began taking in more people than they lost. This change reflected a more general shift in world migration. For three centuries, the primary flow (except for slavery and contract labor) had been from developed Europe to new areas of the globe. Now the flow was reversing, from less to more developed areas. The typical migrants of the past—the Spanish conquistador in Mexico, the Scandinavian farmer in the Dakotas, the English convict in Sydney—now gave way to the Irish factory hand in London, the Italian peasant in New York, the North African worker in France.

Moreover, as transportation became steadily cheaper, migration increasingly acquired a temporary character. What we now call migrant labor originated in this period. By 1850, about one-quarter of the industrial work force in England was Irish. Polish workers streamed into Germany, and Belgians and Italians into France. Now a new set of problems developed. Lowly in status and culturally alien, the new migrant workers encountered resentment and unrest. To protect themselves, the host countries (especially Germany) began to regulate the flow of migrants more strictly, much in the way of contemporary guest worker programs.[40]

Closing the Door to Immigrants

The resentment aroused by migrant labor pointed up the sensitive nature of the new immigration patterns. So long as movement was directed to open spaces, to undeveloped, largely defenseless areas, immigration control was minimal. Unrestricted entry seemed to be natural in the nineteenth-century world of free movement. There was even serious debate over whether states had the *right* to restrict immigration. In 1892 the Institute of International Law proposed that "the free entrance of aliens into the territory of a civilized state should not be curtailed in a general and permanent manner other

40. Zolberg, "Patterns of International Migration Policy: A Diachronic Comparison," in *Minorities: Community and Identity,* ed. C. Fried (Berlin: Springer, 1983), p. 238.

than in the interest of public welfare and for the most serious of reasons."[41] Latin American states often included the right of immigration in their constitutions.

Not that anti-immigration sentiment was lacking. Antagonism to aliens has probably accompanied every major influx of foreigners in history. The United States, for example, gave birth to numerous nativist movements, and efforts to cut off immigration date back almost to Plymouth Rock. In 1654, for instance, Governor Peter Stuyvesant of New Amsterdam protested bitterly against admitting Jewish refugees to his city, where eighteen different languages were already spoken.

In fact, immigration into the United States has always been characterized by some selectivity. It began with the choice of where immigrants were recruited, and was reinforced by shipping regulations that discouraged the transportation of non-Europeans. Naturalization laws excluded nonwhites. And in the late nineteenth century, Congress began to add more specific restrictions. In 1875 it voted to exclude prostitutes and criminals guilty of "moral turpitude." In 1882 this was extended to "convicts, lunatics, idiots, and those likely to become a public charge." At the same time, all Chinese were excluded (a move quickly copied by Australia and Canada). By agreement with Japan in 1908, no Japanese were to be allowed to leave their country for the United States.

Then, around the turn of the century, the massive immigration from eastern and southern Europe aroused a new wave of nativist sentiment. In 1911 an Immigration Commission, chaired by Senator William Dillingham, issued a massive report that viewed the "alien" invasion with alarm and laid the foundation for the discriminatory immigration restrictions of the 1920s. In Britain, too, new restrictions on entry were put in place. The foundation was laid for far-reaching exclusion policies after World War I.

41. R. Plender, *International Migration Law* (Leiden: A. W. Sijthoff, 1972), p. 53.

The late nineteenth and early twentieth centuries represent the closest approximation to an open world in modern times. Every European and American state except Russia regarded the right to emigrate as basic and inalienable. With immigration restrictions at a minimum, real freedom of international movement was a fact. The right of personal self-determination was reasonably secure for residents of Europe and the Americas, if not for other peoples ruled by them. Passports, which had fallen into disuse in much of the West, were required only in the Ottoman Empire, Russia, Romania, Bulgaria, and Bosnia/Herzegovina. In fact, the right to cross frontiers had become so generally accepted that formal guarantees were considered unnecessary. It was only when the right came under serious assault, in the twentieth century, that the need to assert it became more urgent.

3

The New Serfdom

It was a metaphysical absurdity to ask: "What if one wants to leave paradise?"

—Lev Navrozov, Soviet émigré

An Italian peasant seeking to emigrate in the 1920s might have been confused. Had he sought to leave before 1927, his government would have pushed him; after that date, it would have restrained him. In the Soviet Union, a citizen would have found it very difficult to leave—unless he was an opponent of the regime, and in that case, he might be forced to go. In either case, the government was eliminating individual choice in emigration decisions. Still, the Italian peasant and the Soviet citizen would have been more fortunate than a Jew in Nazi Germany. In an age of closing doors, many German Jews would not survive.

After the relatively free movement of the nineteenth century, emigration and immigration in the twentieth have become restricted as never before. In a general assault on the right of personal self-determination, walls have been built to keep people in as well as out, making sanctuary for the oppressed hard to find. Traditional places of refuge began closing their gates at the turn of the century. The symbolism of Ellis Island was replaced by the symbolism of the

Soviet Gulag, the Armenian and Assyrian massacres, Dachau and Auschwitz.

Between the two world wars, more and more regimes instituted coercive emigration policies. These worked both to choke off the outflow of people and to compel it, the two methods being "complementary techniques of control."[1] Techniques for sealing borders were perfected at the time of the most massive dislocations in history (though even larger numbers would be displaced during and after World War II). The tragic irony was that most who moved did not want to, and most who wanted to move could not. It was, indeed, a new serfdom.

Ironically, all of this occurred as the right to leave and remain was gaining legal recognition. In the nineteenth century, these rights had been widely honored in practice without explicit codification; in this century, they have been violated routinely despite growing legal guarantees. As the gap between practice and profession widened, official discussion of emigration policies became cloaked in pretense—hypocrisy being, in La Rochefoucauld's words, the tribute that vice pays to virtue.

Why the sudden change? For one thing, birth rates across Europe began dropping in the late nineteenth century, causing a brake on population growth. In addition, industrial take-off and the introduction of welfare policies reduced the pressures for emigration. Germany, England, and the nations of Scandinavia joined France as countries experiencing net immigration.

In addition, empty space was rapidly disappearing. Most attractive agricultural land in North America, Australia, and elsewhere was now occupied. In fact, the flow from Europe to the New World had slackened even before the enactment of restrictive American laws. Now movement was more likely to take place within—or into—

1. Aristide Zolberg, "International Migrations in Political Perspective," in *Global Trends in Migration: Theory and Research on International Population Movements,* ed. Mary M. Kritz, Charles B. Keely, and Silvano M. Tomasi (New York: Center for Migration Studies, 1981), p. 23.

Europe itself. Italians traveled to France rather than New York or Boston; Poles, too, were more likely to move to Western Europe. Colonial ties provided other channels: Algerians migrated to France, Indians and Caribbean blacks to Britain, Indonesians to the Netherlands. By the 1930s, Europe was gaining more people than it lost.

Meanwhile, immigration was encountering new opposition, the result of cultural antipathies, fear of job shortages, and plain racism. Growing political and economic instability, combined with heightened nationalism, fed the urge to exclude foreigners. Germany in the 1930s was no longer a hospitable environment for the oppressed of Eastern Europe. Furthermore, improved communication and transportation raised fears of even more massive hordes from Asia, the West Indies, and other remote regions.

The role of the state was itself changing. After World War I, countries became increasingly identified with the aspirations of specific nationalities: Poland for the Poles, Turkey for the Turks, Albania for the Albanians. Whereas previously the regulation of emigration had been justified primarily as a matter of protecting the individual—for example, maintenance of family obligations or protection of women and minors—it was now the interests of the state that took precedence.

Many states found themselves in a bind. Falling birth rates and the devastating losses of the Great War caused considerable pressure to conserve or increase national manpower; in some places, serious labor shortages loomed. However, popular resistance to open immigration closed off this traditional method of meeting manpower needs. As a result, governments felt called upon to curtail emigration.

Migration also clashed with prevailing cultural values. The belief in ethnic homogeneity made the notion of choosing one's nationality somewhat suspect. As national loyalty came to be perceived as the cement of society, emigration was increasingly regarded as deviant behavior. This became especially true as international differences sharpened along ethnic or ideological lines, making emigration seem almost traitorous. And, as in earlier periods, the more uniform national identities became, the less diversity was tolerated. Refugees were also a natural by-product of consolidation and national development.

While much of the assault on free movement derived from surging nationalism and the strengthening of the nation-state, the new serfdom was also an expression of contemporary political beliefs. The era of the individual, it was proclaimed, had passed; individual political identity must now be defined solely in relation to the state.

The Collectivist Ethic

As supporters of free trade argue that the flow of goods will regulate itself, so defenders of free movement contend that the unhindered flow of people will find a natural balance. In this view, the accumulation of millions of individual decisions will produce a better social result than any centralized scheme of control. The movement of people thus serves as a "thermostat" of the relative pressures and opportunities existing in different societies.

A contrary school advocates regulating the flow of both goods and people, in the presumed interest of the whole society, which in practice often means a narrow part of it. Governments have come to play an increasing role in directing economic life, even more so than at the peak of mercantilism. (Appropriately, the term *neo-mercantilist* is sometimes used to describe this tendency.) The collectivism of the twentieth century is indeed rooted in the old organistic conception of the state, in which the individual is seen as only a cog in the whole. Modern variants simply take to a logical conclusion the traditional ideology of the benevolent despot who seeks to achieve national prosperity by identifying his own strong-handed leadership with the welfare of society.[2] The twentieth-century version, however,

2. See the discussion of "enlightened despotism's ideology of unbounded material progress in a harmonious community ordered and directed by an omniscient leader and elite," in Marc Raeff, *The Well-Ordered Police State* (New Haven and London: Yale University Press, 1983), p. 254.

takes this model to its brutal extreme in radical ideologies that exalt the state and enforce its prerogatives with the efficiency afforded by modern technology.

Such ideologies may spring from either the left or the right; neither end of the political spectrum has a monopoly on collectivist zeal. What they do share is a determination to submerge the individual. Benito Mussolini proclaimed that "if the nineteenth century was a century of individualism . . . it may be expected that this will be the century of collectivism, and hence the century of the state."[3] Another Fascist idealogue, Giovanni Gentile, claimed that "It may be said that I, as a citizen, have indeed a will of my own; but that upon further investigation my will is found to coincide exactly with the will of the state, and I want anything only insofar as the state wants me to want it."[4] At the opposite political pole, Nikita Khrushchev asserted: "Each person must, like a bee in the hive, make his own contribution to increasing the material and spiritual wealth of society. . . . We are living in an organized socialist society where the interests of the individual conform to the interests of society and are not at variance with them."[5]

Given this stress on the unity of individual and state, collectivist regimes have little room for deviance or dissent; their continued presence must be due to a failure of leadership. Leaders are therefore inclined to deny that the phenomenon exists. One result is a drive for total consensus and a passion for unanimity that is reminiscent of medieval attitudes toward dissenters and heretics. If the gospel as preached is universally valid, the existence of nonbelievers is an affront to the established order. All members of society should be active and believing participants. Such a view, of course, can be used

---

3. Mussolini, "Dottrina del fascismo," *Opera omnia,* 34 (Florence: Fenice, 1951–63): 128.

4. Gentile, *La riforma dell'educazione* (Florence: Sansoni, 1955), p. 25.

5. Quoted in A. Kassof, "The Administered Society: Totalitarianism without Terror," *World Politics* 16 (July 1964): 558.

to justify compelling most citizens to stay, while forcing some to leave.

In this context, leaving a society acquires a new significance. It becomes an act of disloyalty, desertion from a common cause, even treachery aimed at overthrowing the authorities. Thus, laws frequently categorize unauthorized departure from the state as high treason. Similarly, in some cases, stiff exit taxes are imposed on those who migrate to ideologically dissimilar states, but not on those who move to "fraternal societies."

Collectivist regimes seek not only to avoid the embarrassment of mass defection, but also to limit contact with hostile environments. In order to rally the public behind the regime, they promote the image of a homeland beset by enemies on all sides. Hitler painted horrific pictures of the Bolshevist threat to Germany, while the Soviets reciprocally appealed to the threat of Nazism (or, later, German revanchism) and imperialist encirclement. Such regimes are innately hostile to the free flow of people and ideas across national frontiers. The nation in effect exists in a perpetual state of siege and mobilization.

Collectivist regimes further perceive *pluralism*—unassimilated groups and their competing claims of identity—as a threat to internal control. So, like the centralizing monarchies of early modern Europe, modern collectivists both close off emigration to make assimilation appear inescapable and force out those individuals and groups that prove unassimilable.

Closing off free emigration is probably an essential policy for any regime that relies heavily on coercion. So long as the option of leaving remains open, the regime must confront sources of dissatisfaction. Groups that resist regimentation will remain stubborn as long as escape remains an option; only when that option is foreclosed will they come to terms with the prevailing order.[6]

6. Albert O. Hirschman, in *Exit, Voice, and Loyalty: Responses to Decline in Firms, Organizations, and States* (Cambridge: Harvard University Press, 1970), pp. 3–20, 120–21, posits "exit" and "voice" (attempts to change a system from within) as the basic options when one is dissatisfied, and concludes that a one-party system will of necessity be driven to suppress both options.

The opposite technique, expulsion, is used against those the regime does *not* want to, or cannot, assimilate. These are typically ethnic groups or prominent individual dissenters and activists. The idea of the nation-state was from the beginning potentially threatening to minority groups, since it could be used to justify the political supremacy of a country's dominant nationality. By the early twentieth century, and even more after World War I, minorities faced unenviable conditions in all the new nation-states of Eastern Europe (Poland, Czechoslovakia, Hungary, Yugoslavia), as well as in such older states as Germany and Romania. As Hannah Arendt expressed it, "denationalization became a powerful weapon of totalitarian politics," making the mass expulsion of unwanted minorities a common feature of modern politics.[7]

Apart from minority politics, collectivist states also use expulsion as a weapon against dissent. As in earlier periods, expulsion serves as a safety valve draining off sources of disruption. Activists and opposition leaders whose presence encourages resistance are forced out even as the bulk of the population is confined. The problem is how to get rid of a few without planting the idea of exit in the minds of the many. Finding a workable balance can obviously be a ticklish matter, as shown by the fluctuating policies of such states as Cuba. On the whole, the more coercive the regime, the more it tends to limit use of expulsion to extreme cases; such regimes are more dependent on total mobilization of the public as active participants in the new order and are better equipped to deal with dissent by methods other than expulsion. On the other hand, regimes with a less efficient apparatus of control may feel that they have no option but to expel potential challengers to authority.[8]

The migration policies of modern collectivist societies bear

7. Hannah Arendt, *The Origins of Totalitarianism* (New York: Meridian, 1958), pp. 269, 275.

8. Zolberg, "International Migration Policies in a Changing World System," in *Human Migration: Patterns and Policies,* ed. William H. McNeill and Ruth Adams (Bloomington: Indiana University Press, 1978), p. 272.

striking similarities to the classical mercantilism of the absolute monarchs. Both seek to seal in an entire population rather than just specific groups. Both are also concerned with state-building and the preservation of economic strength by keeping skilled personnel at home. But the differences are perhaps more striking. Twentieth-century collectivism is less concerned with increasing numbers than with achieving social homogeneity and mobilizing the public behind the ruling power. The contemporary stress on ideology and ethnicity results in a much reduced tolerance for diversity. More tragically, those who are forced to emigrate have far fewer havens of refuge; while the mercantilists sought to attract immigrants, refugees in the twentieth century often find themselves universally unwanted.

Even more important, perhaps, is that international movement can actually be controlled in the twentieth century. In the past, massive numbers of people exercised their right to leave in defiance of all prohibitions, decrees, and exhortations. Even in the late nineteenth century, millions of illegal emigrants still poured out of countries like Tsarist Russia. Few governments actually had comprehensive physical control of their borders; nor did they have bureaucracies sophisticated enough to pick out legal from illegal migrants as they passed through border posts.

Effective control of international movement was one of the many legacies that World War I left to the modern world. Passports, which had been required by only a few countries, were reintroduced as a wartime measure and never disappeared. Now most countries required a valid passport not only to enter but also to leave. In a 1925 League of Nations survey, forty of forty-three countries fell into this category, the United States and Canada being two of the exceptions.[9]

Governments justified this requirement on the grounds that other states required passports for entry anyway. But the result was to give the state de facto control over the foreign travel of its citizens.

9. International Labour Office, *Migration Laws and Treaties,* vol. 1: *Emigration Laws and Regulations* (Geneva: International Labour Office, 1928), pp. 79–89.

The right to a passport might be universally upheld, but bureaucratic stonewalling could effectively stymie movement. Furthermore, by 1925, at least twenty countries required exit visas as well as passports and set conditions for the visas that clearly infringed on free movement. Overall, the new infrastructure of regulation and border controls facilitated strictures on movement as never before, though some states, of course, made greater use of these means than others.

The Soviet Variant

The Soviet Union is central to any study of modern emigration policies. It was the first modern state to control international movement systematically, and it has since served as an influential model to many other countries. Therefore, the Soviet experience in the interwar period will be examined in some depth. This does not mean that the Soviet Union is necessarily the most egregious practitioner of the new serfdom, nor that such control is unique to Soviet ideology. The reality is more complex.

The story begins well before the Russian Revolution. Hostility toward individual freedom of mobility is deeply rooted in Russian tradition. Current practices—the requirement of residence permits, resistance to frequent job-changing, bars to departures from collective farms, and a refusal to acknowledge renunciations of Soviet citizenship—are modern embodiments of deep-seated attitudes. Even voluntary organizations do not allow for resignation, and members seeking to leave may be expelled for their presumptuousness.[10]

Russian political thought has traditionally lacked any concept or suggestion of limited government. The hold of absolutism was so total that it was not fully formulated as a theory until the nineteenth century, when the first serious challenges to Tsarism finally forced a systematic defense of autocracy. Russians also stressed collectivity more than any Western tradition did. Even radicals like Alexander

10. Valery Chalidze, *To Defend These Rights: Human Rights and the Soviet Union* (New York: Random House, 1974), p. 105.

Herzen saw the solution to despotism not in Western individualism but in a collectivism drawn from Slavic communal institutions and Western utopian socialist ideas.

This stress on the whole was reinforced by Russia's centuries-old suspicion of the outside world and its urge to be closed off from it. Prince Kurbsky, the Russian nobleman who fled from Russia in the late sixteenth century and then engaged in a famous correspondence with Ivan the Terrible, taxed the Tsar with this "unpraiseworthy habit. . . . For you shut up the kingdom of Russia—in other words, free human nature—as in a fortress of hell; and whoever, according to the prophet, goes from your land 'to strange countries', as Jesus the son of Sirach says, you call a traitor; and if he is caught on the frontier, you punish him with various forms of death."[11] Pushkin has Tsar Boris Godunov commanding, a few years later,

> Take steps this very instant
> To fence our Russia off from Lithuania
> With barriers, so that not a single soul
> May pass the line; that not even a hare
> Can scurry here from Poland; that no raven
> Can come winging its way from Krakow.[12]

In the early eighteenth century, Montesquieu's fictitious Persian envoy in Moscow wrote that "the Muscovites may not leave their country, even in order to travel; and so, separated from other nations by the law of the land, they have become attached to their ancient customs, all the more warmly that they do not think it possible to have others."[13]

11. *The Correspondence between Prince A. M. Kurbsky and Tsar Ivan IV of Russia, 1564–1579,* ed. J. L. I. Fennell (Cambridge: Cambridge University Press, 1955), p. 215.

12. Alexander Pushkin, *Boris Godunov,* trans. Philip L. Barbour (New York: Columbia University Press, 1953), p. 71.

13. Charles Louis, Baron de Montesquieu, *Persian and Chinese Letters,* trans. John Davidson (Washington and London: M. Walter Dunne, 1901), p. 109.

When Montesquieu wrote this, most Russians were still fettered by serfdom. But even the nobility was bound to state service throughout most of the Tsarist period and thus could not freely travel abroad. Only at the time of Catherine the Great, toward the end of the eighteenth century, were nobles granted free movement. Foreign travel thus became a privilege of the gentry—much as today it is a prerogative of the Soviet elite.

Some limited emigration did occur beginning in the late eighteenth century, but it was not exactly calculated to make future Russian governments think well of free movement. The flow consisted of cultural expatriates, political exiles (some reflecting Tsarist use of the safety valve), and, later in the century, an increasing number of non-Russian refugees. Those who traveled to the West and back became a channel for "subversive" influences, causing an increasingly Westernized elite to become alienated from the existing order. The activities of exile groups also became a source of growing concern. It is no surprise that the Bolsheviks, having themselves operated as an exile group, would after seizing power become extremely leery of émigré communities.

During the Tsarist period, passports were generally not issued for the purpose of emigration, and remaining abroad for more than five years was, according to the nineteenth-century criminal code, a punishable offense. Those who did manage to obtain passports for temporary travel often did not return, however; furthermore, bureaucratic controls were primitive and the borders fairly porous. For example, Jews often traveled illegally on pilgrimage to Palestine. The government's major sanction was revocation of citizenship and, consequently, the right to return. This also applied to legal passport holders who did not return within a specified period.

Some efforts were made at organized emigration. In 1846, Jacob Isaac Altaras, a French Jew, proposed to the Russian government a scheme for the large-scale resettlement of Russian Jews in Algeria. The Tsarist government at first—in strikingly modern style—demanded a per capita payment for each exit permit. But, once recognizing an opportunity to reduce the Jewish population, it approved the departure of large groups (excluding men of draft age). The project was finally vetoed by the French, who were horrified at the idea of "Judaizing" Algeria.[14]

After the assassination of Tsar Alexander II in 1881, officially inspired waves of persecution made the position of Russian Jews precarious. Nonetheless, emigration was still prohibited. The Minister of Interior, Nikolai Ignatev, declared in 1882 that, given the fact that "emigration does not exist for Russian citizens," talk of mass Jewish emigration was "incitement to sedition."[15]

Large numbers of Jews left anyway, often smuggled out without passports by agents of shipping lines. The sheer scale of the illegal emigration—about two million people between 1880 and 1914—suggests the connivance of at least lower-level Russian officials. Senior officials, too, were probably not entirely averse to the departure of Jews, given the government's clear hostility to them. Very few emigrants were caught or turned back as they left. In fact, the Jewish exodus from Russia clearly seemed the result of deliberate policy, though the Tsarist regime could never accept free emigration in principle. President Benjamin Harrison complained in his Third Annual Message (1891) that "this Government has found occasion to express in a friendly spirit, but with much earnestness, to the Government of the Czar its serious concern because of the harsh measures now being enforced against the Hebrews in Russia. . . . The banishment, whether by direct decree or by not less certain indirect methods, of so large a number of men and women is not a local question."[16]

14. Salo W. Baron, *The Russian Jew under Tsars and Soviets* (New York: Macmillan, 1976), pp. 38, 70; Hans Rogger, "Tsarist Policy on Jewish Emigration," *Soviet Jewish Affairs* 3 (1973): 27.

15. In a conversation with Samuel Poliakov, a Jewish railroad builder with access to high officials, Baron, p. 364; Rogger, p. 28. Rogger stresses the inconsistency of Tsarist policy toward Jewish emigration; on another occasion, for example, Ignatev declared that "the Western frontier is open to Jews."

16. Quoted in Baron, p. 49.

Before coming to power, the Bolsheviks condemned these Tsarist policies. They called for the removal of controls on movement along with other such tools of class oppression. In his "Address to the Village Poor," Lenin castigated such controls as enslavement: "What does this mean, this *freedom to move from place to place?* It means that the peasant must be free to go where he pleases . . . to choose for himself the village or the town he prefers, without having to ask for permission. It means that passports must be abolished in Russia. . . . The peasant is a child who dares not move without authority! Is this not serfdom, I ask you?"[17]

The first program of the Social-Democratic Labor Party—the Marxist movement in Russia—included the demand for "abolition of passports, full freedom of movement and residence."[18] This was clearly consistent with classical Marxism, which identified the state as an instrument of oppression and asserted that human rights would be realized only when the state withered away. Pre-Soviet varieties of Marxism (and many later ones) do not require, or even justify, government control over human movement.

Soviet Marxism, or Marxism-Leninism, is a different story. Whatever Lenin's direct pronouncements on freedom of movement, his views on the state laid the basis for future controls. Even before the Revolution, Lenin had argued in *State and Revolution* that in order to suppress exploitation during the transition from capitalism to communism, "a special machine for suppression, the 'state', is still necessary." He called for the "strictest control" of the economy by the state, and for making all citizens into "hired employees" of the state. In a pamphlet published on the eve of the Bolshevik Revolu-

17. Quoted in Herbert McClosky and John E. Turner, *The Soviet Dictatorship* (New York: McGraw-Hill, 1960), p. 470; see also Roy A. Medvedev, *On Socialist Democracy* (New York: Knopf, 1975), p. 211.

18. Jiri Toman, "The Right to Leave and to Return in Eastern Europe," in *The Right to Leave and to Return,* ed. Karel Vasak and Sidney Liskofsky (New York: American Jewish Committee, 1976), p. 120.

tion, he called for issuing workbooks in order to compel the wealthy to work.[19]

So despite Lenin's attack on Tsarist restrictions and the massive movement of those chaotic first years, the new regime instituted passport controls and, a mere two months after the Revolution, forbade the exit of belligerent nationals. The Bolsheviks also drew up general rules on entry and exit, something neglected under the Tsars.[20]

The Bolshevik attitude toward emigration was also shaped by civil war and foreign intervention. It was feared that those leaving the country would swell the ranks of the White armies and other enemies abroad. From there it was a short step to equating the wish to emigrate with opposition to the socialist state. From the beginning, the Soviet government refused to recognize any legitimate grounds for leaving, except for prior citizenship in another state.

In 1918, the Brest-Litovsk Treaty obligated the Soviets to allow the emigration of those, mainly non-Russians, who wished to opt for German citizenship, but the regime tried to reduce the flow by allowing only one month for the process to take place. A similar maneuver was used against foreign citizens in the Ukraine. At the same time, some groups were allowed, or even helped, to leave the country. In the early 1920s, for instance, a limited number of Jews were allowed to join their families abroad. In fact, a small stream of Zionists was permitted to emigrate to Palestine until the mid-1930s.[21]

19. V. I. Lenin, *The State and Revolution* (Moscow: Foreign Languages Publishing House, n.d.), pp. 144, 155, 161; Lenin, *Can the Bolsheviks Retain State Power?* (Moscow: Progress, 1971), p. 24.

20. Yuri Felshtinsky, "Legal Foundations of the Immigration and Emigration Policy of the USSR, 1917–27," *Soviet Studies* 34 (July 1982): 328.

21. Gitelman, *Jewish Nationality and Soviet Politics: The Jewish Sections of the CPSU, 1917–1930* (Princeton: Princeton University Press, 1972), pp. 235–36; Julius Margolin, "Russian-Jewish Immigration into Israel," in *Russian Jewry, 1917–1967,* ed. Gregor Aronson, Jacob Frumkin, Alexis Goldenweiser, and Joseph Lewitan (New York: Thomas Yoseloff, 1969), pp. 541–44.

From the outset, however, the clear intent of the regime was to curtail outward flow as much as possible. In 1919, travel abroad required approval from both the People's Commissariat for Internal Affairs (NKVD) and the People's Commissariat for Military Affairs; a year later the consent of the Special Department of the Cheka (the secret police) was added. Workers were forbidden to leave their workplace without the consent of their employer. Then, in 1922, both Russia and the Ukraine issued general rules for travel that foreclosed virtually all departures. Legal emigration had become all but impossible.[22]

The one obstacle to complete control was the regime's inability to seal its borders. For those who made it across, the government had to content itself with punishing family members who remained. The authorities also used amnesties and other means to entice Russians back from abroad, especially former soldiers who might be recruited by the White army. In 1923 all Russians of military age were ordered to return home or face penalties.[23]

This does not mean, of course, that the Soviet government welcomed all comers with open arms. Control of entry was no less strict than control of exit. Wary of those who might be hostile to the Revolution, the government carefully screened all returning Russians. As for immigration by non-Russians, the Soviets accepted only committed Communists come to build the new society; once arrived, they were prohibited from having any contact with their home countries. Even this immigration, however, was gradually reduced, due in part to economic strains, and by 1927 it had practically ceased.[24]

By the end of the 1920s, the Soviet government finally achieved what it had clearly been seeking from the start: to seal itself off entirely from a hostile environment. While a system of border guards

22. Felshtinsky, pp. 337–40; Neil Harding, "Socialism, Society, and the Organic Labor State," in *The State in Socialist Society,* ed. Neil Harding (Albany: State University of New York Press, 1984), p. 32.

23. Felshtinsky, p. 341.

24. Ibid., pp. 328–36.

was established in 1918, effective control began with the founding in 1923 of a special corps of the GPU (successor to the Cheka). To ensure dedication and loyalty, border guards were specially selected, trained, and rewarded. By 1928, illegal departure had become almost impossible.

But even then, new, stricter regulations were introduced.[25] In 1929, for example, the government decreed that any Soviet official serving abroad who went over "to the camp of the enemies of the working class and the peasants," and who refused to return to the Soviet Union, would be executed within twenty-four hours of being apprehended.[26]

Strict internal controls were imposed in the early 1930s as Stalin's first Five-Year Plan and forced collectivization gathered force. To allocate scarce housing and to weed out "nonproductive" elements, the government in 1932 introduced the internal passport. Together with the residence permit required to live in certain cities and towns, the passport seriously restricted mobility. And, while members of collective farms did not need passports (a requirement introduced only in recent years), they could not leave their farms without permission from the authorities.

By the time the Soviet Constitution of 1936 was promulgated, there was virtually no legal emigration from the Soviet Union. The only exception was families seeking reunification and members of some nationalities with strong ties abroad. During the 1930s, for example, some Greek and Armenian family reunifications took place, and some Crimean Tatars were allowed to emigrate until about 1935. During the purges of the late 1930s, the Soviet government forced out some persons of Polish origin who had been in Russia since before the Revolution.[27]

25. Ibid., pp. 340–43.

26. Rudolf Turovsky, "Freedom of Movement: Right of Exit," *Journal of the International Commission of Jurists* 47 (1962): 87.

27. Eugene M. Kulischer, *Europe on the Move: War and Population Changes, 1917–1947* (New York: Columbia University Press, 1948), p. 97.

In all, the numbers were small. The only Soviet citizens allowed to depart for temporary travel during these years were those carrying out official missions. This put Soviet policy more or less in line with Plato's idea that foreign travel should be limited to older citizens of proven loyalty who would function as members of official delegations.

There was, however, a small trickle of clandestine emigration. Through the early 1930s, a few people—prodded largely by the forced collectivization of 1929 to 1932—crossed successfully into Romania and the Baltic states. Others made it into Sinkiang, Persia, and Manchuria, with a group of Mennonites reaching Harbin in 1930. Apparently the largest group to leave were tens of thousands of Kazakhs, a Central Asian people, who crossed a poorly guarded frontier into China around 1933.[28]

While holding the bulk of the population captive, the Soviet government also used expulsion as a weapon of control. Lenin had recommended that hostile leaders be sent into exile, and the criminal code issued in 1922 provided eternal exile for those guilty of "propaganda or agitation on behalf of the international bourgeoisie." Last used as a formal punishment against Trotsky in 1929, this provision was abolished in 1935.[29] But this did not end expulsion of individuals judged a threat to the regime, nor the more subtle application of pressure on individuals or groups who were *encouraged* to apply for exit visas.

How were these policies justified in light of the earlier support for free movement? Building on Lenin, Soviet ideologists argue that once the working class has seized power, the interests of the individual and the state are identical. All justification for placing limitations on state power are thus eliminated. Human rights are invested in the collectivity, the state, rather than the individual. As Vladimir Kartashkin, a leading Soviet jurist, puts it, "Freedom of the individual is understood as freedom of man in a society, State, collec-

28. Ibid.; John Hope Simpson, *The Refugee Problem: Report of a Survey* (London, New York, Toronto: Oxford University Press, 1939), p. 84.
29. Felshtinsky, pp. 341–42; 347*n*91; 348*n*100.

tivity, and not as freedom from them." Consequently, the individual needs to "compare his behavior with the interests and requirements of the whole society." To put his interest above that of society would be an act of egoism and irresponsibility: "Personal freedom should be differentiated from personal arbitrariness which disregards the interests of the society as a whole and hence the interests of the collectivity. To avoid the transformation of freedom into its opposite—arbitrariness—it is necessary to promote responsible behavior in every individual, that is a behavior co-ordinated with the requirements of the law and public morals."[30] In this perspective, an individual's right to choose whether to remain a part of society or not seems an ultimate act of personal "arbitrariness."

One corollary of this view is that there exist no universal standards of human rights, only domestic standards determined by the particular circumstances of each state. The protection of human rights therefore becomes an exclusive matter of domestic jurisdiction, insulated from any standards issued by international bodies. For Soviet jurists, international law governs only relations among governments, not relations between a government and its own people. Soviet authorities roundly condemn any attempt to extend international law into "domestic questions." G. E. Tunkin, perhaps the most prominent Soviet expert on international law, asserts that "this 'intrusion' of the regulatory influence of international law into the domain of human rights does not mean that human rights are directly regulated by international law nor that they have ceased basically to be the domestic affair of a state."[31]

The frequent Soviet invocation of national sovereignty is thus

30. Vladimir Kartashkin, "The Socialist Countries and Human Rights," in *The International Dimensions of Human Rights,* vol. 2, ed. Karel Vasek (Westport, Conn.: Greenwood, 1982), p. 633.

31. G. E. Tunkin, *Theory of International Law,* trans. William E. Butler (Cambridge: Harvard University Press, 1974), p. 82; see also quotations from Soviet jurists in Mitchell Knisbacher, "Aliyah of Soviet Jews: Protection of the Right of Emigration under International Law," *Harvard International Law Journal* 14 (1973): 91.

not simply a convenient tactical response by a regime under attack in international forums. It is instead a natural outgrowth of Soviet views on the role of the state. This became clear almost from the start of the Revolution. In the struggle to survive, the new Soviet regime quickly enlisted the coercive apparatus of the state. The stress was on unity and discipline, on the need to mobilize every available resource on behalf of the Revolution. Trotsky declared that the road to socialism "lies through a period of the highest possible intensification of the principle of the State . . . the most ruthless form of State, which embraces the life of the citizen authoritatively in every direction."[32]

The state's power was further reinforced by Soviet perceptions that the logic of the modern industrial order required hierarchy and organization. Soviet theorists evolved what has been called "the organic labor state," in which the whole of society is regarded primarily as an instrument for production. All citizens are to be judged and rewarded by the amount of "socially useful work" they perform.[33]

Simultaneously, the Soviet Union moved to control emigration for both practical and ideological reasons. The mobilization of the organic labor state was not feasible while the door remained open. Given the low standard of living imposed by Stalinist economic planning, allowing massive emigration would have forced the regime to reverse its economic priorities.

In the Soviet case, however, the ideological impulse is at least as important as practical considerations. A large-scale exodus would have constituted an unacceptable blow to Soviet self-esteem. Soviet leaders saw themselves as engaged in an ongoing struggle with hostile forces throughout the world. That some Soviet citizens might prefer to live elsewhere, especially in the capitalist West, was highly threatening. Admitting the loss of ideological battles would undermine the legitimacy of the prevailing faith.

32. Quoted in Harding, p. 26.
33. Harding, pp. 1–50, provides an excellent account of this entire frame of mind.

Soviet authorities could not, therefore, accept emigration as a routine process. As *Moskovskaya Pravda* put it more recently, the decision to emigrate is "unnatural and like burying someone alive."[34] Lev Navrozov, a Soviet émigré of the 1970s, captured the underlying mentality when he noted that "it was a metaphysical absurdity to ask: 'What if one wants to leave paradise?'"[35]

Behind both practical and ideological concerns was the actual fear that a lowering of barriers would produce a massive outflow of people. Here is how Khrushchev describes the first post-Stalin liberalizations: "We were scared, really scared. We were afraid the thaw might unleash a flood, which we wouldn't be able to control and which could drown us. How could it drown us? It could have overflowed the banks of the Soviet riverbed and formed a tidal wave which would have washed away all the barriers and retaining walls of our society."[36]

Such sentiments may help explain why Soviet authorities go to such great lengths to discredit those who leave, demanding that friends and relatives denounce them and convening mass assemblies to humiliate them publicly. As in a religious rite of purification, it is important to isolate apostasy and delegitimize it. Even fellow-workers who are sympathetic may feel impelled to participate in such ceremonies in order to eliminate all doubts about *their* loyalty.[37] Furthermore, anyone seized attempting to leave illegally is regarded as not just a deserter, but a traitor. As *Izvestiya* observed in 1963 regarding the case of an eighteen-year-old boy caught crossing the

34. Quoted in *Alert* (newsletter of the Union of Councils for Soviet Jews), May 6, 1983.

35. Lev Navrozov, "Getting Out of Russia," *Commentary* 54 (October 1972): 45.

36. Reported in *Pravda* and *Izvestiya,* March 10, 1963; translation in *Current Digest of the Soviet Press* 15, no. 11 (April 23, 1963).

37. Victor Zaslavsky and Robert J. Brym, *Soviet-Jewish Emigration and Soviet Nationality Policy* (New York: St. Martin's, 1983), p. 141.

border, "He betrayed his parents and his comrades. Now he must answer to Soviet justice."[38]

Such cases are governed by two different Soviet laws. The first simply makes it an offense to leave without a passport, punishable by one to three years in prison. This is generally applied in cases where the person returns or intends to return, especially if travel has only been to another East-bloc country. If, however, the culprit intended to flee to a capitalist state, or refuses to return from one, he is usually charged with "treason against the nation, that is to say a deliberate act performed by a citizen of the USSR to the detriment of national independence, territorial defence or military power of the USSR."[39] Thus the defendants in the 1970 Leningrad trial, who had planned to hijack an airplane to fly to Sweden, were convicted of treason. The penalties are accordingly Draconian: some of the defendants were initially condemned to death.

To remove the temptation of treason, the Soviet government invests heavily in border controls. The relevant statute, running to over six thousand words, includes a lengthy definition of the border, all the rules pertaining to it, and provisions excluding all nonresidents from the border region; penalties for violations are described in unusual detail.[40]

To allow unchecked movement would run counter to all the basic instincts of the Soviet system as it has evolved over the years.

38. *Izvestiya,* February 6, 1963, quoted in Mary Jane Moody, "Tourists in Russia and Russians Abroad," *Problems of Communism* 13 (Nov.–Dec. 1964): 9.

39. From the Criminal Code of the Russian Soviet Federated Socialist Republic, 1961. Earlier codes, and provisions of other Soviet republics, are similar. Quoted in Turovsky, p. 88; the Soviet legal position is summarized by Henn-Juri Vibopuu, "Freedom of Movement of Persons and Ideas in Soviet Doctrine and Practice," *Osteuropa Recht* 30 (February 1984): 116–29; see also Moody, p. 9, and William Korey, *The Soviet Cage: Anti-Semitism in Russia* (New York: Viking, 1973), p. 215.

40. "The Law on the USSR State Border," *Current Digest of the Soviet Press* 34, no. 51 (January 19, 1983): 15–20.

In the Soviet view, exit permits are not a right but a *concession* by the state. In order not to create any expectations, Soviet policy is deliberately ambiguous. There is no law on the subject, only unpublished administrative decisions and guidelines.[41] And concessions are usually granted only to serve foreign policy ends or to get rid of problem cases.

Fascist Italy

Beginning in the late nineteenth century, Italy encouraged emigration, even aided it. This was a logical response to heavy population pressures, high unemployment, and the threat of growing social unrest. A government agency set up in 1901 attempted to coordinate emigration and bargain with countries to which Italian laborers were headed in order to secure better terms for their employment and thus more remittances home. In 1913 this agency was granted the authority to suspend emigration if its negotiating efforts required it. Contracts were eventually concluded with French and German agencies that regularized the flow of workers and their working conditions.[42]

The Fascist government that took power in 1922 at first followed the same basic approach, save for trying to milk greater concessions from other nations dependent on Italian labor. To make emigration more fully serve foreign policy goals, the Fascists placed the responsible agency in the Foreign Ministry. Benito Mussolini's ambition was, as he put it, to strengthen the ties of emigrants to the mother country and to use this connection to pursue the "spir-

41. On Soviet law and procedures, see George Ginsburgs, "Emigration and Immigration," in *Encyclopedia of Soviet Law,* ed. F. J. M. Feldbrugge (Dobbs Ferry, N.Y.: Oceana, 1973), pp. 245–46; and Zvi Gitelman, *Becoming Israelis: Political Resocialization of Soviet and American Immigrants* (New York: Praeger, 1982), pp. 96–97.

42. Gary Cross, *Immigrant Workers in Industrial France: The Making of a New Laboring Class* (Philadelphia: Temple University Press, 1983), p. 102.

itual and cultural penetration of other countries."[43] In this way, emigration could be rationalized as expanding Italian influence abroad rather than draining the country's human resources. To nurture outposts of Italian influence abroad, Rome increased its activities among expatriate communities and tried to preserve their Italian character. Women were directed to return to the homeland for childbirth, and all were urged to return periodically for a "bath of Italianization."[44]

By 1927, however, as the birth rate began dropping, the Fascists decided that national power and prestige required maximum population growth. Thus, despite lingering concern about over-population, the government launched a massive effort to promote larger families. Tax incentives and penalties were used to increase the birth rate. Still it continued to drop. As a result, emigration increasingly came to seem a threat to national vitality. The vision of building outposts of influence abroad faded as it became clear that the pressures for assimilation in foreign lands were too strong. The turning point was marked in a speech by Dino Grandi, Undersecretary of Foreign Affairs, before the Chamber of Deputies on March 31, 1927:

> We as Fascists must have the courage to declare that emigration is an "evil" when, as at present, it is directed towards countries under foreign sovereignty. Emigration is necessary, but towards Italian countries and possessions. . . .
>
> Why should our race form a kind of human reservoir for the replenishment of the small or declining populations of other nations? Why should our mothers continue to bring into the world children who will grow up into soldiers for other nations?

43. Quoted in Philip V. Cannistraro and Gianfausto Rosoli, "Fascist Emigration Policy in the 1920s: An Interpretive Framework," *International Migration Review* 13 (Winter 1979): 676.

44. Kulischer, p. 219.

> Fascism will cease to encourage emigration, which saps the vital forces of race and State.[45]

Concrete measures soon followed. In June 1927 circulars were issued ordering prefects to follow strict guidelines in issuing passports. Beginning in 1928, passports for permanent emigration were issued only upon receipt of a letter of invitation from a relative (later limited to immediate family). Another new policy required that temporary labor migration be regulated by collective contracts, which would not only guarantee the terms of employment but also help ensure the laborers' return.[46]

In this as in other areas, Italy mastered the concepts and rhetoric of Fascism; in execution, however, it lagged far behind Nazi Germany. In 1930, as Italy's economic crisis inspired greater ingenuity in evading border controls, severe penalties were set for illegal migration. Paradoxically, at the same time, Italy continued to encourage the emigration of professionals and intellectuals, on the grounds that their presence abroad enhanced Italian prestige. Perhaps more to the point, their departure also rid the country of many prominent anti-Fascists.

Was the Italian policy a success? An Italian scholar writing in 1931 claimed that net emigration in 1928–29 dropped by 62 percent compared to earlier years.[47] However, much of the plunge was due to economic forces rather than government policy; furthermore, the numbers rose sharply in 1930.[48] During the decade that followed, most opportunities for immigration disappeared anyway. Nonetheless, some movement out of Italy continued.

The German Solution

Beginning in the late nineteenth century, Germany, unlike Italy, took in more people than it lost. Thus, when the Nazis came to

45. Quoted in Attilio Oblath, "Italian Emigration and Colonisation Policy," *International Labour Review* 23 (June 1931): 808; see also Cross, p. 113.

46. Oblath, pp. 809–10; Cross, p. 114.

47. Oblath, p. 823.

48. Cross, p. 115.

power in 1933, they did not share the Soviet or Italian fear of hemorrhaging population. They were much more concerned with purging society of unwanted elements. The main targets were political opponents and members of "inferior" population groups, mainly Jews, Slavs, and Gypsies.

A wave of emigration occurred in the initial panic over the Nazi takeover. Thereafter, Jewish emigration, in particular, fluctuated in response to varying pressures. Major flows took place after passage of the Nuremberg Laws in 1935, and the persecutions of Kristallnacht in 1938. About 30 percent of German Jews left before Kristallnacht, and another 30 percent between then and the outbreak of the war. Of those who remained, about three-quarters were over the age of forty. The major obstacle that they faced was the scarcity of viable destinations. The traditional countries of refuge in the West were largely closed off. Even entry to Palestine was severely limited during this period. Other available opportunities—for example, as rural settlers in South America—held little appeal for urban middle-class German Jews.[49]

At first, the Nazis tried to push the Jews into the few channels left open. Gestapo head Reinhard Heydrich, who was responsible for Jewish affairs, declared in January 1935 that "the activity of the Zionist-oriented youth organizations that are engaged in the occupational restructuring of the Jews for agriculture and manual trades prior to their emigration to Palestine lies in the interest of the National Socialist state's leadership."[50] Along the same lines, in April 1935 a directive banned propagation of the view that Jews should remain in Germany. On May 15, 1935, *Schwarze Korps,* a publication of the SS, published a scathing attack on assimilationism among German Jews that was startlingly reminiscent of the Spanish Inquisition's attitude toward the *conversos* who threatened Christendom: "The assimilation-minded Jews deny their race and insist on

49. Lucy S. Dawidowicz, *The War against the Jews* (New York: Bantam, 1976), p. 255.

50. Quoted in Dawidowicz, pp. 112, 257.

their loyalty to Germany or claim to be Christians, because they have been baptized, in order to subvert National Socialist principles."[51] During this period, the SS espoused a policy of *Entjudung,* or de-Jewification, and brought pressure on Jewish leaders to promote emigration. Even Hitler approved emigration to Palestine in order to create "only *one* center of Jewish trouble in the world."[52] At first, Jewish emigrants were even allowed to take most of their property with them.

In 1938–39, increased pressure was placed on Jews to leave, partly as a consequence of Adolf Eichmann's successful program in Vienna, following the Anschluss in 1938, which combined terror and bureaucratic efficiency to hasten the departure of Austrian Jews. In January 1939, Heydrich established a Reich Central Office for Jewish Emigration to promote the departure of Jews "by every possible means."[53]

One reason the Nazis favored the forced emigration of German Jews was to arouse anti-Semitism elsewhere. In a 1938 circular, the Foreign Ministry stated that "the emigration movement of only about 100,000 Jews has already sufficed to awaken the interest of many countries in the Jewish danger. . . . the influx of Jews in all parts of the world invokes the opposition of the native population and thereby forms the best propaganda for the German Jewish policy."[54]

The Nazis then moved to the next logical step in their program. As "emigration" had been a euphemism for "expulsion," now "evacuation" became a euphemism for "deportation," which actually meant something even more sinister.[55] In 1938 the German government expelled Jews of Polish origin back across the Polish border. After the conquest of Poland, Jews in areas annexed by Germany

51. Ibid., p. 113.
52. Ibid., pp. 114–15.
53. Ibid., p. 140.
54. Quoted in Arendt, p. 269.
55. Dawidowicz, pp. 141–42.

were forced to move to other sections of Poland. In 1940 the Nazis began deporting German Jews to Poland. It also forced Jewish populations in occupied territories to live in ghettos—a policy that, among other things, was designed to depopulate Jewish centers through starvation and disease.

All along, however, the Nazis had underlying objections to emigration as a solution. Allowing Jews to leave strengthened their communities abroad, which were still seen as part of the enemy camp. In other words, emigration was not a final solution. Many devout Nazis could not abide the idea of a Jewish state built with German help. Thus, the German government responded sympathetically to Arab requests, from 1937 on, for help in opposing a Jewish state in Palestine. Furthermore, the Nazi Party never fully accepted the SS position on encouraging Jewish emigration to Palestine and elsewhere.

Gradually, the Nazi regime clamped down on Jewish emigration. After June 1938, emigrants were prohibited from taking any capital with them. This, of course, had the effect of discouraging emigration by all but the most desperate.[56] The final prohibition took place on October 31, 1941. It clearly coincided with the ultimate decision, taken during the same period, to exterminate the Jewish people.

Emigration Policies Elsewhere

Classical liberal thought, in reaction to absolutism, assigned a limited and largely negative role to the state. Even when Western societies began carving out a more active role for the state, there was one crucial difference: democratic states did not impose the values of one group on the rest of society. Instead, they featured intricate interactions and compromises among their various constituencies. Neither class nor race became the exclusive point of reference, as each did in the modern totalitarian state.

56. David S. Wyman, *Paper Walls: America and the Refugee Crisis, 1938–1941* (Amherst: University of Massachusetts Press, 1968), p. 28.

Nevertheless, the collectivist ethic did cast its shadow over the emigration policies of liberal democratic societies. Though there were no wholesale expulsions or denials of exit, the right of personal self-determination was challenged in specific and limited ways.

Throughout the interwar period, the right of emigration continued to lack formal acknowledgment from liberal democratic theorists. While the right had received de facto recognition during the nineteenth century, law and theory lagged behind. A leading textbook of international law argued in 1928 that "emigration is in fact entirely a matter of internal legislation of the different States. . . . the Law of Nations does not, and cannot, grant a right of emigration to every individual, although it is frequently maintained that it is a 'natural' right of every individual to emigrate from his own State."[57]

There were exceptions. A widely circulated 1924 opinion by the French scholar Paul Fauchille argued that emigration was a natural right that should be restricted only to prevent departures from reaching "excessive proportions" or to protect would-be emigrants.[58] Similarly, the U.S. representative at a 1930 conference on the codification of international law stated: "For a century past, it has been the policy of my country that the right of expatriation is an inherent and natural right of all persons. It is true that allegiance is a duty, but it is not a chain that holds a person in bondage."[59] Nevertheless, efforts to codify free emigration in legal documents failed at this conference and elsewhere.

The League of Nations made some efforts to facilitate movement. Many League members hoped to liberalize, if not abolish, the passport system left in place by the World War. But League reso-

57. Lord McNair, in Oppenheim's *International Law*; quoted in Stig Jagerskiold, "Historical Aspects of the Right to Leave and to Return," in Vasak and Liskofsky, p. 10.

58. Paul Fauchille, "The Rights of Emigration and Immigration," *International Labour Review* 9 (March 1924), esp. pp. 321–22.

59. League of Nations, Acts of the Conference for the Codification of International Law, Meetings of the Committees: *Nationality* 80 (1930).

lutions passed at conferences in Paris in 1920 and Geneva in 1926 achieved very modest results. The major League accomplishment was the provision of so-called Nansen passports for the growing number of stateless refugees (see the following section).

Ironically, as personal self-determination gained at least some legal and moral recognition, free movement in practice lost ground. Some of the new controls on international movement resulted from agreements between sending and receiving nations. Italy, not surprisingly, was a leader in this effort. Following the failure of direct talks with the United States, the Italians in 1924 organized an International Conference on Emigration and Immigration. "It is time," Mussolini declared, "that the agreements for international protection of workers be joined to economic agreements settling the exchange of resources."[60]

Italy argued that, in contrast to the unregulated conditions of the nineteenth century, the complexity of modern industrial society required bilateral agreements to protect the workers involved and to secure suitable concessions for the country supplying the labor. On these grounds, Italy extracted favorable agreements from France and Brazil, leading others to imitate it. Poland and Spain began to control emigration with an eye to gaining concessions. Eventually, both countries entered agreements with France. Paris also signed contracts with Czechoslovakia, Yugoslavia, Romania, and Austria.[61] The laissez-faire era in international labor migration had come to a close.

Meanwhile, states were expanding internal restrictions on movement. Some regulations simply formalized limits that had long been respected in practice; others, reflecting the new collectivist spirit, extended controls into new and debatable areas. A 1928 survey of emigration laws, published by the International Labour Office, gives a clear overview of these trends.[62] Few countries admitted to

60. Cannistraro and Rosoli, pp. 680–81.

61. Cross, pp. 119–21; Fauchille, pp. 332–33.

62. International Labour Office (see n. 9). Information in this section is from pp. 32–99.

general denial of emigration. In fact, of those surveyed, only Haiti and Japan expressly prohibited emigration, apart from certain specified cases. In the Japanese case, moreover, the laws reflected more an attempt to control migration than to oppose it per se. In fact, Japan, facing overpopulation, encouraged emigration during these years. But, true to the traditional Asian focus on collective planning, the Japanese government was promoting organized emigration under its own aegis. The idea was to establish Japanese enclaves abroad that would maintain close ties with the homeland.[63] Except for small settlements in Brazil, Paraguay, and Peru, however, Japan found most doors closed, forcing it eventually to direct itself to developing the "Great East Asia Co-Prosperity Sphere." As one Japanese writer asserted, "There are only three ways left to Japan to escape from the pressure of surplus population . . . emigration, advance into world markets, and expansion of territory. The first door, emigration, has been barred to us by the anti-Japanese immigration policies of other countries. The second door . . . is being pushed shut by tariff barriers and the abrogation of commercial treaties. What should Japan do when two of the three doors have been closed against her?"[64]

However, if few countries denied the right to leave explicitly, they all controlled it in practice. Most governments required all citizens to obtain official permission to leave, making emigration an act of grace on behalf of the authorities rather than an exercise of an individual right.

Not that all of the specific limitations were controversial. Most countries required emigrating minors to obtain parental consent, while the sick, infirm, and elderly were often kept from leaving altogether. Many countries and colonies required financial guarantees

63. Akira Iriye, "The Failure of Economic Expansion: 1918–1931," in *Japan in Crisis: Essays in Taisho Democracy,* ed. Bernard S. Silberman and H. D. Harootunian (Princeton: Princeton University Press, 1974), pp. 250–61.

64. Quoted in *Sources of the Japanese Tradition,* compiled by Ryusaku Tsunoda, Willliam Theodore de Bary, and Donald Keene (New York: Columbia University Press, 1958), pp. 796–97.

or deposits in order to screen out the destitute from any potential emigrants. Hungary and Romania, for example, required proof of employment or support in the country of destination. In addition, most countries still limited the right of women to travel without family consent (though in some countries, like the United States, such restrictions were directed primarily at the white slave trade).

Most countries further prohibited the departure of individuals involved in legal proceedings; many also restricted men of military age. Family obligations, such as maintenance agreements, were also grounds for denying visas. China required those working abroad to remit 20 percent of their wages to families at home.

More troubling, new types of restrictions were beginning to be justified on grounds of national security or national interest. Five countries reserved the right to restrict or prohibit emigration in the name of "public safety." Two states, Romania and Spain, restricted "collective" emigration—meaning emigration of organized groups—in order to prevent the depopulation of a particular region through mass departures. Germany and Italy, among others, restricted departures by members of certain occupations. A larger number legislated restrictions on the provision of financial inducements from abroad in order to encourage emigration.

The unkindest cut of all, however, was the growing tendency to restrict emigration on the grounds that immigration opportunities had closed. During this period, as noted, most of the traditional countries of refuge had reduced immigration flows to a trickle. The national-origins quotas of the United States, in particular, had a devastating impact on countries like Italy. As immigration openings dwindled, several source countries decided to limit exit permits to a like number. In this way, they could regulate movement according to their own preferences, rather than allow the country of destination to impose its own. Would-be emigrants, facing a world of vanishing openings, were thus denied even the right to test what hospitality might remain. They had only one solace: expulsion might be worse.

The Century of Refugees

World War I, presumably a victory for national self-determination, left as its ironic legacy a continent riven by ethnic tensions. The old multinational empires had given way to new nation-states, but every new border was disputed. No lines existed that would cleanly divide Europe's tangled nationalities into neat homogeneous units. A host of ethnically diverse states came into being at the very moment that national identity was coming to the fore of international politics. Virtually every state contained minority groups that identified with neighboring states, or residual groups that identified with no existing state at all.

As in the earlier phase of European nation-building, the process of integration placed tremendous pressures on recalcitrant groups. Once again, the flow of refugees became a reliable index of social and political turmoil. By one count, over one hundred million people were forced to move between 1912 and 1969.[65] Official tallies, of course, were lower; ethnic tensions were usually so sensitive that, for the record, refugees were often considered voluntary migrants. Furthermore, nations were frequently slow to grant refugee status, since it conferred certain rights and privileges (such as asylum). But, by any reasonable count, those expelled or forced to leave by political, social, economic, or religious pressures account for the bulk of migration in this century. They also dwarf the total human movement, involuntary or otherwise, of any previous century.

In the period immediately following World War I, the largest single group of refugees was the 1.5 million people forced to leave

65. Gunther Beijer, "Modern Patterns of International Migratory Movements," in *Migration,* ed. J. A. Jackson (Cambridge: Cambridge University Press, 1969), p. 18; see also Beijer, "The Political Refugee: 35 Years Later," *International Migration Review* 15 (Spring–Summer 1981): 26–34. Kingsley Davis, "The Migration of Human Populations," *Scientific American* 231 (September 1974): 102, gives a figure of 71.7 million for forced population displacement in the 1913–68 period. The definitive study of this movement, published as this study was nearing completion, is Michael R. Marrus, *The Unwanted: European Refugees in the Twentieth Century* (Oxford: Oxford University Press, 1985).

Russia, where an estimated 350,000 Assyrians, Greeks, Turks, and others fled southern Russia alone. In Eastern Europe and the Balkans, the establishment of new borders resulted in the flight of 250,000 Bulgarians from Greece, Serbia, and Romania; 50,000 Greeks from Bulgaria; 200,000 Hungarians from Romania; and 20,000 Serbs from Hungary. The new Poland took in 570,000 Polish refugees, and over one million ethnic Germans were forced out of areas annexed by other countries at the end of the war.[66]

Turkey deserves special mention. Before and during the World War, the new Ottoman government of the "Young Turks" had embarked on a program of Turkification—with drastic results for non-Turks. As Dr. Nazim Bey, the main Ottoman theoretician, argued, "There exists a very simple method: expel the foreigners and replace them with Turks of pure race. . . . Within twenty years we will have created an empire which essentially is Ottoman."[67] Under this policy, the Ottomans removed over 2 million "aliens" within a decade.

Most notorious, of course, was the treatment of the Armenians. Massacres took place in 1894–96, 1904, and 1909. The worst, however, came under the duress of war in 1915. Fearful of Armenian defection to the advancing Russian army, the Ottoman government disarmed the Armenian population and began a brutal deportation from border areas to the Syrian desert. Armenians in the Van area near the Russian border rose in rebellion and resisted deportation until rescued by the advancing Russian army, which both reinforced Turkish doubts about Armenian loyalty and sparked intensified deportations and massacres elsewhere in Turkey. By 1923, when a new secular Turkish state was established, an estimated 600,000 to

66. Louise W. Holborn, *Refugees: A Problem of Our Time. The Work of the UN High Commissioner for Refugees, 1951–1972* (Metuchen, N.J.: Scarecrow, 1975), pp. 3–4; Beijer, "The Political Refugee," p. 28.

67. Quoted in Kurt Glaser and Stefan T. Possony, *Victims of Politics: The State of Human Rights* (New York: Columbia University Press, 1979), p. 417.

1,000,000 Armenians had perished, and some 320,000 had been forced into exile.[68]

The position of the Greek minority in Turkey also became precarious following the defeat of an invading Greek army in 1922. Some one million refugees fled to Smyrna, a largely Greek city on the Turkish coast, where they were rescued by an armada of Greek ships. When the Turks announced they would tolerate no more Greeks on Turkish soil, Greece proposed an exchange of minorities. (About 190,000 Greeks remained in Turkey, and 356,000 Turks in Greece.) In 1923 the two nations concluded an agreement providing for the compulsory transfer of both populations; it was quickly effected. To some contemporary observers, the exchange set a dangerous precedent. British Foreign Secretary Lord Curzon condemned the action as "a thoroughly bad and vicious solution for which the world will pay a heavy penalty for a hundred years to come."[69]

One sign of the times was the emergence of a new society composed predominantly of refugees. The Jewish community of Palestine grew from about 65,000 on the eve of World War I to about 650,000 in 1948, spurred mostly by refugee flows from Russia and Poland in the 1920s and from Central Europe (largely Germany and Austria) in the 1930s. It was less Zionist ideology than sheer human displacement and lack of alternative destinations that laid the foundations for a Jewish state.

As the scale of the problem grew, the will to resolve it faded. Soon after Hitler's accession to power in 1933, the League sponsored an autonomous High Commission for Refugees Coming from Germany, and in 1936 this body was brought directly under League

68. Simpson, pp. 29–37; Holborn, pp. 3–4; Beijer, "The Political Refugee," p. 28.

69. Quoted by Alfred-Maurice de Zayas, "Population, Expulsion, and Transfer," in *Encyclopedia of International Law*, vol. 8 (Amsterdam: North Holland, 1984); see also Simpson, p. 15; and G. J. L. Coles, "The Problem of Mass Expulsion" (background paper prepared for the Working Group of Experts on the Problem of Mass Expulsion, International Institute of Humanitarian Law, San Remo, Italy, April 16–18, 1983), pp. 16–17.

control. In 1938 it was amalgamated with the "Nansen Office," a League of Nations agency directed by the Norwegian explorer Fridtjof Nansen which dealt with the problem of providing travel documents to stateless refugees. However, the High Commission dealt principally with the legal, not the humanitarian, aspects of the problem, and at the end of the 1930s its mandate covered only about 800,000 refugees. The Commission's first head, James G. McDonald, resigned in frustration at the end of 1935, calling for "friendly but firm intercession with the German Government" in order to get at the source of the refugee problem.[70]

A Convention Relating to the International Status of Refugees, passed by the League in 1933, was ratified by only eight states. Its only real significance was to serve as a precedent for the Convention of 1951, which finally granted international recognition to the rights of refugees. Likewise, the High Commissioner for German Refugees served as a model for the later establishment of the U.N. High Commissioner for Refugees. As the leading study by Louise Holborn attests, these earlier efforts "focused international attention upon finding solutions to the problems, . . . established important legal precedents for future international agreements regarding the status of refugees. . . . and gained recognition for the concept of international protection for refugees exercised by an international agency on behalf of the community of nations."[71] But that is about all that was accomplished.

What most frustrated the League's efforts was the general crackdown on immigration. Before the war, immigration limits were aimed at excluding certain groups and categories; now, the overall flow was cut to a fraction of what it had once been. This reflected both growing antipathy to aliens (a corollary of the new nationalism) and increasing economic pressures brought on by the worldwide depression.

70. Wyman, p. 32.
71. Holborn, p. 17.

While the United States had excluded all Asians before the war and imposed a literacy test on would-be entrants in 1917, the real turning point came in 1921, when a tight national-origins quota system was enacted as a temporary measure. Total immigration was capped at about 350,000; immigration from each country in a given year was limited to 3 percent of all nationals from that country living in the United States as of 1910. One immediate effect was drastically to cut immigration from southern and eastern Europe. In 1924 the measure was made permanent and the total quota reduced to 150,000. This reduced to a trickle the numbers from outside the traditional sources of immigration in northwestern Europe (the British Isles, Germany, Scandinavia). In addition, the Hoover administration in 1931 required immigrants to have sponsors guaranteeing that they would not become a public charge. This cut actual entries well below even the very limited quotas.

There was an underlying inconsistency in the American approach to immigration. When immigration was relatively open in the nineteenth century, Chinese laborers had been brought into the country, presumably on a temporary basis and without the right of naturalization. After the exclusion of the Chinese, their place was taken primarily by Mexicans, whose entry into the country was not limited. This flow was not hindered by the legislation of the 1920s: while supposedly cutting immigration severely, the U.S. government actually moved to ease the import of cheap labor from Mexico and elsewhere.[72]

Following the American lead, more than twenty states during this period adopted highly restrictive immigration laws.[73] In the

72. Aristide Zolberg, "International Migration and Foreign Policy: When Does a Marginal Issue Become Substantive?" in *Immigration and Refugee Policy* (In Defense of the Alien, vol. 6), ed. Lydio Tomasi (New York: Center for Migration Studies, 1984), p. 212.

73. R. Plender, *International Migration Law* (Leiden: A. W. Sijthoff, 1972), pp. 55–60; United Nations, Department of Social Affairs, *The Determinants and Consequences of Population Trends* (New York: United Nations, 1953), pp. 121–22.

1930s, European countries kept out all but a very small number of self-supporting immigrants. British policies favored immigrants from northwestern Europe and the dominions; Asians were excluded by various means. Even France, a country that had traditionally welcomed immigration, imposed quotas. In Latin America, too, restrictive policies became general after 1929. Numbers were reduced through quotas, high fees, and a ban on all but rural settlers; Asians were generally excluded altogether. In Asia itself, most countries erected high barriers against the entry of Indians and Chinese.

This, then, was the striking new aspect of the refugee situation: the absence of refuge. In the long history of expulsion and flight, haven had always been available somewhere. Now, with the new stress on national belonging, many were in the unprecedented position of belonging nowhere. A new phenomenon—stateless refugees—appeared on the scene. These were the denationalized who could acquire no new nationality. They were, in Hannah Arendt's phrase, "the most symptomatic group in contemporary politics,"[74] As the Zionist leader Chaim Weizmann told a British commission of inquiry on Palestine in 1936, for refugees the world "is divided into places where they cannot live and places into which they cannot enter."[75]

The supreme embodiment of this new spirit, and a fitting climax to the era, was the futile Evian Conference of 1938. The meeting was suggested by President Franklin D. Roosevelt shortly after the Nazi takeover of Austria, as a means of aiding the departure of political refugees from Germany and Austria. Thirty-two nations from Western Europe, the Americas, and the British Commonwealth attended. They gathered with reasonable hopes that a place of refuge could be found for the victims of Hitlerism. Only a few hundred thousand people were at issue, and by this time the Nazi regime was widely viewed with repugnance.

Appearances were deceiving, however. The United States was

74. Arendt, p. 277.
75. Great Britain, Palestine Royal Commission, *Minutes of Evidence,* November 25, 1936 (London, 1937).

able to secure such wide participation in the conference only by promising that no nation would be asked to accept additional immigrants. In fact, internal documents of the State Department now show that the principal aim in promoting the conference was precisely to head off any pressure to increase American quotas.[76] In that, the department was only responding to American public opinion; a *Fortune* poll at the time showed that 67.4 percent favored keeping refugees out, 18.2 percent supported the Roosevelt policy of admitting them within quotas, and only 4.9 percent favored raising quotas.[77]

Conference organizers also feared that showing generosity toward refugees would encourage more expulsions elsewhere. Romania, in fact, asked to be included as a "supply-side" participant, to find destinations for those of whom it wished to be rid. The State Department declined the offer. The British, for their part, agreed to participate only after being assured that the matter of immigration into Palestine—which they were then curtailing—would not be raised.

All of this enabled Hitler to taunt the democracies for their hypocrisy: "I can only hope and expect that the other world, which had such deep sympathy for these criminals, will at least be generous enough to convert this sympathy into practical aid. We, on our part, are ready to put all these criminals at the disposal of these countries, for all I care, even on luxury ships."[78]

At the conference, held at Evian-les-Bains, France, from July 6 to 15, 1938, one country after another rose to explain why it could not accept any additional refugees. Most pleaded lack of absorptive capacity; even Canada and Latin American states announced that they had room only for agricultural settlers. Some were more frank

---

76. See in particular the archival-based studies by Arthur D. Morse, *While Six Million Died* (New York: Random House, 1968), p. 212; and Wyman, pp. 44–47.

77. Morse, p. 212.

78. Quoted by Morse, p. 212.

about the threat to national homogeneity. Australia, for example, declared that as a country with no racial problems it did not desire to import such problems. The major American concession was an announcement that the United States would, for the first time, accept the full *existing* legal quotas for refugees from Germany and Austria. The Dominican Republic announced that it would take 100,000 refugees, but it was estimated that the country could absorb only 5000; ultimately, only a few hundred were resettled there. Some Latin American countries actually tightened entry restrictions in the wake of the conference.

The sole concrete measure taken at the conference was the establishment of a new Intergovernmental Committee on Refugees. The head of this body, George Rublee, negotiated with the German government to arrange a more orderly exodus, but, due to German financial demands and various other delays, the discussions were overtaken by the outbreak of the war. The major problem still remained: finding a place to resettle those let out. At the rate of immigration permitted at the time, it would have taken sixteen years to place all of the 660,000 seeking to leave German-controlled territory. The U.S. government investigated a succession of colonization schemes in Angola, Ethiopia (asking Mussolini's cooperation!), Kenya, British Guiana, Northern Rhodesia, Tanganyika, Venezuela, and the Philippines—each more unrealistic than the last. A Jewish periodical commented sardonically: "Powerful nations, enjoying sovereignty and freedom, have only their own countries to fall back upon. But Jewish refugees have a choice of many lands to pick from. If one prefers the humid heat of the jungles of Guiana, he is welcome to it. If someone else's taste runs to tsetse flies and similar blessings of East Africa, they are at his disposal. Verily, it is good to be a refugee."[79]

The Germans regarded Evian as exoneration for their policies.

79. S. Ethelson, "It Is Good to Be an Orphan," *Jewish Workers' Voice* 4 (December 1938): 22; quoted by Wyman, p. 58.

A few weeks after the conference, Minister of Propaganda Josef Goebbels, responding to Western nations' expressions of outrage over the excesses of Kristallnacht, called their bluff. "If there is any country that believes it has not enough Jews," he declared, "I shall gladly turn over to it all our Jews."[80]

In short, the Evian conference simply confirmed that the final lifeline—the right to flee—no longer existed. Observers seeking symbolism pointed out that Evian is a source of still water, and that Evian backward spelled "naive." In any event, the futility of Evian was a final tribute to the global retreat before the new serfdom, not to mention the new barbarism.

80. Quoted by Morse, p. 237; see also Marrus, pp. 170–72.

4

Recognition and Retrogression

> *Greater numbers of people are effectively confined behind their national boundaries today than in previous periods of history.*
>
> —*Judge José D. Inglés, U.N. Special Rapporteur, 1963*

Forced Movements after World War II

If any event could, surely the Second World War would have discredited the control of international movement. The German and Italian regimes, along with their petty imitators in Central and Eastern Europe, were swept away, and many hoped it was for good. Yet, immediately following the war's end, some 14 to 15 million Germans were expelled from Eastern Europe, and over 2 million liberated Soviet prisoners of war were forcibly repatriated to their homeland. Hitler's defeat was accompanied, paradoxically, by widespread imitation of his methods.

One reason was that the war had heightened sensitivities to the importance of national consolidation and homogeneity. New attention was focused, in particular, on the German populations scattered throughout Eastern Europe. Many of these communities had existed as isolated minorities for centuries; others were created by the border changes attending two world wars. The Nazis manipulated these populations as part of their expansionist efforts. In fact,

95

Hitler's ambitions regarding two German minorities—in Czechoslovakia's Sudetenland and the Polish corridor—had helped precipitate the war. Such events fostered a grim determination among Eastern Europeans to be rid of these "fifth columns." This was true not only of the Soviet-style governments that ultimately took power, but also, in Czechoslovakia and Hungary, of the short-lived regimes that preceded them.

Further problems arose from the political and strategic implications of the Allied victory. Poland was a good example. Stalin had made it clear that he would not give up the eastern provinces of Poland that the Soviet Union had annexed by agreement with Hitler in 1939, and Western leaders agreed in principle to compensate Poland with German territory to the west. However, the areas in question—East Prussia, Pomerania, and Silesia—had been predominantly German for centuries, and given the problems with Danzig and the Polish corridor that had triggered the war, neither the Polish government nor its Soviet sponsors contemplated saddling Poland with several million additional Germans.

Germany had itself established unfortunate precedents. During the war it had expelled over a million Poles from annexed areas of Poland, kicked out 100,000 French from Alsace-Lorraine, and transferred about 5 million slave laborers from occupied areas to Germany. These acts were later defined as war crimes at the Nuremberg trials. There were also other precedents: the Soviet Union had deported about 2 million people from the Polish, Baltic, and Bessarabian territories it annexed in 1939, and it had forcibly relocated some 800,000 ethnic Germans, 250,000 Crimean Tatars, and about a million other combined Meshketians, Chechens, Ingushi, Karachai, Balkars, and Kalmyks. Nor should it be forgotten that, after Pearl Harbor, both the United States and Canada had forcibly relocated their West Coast Japanese populations on the flimsiest of grounds.

An even earlier precedent was the compulsory transfer of populations between Greece and Turkey in the 1920s. Winston Churchill, bringing himself to face the inevitable in Poland, argued that "the disentanglement of populations which took place between Greece and Turkey after the last war . . . was in many ways a success, and has produced friendly relations between Greece and Turkey ever since." Others recalled the criticism of Lord Curzon (see above, p. 88), and noted that the transfer of just over one million Greeks from Turkey took several years and involved "an appalling amount of misery and hardship."[1] Also, the friendly relations between the two states did not prove very durable.

The resettlement of German populations from Poland, Czechoslovakia, and Hungary was governed by the protocol agreed to at the Potsdam Conference at the end of the war, in July 1945. Article 13 stated: "The Three Governments, having considered the question in all its aspects, recognize that the transfer to Germany of German populations, or elements thereof, will have to be undertaken. They agree that any transfers that take place should be effected in an orderly and humane manner."

The British and Americans agreed to this article in part to bring some order to the widespread expulsions and flight that were already taking place in areas of Poland and Czechoslovakia liberated by the Soviet army. The reestablished authorities in these areas had been trying to create facts by getting rid of as many Germans as possible before postwar negotiations even began. Churchill and Roosevelt hoped, through agreement, to contain the flow. Article 13 sought to tie the "transfers" of German populations, as it called them, to the absorptive capacity of occupied Germany; it declared a moratorium on further expulsions pending a determination of this capacity. In addition, the Western allies refused to recognize the new western border (the Oder-Neisse line) that Poland was trying, with

1. Churchill in the House of Commons, December 15, 1944, and Lord Bishop of Chichester in the House of Lords, January 30, 1946, both quoted in Alfred M. de Zayas, *Nemesis at Potsdam: The Anglo-Americans and the Expulsion of the Germans: Background, Execution, Consequences,* 2d rev. ed. (London and Boston: Routledge and Kegan Paul, 1979), pp. 11–12.

Soviet backing, to claim, and thus they disputed the right of Poland to transfer all Germans up to this line.

Nevertheless, Western agreement to the underlying premise of Article 13 threw a cloak of respectability, if not legality, over the expulsion enterprise. In practice, there was no moratorium; the exodus from the three countries continued, augmented by similar flows from Romania, Yugoslavia, and Bulgaria. Little or no distinction was made between recent German settlers—whose expulsion as German citizens may have been legal—and native-born Germans with local citizenship. Nor was any serious effort made to distinguish between Nazi supporters and others.

Finally, the transfer was far from "orderly and humane," as promised in the Potsdam protocol; in fact, some 2 million refugees did not survive it.[2] The total number expelled is estimated at 14 to 15 million; after the dust settled, only about 2.6 million ethnic Germans remained in all of Eastern Europe (outside the Soviet Union), and many of these would leave in subsequent years.[3]

Thus the regimes of the region, Communist and non-Communist alike, demonstrated that the war had reinforced, rather than discredited, the totalitarian aversion to pluralism. The author of a leading study, Alfred de Zayas, comments: "Indeed, if the Allies fought against the Nazi enemy because of his inhuman methods, could they then adopt some of those same methods in retribution? Who was it then, who succeeded in imposing his methods on the other? Whose outlook triumphed?"[4]

The regimes of Eastern Europe were hardly the only perpetrators. As the end of the war approached, both the United States and

2. de Zayas, "The Legality of Mass Population Transfers: The German Experience, 1945–48," *East European Quarterly* 12 (1978): 7–20, 143–60.

3. de Zayas, *Nemesis at Potsdam,* pp. xix, xxv, 187; Kurt Glaser and Stefan T. Possony, *Victims of Politics: The State of Human Rights* (New York: Columbia University Press, 1979), pp. 421–32; Michael R. Marrus, *The Unwanted: European Refugees in the Twentieth Century* (Oxford: Oxford University Press, 1985), pp. 325–31.

4. de Zayas, *Nemesis at Potsdam,* p. xxi.

Britain gained control over large numbers of Soviet soldiers who had been captured by Germany early in the war and who now wore German uniforms. The United States and Britain forcibly repatriated them, in violation of the traditional right of asylum and of the Hague and Geneva conventions governing prisoners of war.[5] According to the two conventions, those captured in German uniform should have been regarded as German prisoners of war and thus protected against forced return to the Soviet Union. Throughout the war, the United States and Britain had insisted on the principle of "not looking behind the uniform," since both had in their armed forces soldiers who would otherwise be vulnerable to charges of treason (Japanese and Germans in U.S. forces; French, Dutch, Norwegians, and other Europeans in the British).

The Soviet Union, however, was not a party to the Geneva Convention, and Soviet soldiers were under standing orders not to be captured. Those taken prisoner were regarded by their own government with great suspicion for having deserted, or, at the least, for having been contaminated by exposure to the enemy. Even those who escaped from the Germans and fought their way back to Soviet lines were sometimes punished or liquidated.[6] When his own son Yakov was captured, Stalin responded by jailing his daughter-in-law and refusing a German offer to exchange Yakov for Hitler's nephew, then in Russian hands. Overall, as many as a million Soviet soldiers agreed or were coerced to fight for the Germans, while others worked in labor battalions. Soviet civilians were also transported westward as laborers. In the Soviet view, most, if not all, were guilty of "collaboration."

After D-Day, when these Russians began falling into Allied hands, the British government made an immediate decision to return all Soviet citizens to their country, whether they wished to go or

5. de Zayas, "Repatriation," *Encyclopedia of Public International Law,* vol. 8 (Amsterdam: North Holland, 1984); Marrus, pp. 313–17.

6. See the cases described by Nikolai Tolstoy, *The Secret Betrayal* (New York: Charles Scribner's Sons, 1977), p. 397.

not. Notwithstanding the Geneva Convention and Churchill's feeling that "these men were tried beyond their strength,"[7] the sight of the Soviets in German uniforms weighed heavily with the British. London was also concerned about how the Soviets might treat British soldiers that they had liberated from German camps. In addition, it wanted to avoid having to deal with another large group of refugees. Above all, British diplomats were eager to maintain close cooperation with Stalin's Russia in ending the war and building the postwar order. The British Foreign Office consistently opposed any course of action likely to offend Soviet sensitivities. As Foreign Secretary Anthony Eden wrote to Churchill and the War Cabinet, "We cannot afford to be sentimental about this." On September 4, 1944, the War Cabinet accepted Eden's position.

Initially the United States followed the British lead, with one important difference. Any Russian captured in German uniform could avoid deportation if he had the presence of mind to insist he was indeed German, or in any event not a Soviet citizen.

Most Russians' fate, however, was determined at the Yalta Conference in February 1945, where the British and American governments agreed that "all Soviet citizens liberated by Allied armies" would be separated from other prisoners of war and "handed to Soviet authorities in places reached by agreement." While the agreement did not explicitly make repatriation compulsory, it was interpreted that way. After the end of the war, when German retaliation was no longer feared, the United States even stopped automatically recognizing the protection of the German uniform for those who claimed not to be Soviet citizens. Such claims were now investigated, and exemptions were limited to those who became Soviet citizens by virtue of border changes after 1939—a category that included most Balts and many Poles.

The bulk of Soviet citizens were returned under this policy during May and June, but by late summer there had developed

7. Ibid., p. 54.

widespread resistance to forced repatriation, especially among those who had fought in the German army. In one incident, at Fort Dix in New Jersey, Russian prisoners barricaded themselves within their barracks and began a mass suicide that was halted only by a tear-gas attack. The British had even more trouble in delivering to Soviet authorities in Austria some Cossack units, including among them pre-Soviet émigrés who were being "repatriated" to a regime that did not even claim them as citizens. In one case the handover was accomplished only by deceiving the Cossacks into believing they were attending a conference with British authorities to discuss their future.[8]

Stuck with the unpleasant duty of delivering desperately resisting people into Soviet hands, the military eventually balked. In August, Field Marshal Harold Alexander, supreme Allied commander of the Mediterranean theater, stalled any further operations under his command by asking for a policy review. Since Alexander exercised a joint command, the British government could not simply order him to obey his orders; they first had to seek American approval.[9] In the meantime, General Dwight D. Eisenhower also asked for a policy review, and on October 4 he suspended all forcible repatriations from the American occupation zone in Germany. Field Marshal Bernard Montgomery soon followed suit in the British zone. For most, though, the change came too late, for they had already been returned to their "homeland."

Many diplomats, especially in the British Foreign Office—more concerned about relations with the Soviet Union than with violations of individual rights or traditions of asylum—urged the

8. News of such incidents was suppressed, a suppression noted at the time by George Orwell and attributed by him to the "poisonous effect of the Russian *mythos* on English intellectual life." Orwell, "The Prevention of Literature," *Polemic,* no. 2 (January 1946), in *The Collected Essays, Journalism, and Letters of George Orwell,* vol. 4, ed. Sonia Orwell and Ian Angus (London: Secker and Warburg, 1968), p. 62.

9. Nicholas Bethell, *The Last Secret* (New York: Basic, 1974), pp. 176–81.

continuation of forced repatriation. Only after prolonged debate did the U.S. government, in December, decree a "compromise" that limited such repatriation to those still on active service in the Red Army, those captured in German uniform, and those who could be proved guilty of treasonable acts. Civilians, at least, would now escape the dragnet. The British eventually accepted the same guidelines.

Under this new policy, isolated instances of forced repatriation involving Russians who had served in the German army continued until 1947. Altogether, some 2,272,000 Soviet citizens were returned, with or without force, to Soviet control; only 250,000 to 500,000 managed to remain in the West.

It is noteworthy that the experience with the Soviet prisoners of war may have influenced the firm stand taken a few years later by the U.N. Command in Korea, under U.S. direction. North Korean and Chinese demands for compulsory repatriation of prisoners were rejected, and an armistice agreement was delayed until the principle of voluntary repatriation was accepted. Subsequently, 21,000 North Koreans and Chinese chose not to return to their homelands.

The New Refugee Flood

The expulsion of German minorities and the forced repatriation of Soviet citizens marked only the beginning of coerced population movements in the postwar period. During the decade after 1945, about 45 million people relocated under duress—about as many as had migrated overseas from Europe during the entire nineteenth century. [10]

These movements had various causes—border changes, the creation of new states, the rise of new regimes, communal strife, and governmental efforts to promote uniformity. Among the more notable movements:

10. Brinley Thomas, "Migration: Economic Aspects," *International Encyclopedia of the Social Sciences 1968,* 10:293.

1. Some 300,000–400,000 Finnish Karelians and about one million Poles fled areas annexed by the Soviet Union, while about 500,000 Ukrainians, White Russians, and Lithuanians were evacuated from Poland to the Soviet Union.

2. From 1949 to 1952, Bulgaria, which generally did not permit emigration, pushed out about 175,000 ethnic Turks before closing the exit gates for good.

3. The violence accompanying independence in South Asia forced a massive flight of Moslems from India and of Hindus from Pakistan; in all, some 14 to 15 million refugees moved in 1946–47.

4. In 1948–49, about 750,000 Palestinian Arabs fled the territory that became the State of Israel: in subsequent years, a like number of Jews were forced from Arab states.

5. The establishment of Chinese authority over Tibet produced two waves of refugees from that country, in 1950 and 1959, totaling about 85,000.

6. As colonial rule ended, Dutch refugees came back to the Netherlands from Indonesia, and French and Italians returned from North Africa (primarily Algeria in the one case and Libya in the other).

7. The divisions of Korea in 1945 and of Vietnam in 1954 were both followed by substantial flows of refugees from north to south.

The movement continued unabated in the late 1950s, the 1960s, and later. Hungary produced refugees in 1956, Czechoslovakia in 1968, and Cuba after 1959. Turkey's partial occupation of Cyprus in 1974 produced movement between the divided island's two sectors, and the Communist victories in Indochina a year later provoked a mass exodus. Numerous upheavals in Africa produced an estimated 3 million refugees by 1980. More recently, refugees have fled Bangladesh, Afghanistan, and Ethiopia. (As this exceedingly brief sketch indicates, much of the displacement over the last four decades has occurred in Third-World countries; these movements will receive greater attention in chapters 5 and 6.)

How much of this movement resulted from deliberate government policy? The question is not an easy one, for few governments are as open as, say, Idi Amin was in expelling Asians from Uganda. But the hand of government has been apparent time and again. Bulgarian Turks, Iraqi Jews, and Vietnam's Chinese all felt they had little choice but to flee. In Indonesia and some African states, governments created or condoned the pressures that forced unwanted groups to flee. In still other cases, such as those of India, Pakistan, and the Palestinian Arabs, the displacement was, from the government's perspective, an acceptable, even desirable, by-product of war.

Since blatant expulsion of a state's own citizens is no longer internationally respectable, most of the refugee flows of recent history are portrayed as voluntary movements. The legal right to remain in one's country, or to return to it, has acquired a strong standing in rhetoric and law, precisely as it has been flouted in practice on an unprecedented scale. Here is a typical statement of the norm, made by Albert Schweitzer upon receiving the Nobel Peace Prize in 1954: "The most grievous violation of the right based on historical evolution and of any human right in general is to deprive populations of the right to occupy the country where they live by compelling them to settle elsewhere."

States no longer claim the right to expel citizens who have committed no crime. Even exile, as a legal punishment of citizens convicted of a crime, has fallen into disuse. A 1964 U.N. study found that only five countries (Costa Rica, France, Haiti, Lebanon, and Peru) still maintained exile as a legal punishment; a more recent survey of Latin America—the home of exile—found that the expulsion of residents for a crime was still legally possible in some twelve Latin American states, though in some instances it was limited to aliens.[11]

11. United Nations, Department of Economic and Social Affairs, *Study of the right of everyone to be free from arbitrary arrest, detention and exile,* prepared by a committee of the Commission on Human Rights (E/CN.4/826/Rev. 1, 1964) (New York, 1964), p. 203; Hurst Hannum, *The Right to Leave and Return in International Law and Practice* (Washington: The Procedural Aspects of International Law Institute, 1985), p. 79.

This does not mean, of course, that exile is not used *illegally* against citizens. Military regimes in Argentina, Bolivia, Chile, and Uruguay have exiled, or prevented the return, of thousands of their citizens in recent years. Paraguay may have forced out, and not readmitted, as many as one million people over the last thirty years. Other Latin American states that have expelled citizens not guilty of a crime include Guatemala, Haiti, Panama, and Peru. [12] But exile, as the legal punishment of individual citizens, has virtually ceased to exist. Only aliens can be legally expelled, and even they enjoy certain protection. [13] International legal experts argue that aliens who are in a country legally can only be deported for cause, on a case-by-case basis.

The illegality of expelling nationals is so commonly assumed that international documents, rather surprisingly, do not explicitly forbid it. It is simply taken for granted. Nevertheless, the right to remain, and not to be forced out of one's country, is implicit in the body of conventions and agreements developed during and after World War II. For instance, Sadruddin Aga Khan, the former U.N. High Commissioner for Refugees, in his "Study on Human Rights and Massive Exoduses" submitted to the U.N. Commission on Human Rights in 1981, concluded that the actions causing recent refugee flows violated most of the articles of the Universal Declaration of Human Rights. [14] This declaration, adopted by the U.N. General Assembly in 1948, provides in article 13(2) that "everyone has the right to leave any country, including his own, and to return to his country." If one has the right to return, he certainly has the right not to leave in the first place.

Article 9 of the Universal Declaration is also relevant, asserting

12. Ibid., pp. 110–13.

13. This is the position of most legal authorities; see Guy S. Goodwin-Gill, *International Law and the Movement of Persons between States* (Oxford: Clarendon, 1978), p. 201.

14. Aga Khan, *Study on Human Rights and Mass Exoduses,* United Nations, Economic and Social Council, Commission on Human Rights (E/CN.4/1503, December 31, 1981) (New York, 1981), pp. 17–30.

that "no one shall be subjected to arbitrary arrest, detention, or exile." It would appear that this permits exile so long as it is not arbitrary. However, this applies only to exile as the legal punishment of a person convicted of a specific offense; moreover, implementation is conditional on the willingness of another state to admit him.

Finally, article 15 states:

1. Everyone has the right to a nationality.
2. No one shall be arbitrarily deprived of his nationality nor denied the right to change his nationality.

States can, therefore, deprive citizens of their nationality—if they do not do so "arbitrarily." As some legal experts have pointed out, international law does not forbid denationalization across the board. But this does not mean that the state can then automatically expel those denationalized, since no other state has an obligation to admit them. Nor, by the same token, can it denationalize citizens simply in order to prevent their return.[15] In the past denationalization was often a prelude to expulsion; Eastern European states, for example, denationalized their German populations before expelling them. Czechoslovakia also denationalized its Hungarian minority, clearly in preparation for their expulsion, and forced out some 100,000, but it was eventually forced to reverse its course when Hungary refused to cooperate.

Other recent international documents include similar provisions. The International Covenant on Civil and Political Rights, which has been ratified by most Western and Soviet bloc states (though not by the United States), provides that "no one shall be arbitrarily deprived of the right to enter his own country." Regional agreements, especially the European and American Conventions on

15. P. Weis, *Nationality and Statelessness in International Law* (Westport, Conn.: Hyperion, 1956), pp. 123–29; Hannum, pp. 73–76.

Human Rights, go even further in forbidding the expulsion of citizens, arbitrary or otherwise.[16]

Efforts to *prevent* expulsion, then, enjoyed some success in law but much less in practice. More progress was made in providing *after the fact* relief to those who fled or who were forced out. The fitful efforts of the 1930s, reinforced by the atrocities of World War II and its aftermath, culminated in the codification and general acceptance of a bill of rights for refugees. The main instrument was the Convention Relating to the Status of Refugees, which was signed in 1951 and which has been in force since 1954.

According to the 1951 convention, a refugee is one who, "owing to a well-founded fear of being persecuted for reasons of race, religion, nationality, membership of a particular social group or political opinion, is outside the country of his nationality and is unable, or owing to such fear is unwilling to avail himself of the protection of that country." While this was broader than previous definitions, it left open the status of those fleeing from pressures that were not persecution in the strict sense—economic deprivation, war or civil strife, foreign occupation. Also, the convention did not cover internal refugees who flee to a different region within their own country.

The new convention was accompanied by more efficient machinery for protecting refugees. In 1947, the United Nations had established, over Soviet opposition, an International Refugee Orga-

---

16. At a 1952 session of the Institut de Droit International, most of the international legal experts present reaffirmed that population transfers between countries must be voluntary. To this de Zayas adds three other standards that must be met under prevailing legal norms: the clear sovereignty of the governments (transfers from occupied territories being illegal according to the Geneva Convention of 1949); the availability of a country willing and able to receive those transferred; and orderly and humane procedures, including compensation for immovable property. Clearly, few if any cases in modern history meet these standards. On the Institut de Droit International, see de Zayas, "The Legality of Mass Population Transfers," p. 6; on de Zayas's own arguments, see ibid., pp. 1–7.

nization (IRO), with a mandate more for resettlement than repatriation. Three years later, the IRO was replaced by the United Nations High Commission for Refugees (UNHCR), which, together with the 1951 Convention, at last provided an institutionalized framework for dealing with refugees. The mandate of the UNHCR was to protect refugees and seek solutions for their plight, whether through resettlement in place, assimilation elsewhere, or voluntary repatriation. The high commissioner was to work with both governments and private humanitarian organizations; his work was supposed to be nonpolitical and limited to refugees as defined in the convention. In fact, the scope of the UNHCR's protection has been extended in practice to include all persons uprooted by "external aggression, occupation, foreign domination or events seriously disturbing public order."

The most serious unresolved problem in refugee rights, however, has been squaring the refugee's right to asylum with the authority of sovereign states to control the entry of aliens. The 1951 convention, in article 33, contained a commitment to what is known as the principle of nonrefoulement: "No Contracting State shall expel or return (*refouler*) a refugee in any manner whatsoever to the frontiers of territories where his life or freedom would be threatened on account of his race, religion, nationality, membership of a particular social group or political opinion."

This still does not entail any obligation to provide permanent asylum, nor to admit any particular refugee seeking entry. Nevertheless, once refugees are present within a country's territory, and their status as refugees is conceded, they acquire a number of important rights. And, generally speaking, the host country is obligated to facilitate their adjustment and assimilation.

By the end of 1983, the Refugee Convention had been ratified by over 90 countries. No Soviet bloc countries were among them, however, on the grounds that the agreement intruded into areas of internal competence and that, in any event, the solution to refugee problems is repatriation. In addition, very few countries in Asia or the Arab world ratified the convention, despite (or because of) the large refugee flows in those regions. The United States, after years of hesitation, finally accepted the convention by ratifying a protocol to it in 1968.

Efforts were also made to deal with the problem of statelessness. A Convention Relating to the Status of Stateless Persons was adopted in 1954, and it entered into force in 1960; it granted to any stateless person, in "the country in which he finds himself," the same rights as a refugee. The next step was a Convention on the Reduction of Statelessness, signed in 1961, which obligated signatories not to denationalize their citizens if such an act left them stateless. These efforts have not stirred a broad response, however. As of 1984, the 1954 convention had been ratified by fewer than three dozen states, most of them in Europe: the 1961 convention, which did not come into force until 1975, had been accepted by only eleven states. The United States has not signed or ratified either agreement.

The major obstacle, predictably, has been political. Nations likely to face massive inflows—Thailand, Pakistan, Hong Kong—are leery about accepting obligations to refugees. Governments are also reluctant to recognize refugees from friendly countries, as demonstrated by the recent U.S. reaction to fugitives from El Salvador. Countries may also fear strained relations with the government from which refugees are fleeing. Reflecting such reservations, none of the above agreements nor other related documents affirm an individual's right to permanent asylum; to the contrary, all speak of the state's sovereign right to *grant* asylum.[17] Thus, a U.N. effort in 1977 to draft a convention on asylum with fuller protection failed. Given the growing political pressure exerted by mass movements, most states were simply unwilling to sign a piece of paper that required them to receive all comers entitled to asylum.

Despite such shortcomings, the post–World War II world man-

17. Florentino Feliciano, *International Humanitarian Law and Coerced Movements of Peoples across State Boundaries* (San Remo: International Institute of Humanitarian Law, 1983), pp. 17–18.

aged to provide new homes for numbers vastly greater than the modest figures that, only a few years before, had thrown the system into paralysis. This did not occur without opposition and struggle, nor without some lapses. But, in comparison to the earlier response, it represented a quantum leap forward in humanitarianism.

The key to this success was resettlement rather than repatriation. The right of return, no matter how justified in principle, may be impractical in execution when the causes of the original refugee flow remain. Even defining the country of origin may be a problem when boundaries and regimes have changed; the predominant view is that the right of return applies to those who have been citizens or permanent residents of a country, but not to others. Other complications include continuing states of war, de facto population exchanges, and questions of national loyalty. Repatriation turned out to be practical in only a handful of postwar cases—for instance, in Italy's South Tyrol, where some German speakers had left under a 1939 option; in Algeria, where the end of colonial rule enabled opponents of the French regime to return; and in Uganda, where Idi Amin's downfall allowed his political adversaries to come home.

Integration in place was made easier by the fact that most refugees found themselves among related peoples. This was true of the Hindus who fled to India and the Moslems who moved to Pakistan; the Germans who found themselves back in Germany; the Karelians in Finland; the Bulgarian Turks in Turkey; and the Dutch, French, and Italians who returned from overseas colonies. North Vietnamese and North Koreans moved to a different state within their homeland, and Jews fleeing the Arab world found themselves among fellow Jews in Israel. And although Palestinian Arab refugees refused in principle to consider integration in place, and received citizenship only in Jordan, they, too, ended up in a culturally familiar setting among kindred people.

In the United States, the resettlement of refugees was facilitated by ideological considerations. After World War II, opposition to refugee admissions was overcome in a campaign waged by private organizations that appealed not only to such traditional concerns as American charity and the historical role of refugees in American society, but also to sympathy for those managing to flee from behind the "Iron Curtain." Motivated largely by the desire to aid refugees from Communism, Congress passed a series of acts admitting a total of about 400,000 displaced persons from Europe.

However welcome these measures were, they were remedies after the fact, not means of preventing refugees in the first place. Despite the shocks caused by massive dislocations, little international attention was focused on their causes. The U.N. high commissioner has utilized his good offices to enter into some discussions on preventive steps, but his mandate on politically sensitive issues remains highly restricted. Thus advances in legal recognition and instruments were not matched by changes in behavior.

Building Walls: Phase Two

Like refugee rights, the right to leave finally achieved clear legal recognition during this same period; and, like refugee rights, it was denied on an unprecedented scale. As the gap between legal standards and actual practice grew, nations were forced to find new subterfuges to hide their coercive policies.

In the debate over the Universal Declaration of Human Rights of 1948, the Soviet representative on the Commission for Human Rights objected to including the right to leave, on the grounds "that it would encourage emigration."[18] In the General Assembly debate the Soviet Union proposed that the language in article 13(2)— "everyone has the right to leave any country, including his own"— be qualified by the phrase, "in accordance with the procedure laid down in the laws of that country." The Soviet representative explained that states should not be asked to change existing laws, as this would constitute interference in domestic affairs. He added that

18. Jiri Toman, "The Right to Leave and to Return in Eastern Europe," in *The Right to Leave and to Return,* ed. Karel Vasak and Sidney Liskofsky (New York: American Jewish Committee, 1976), pp. 121–22.

"in the Soviet Union . . . no law prevented persons from leaving the country, but anyone desiring to do so had, of course, to go through the legally prescribed formalities."[19]

Other countries objected that the proposed amendment would empty the right of any real content. Only Poland and Saudi Arabia spoke in support, and the Soviet amendment was defeated by a vote of 24–7, with 13 abstentions. The final version was adopted by a 44–6 vote, with 2 abstentions. The vote to accept article 13 as a whole was unanimous, but three Soviet bloc delegates abstained and later announced that they had misunderstood the vote and had intended to oppose its adoption.[20] The Soviet bloc nations also abstained on the final vote on the Universal declaration as a whole—which, in any event, was not considered a legally binding document.

However, member states, including those in the Soviet bloc, have on occasion voluntarily accepted the obligations of the Universal Declaration of Human Rights. The right to leave also appears in other documents, such as the International Convention on the Elimination of All Forms of Racial Discrimination, adopted in 1965. Perhaps most important is the International Covenant on Civil and Political Rights, which was adopted in 1966 and which has been in force since 1976. Article 12 of the covenant provides:

> 1. Everyone lawfully within the territory of a State shall, within that territory, have the right to liberty of movement and freedom to choose his residence.
> 2. Everyone shall be free to leave any country, including his own.
> 3. The above-mentioned rights shall not be subject to any

19. José D. Inglés, *Study of Discrimination in Respect of the Right of Everyone to Leave Any Country, Including His Own, and to Return to His Country,* United Nations, Economic and Social Council, Commission on Human Rights, Subcommission on Prevention of Discrimination and Protection of Minorities (E/CN.4/Sub. 2/229/Rev. 1, 1963) (New York, 1963), p. 85.

20. Ibid., p. 87.

restrictions except those which are provided by law, are necessary to protect national security, public order (*ordre public*), public health or morals or the rights and freedoms of others, and are consistent with the other rights recognized in the present Covenant.

4. No one shall be arbitrarily deprived of the right to enter his own country.

The overall right spelled out here is restricted by paragraph 3, which permits limits on the right of movement on the broad grounds of national security and public order. The drafters even added the French concept of *ordre public,* which is broader than the English "public order," implying not just the absence of disorder but public policy generally. John Humphrey, a Canadian serving as director of the U.N. Division of Human Rights, later wrote that he was shocked by the use of the French concept, which he found dangerously far-reaching.[21] These permissible exceptions appear frequently in other human rights provisions and thus do not represent a special attack on the right of movement; nevertheless, their inclusion provides a toehold for governments seeking to justify limits on emigration. When ratifying the covenant, for example, the Soviet Union announced that these restrictions "gave it specific authority to limit the right of emigration, the free flow of ideas and other individual liberties."[22]

Despite this strong protection of the right to leave in law, some states were blatant in their disregard of it in practice. The Shah's Iran, for example, openly announced that it denied passports "when the applicant has no good reasons for leaving the country." And Spain under Franco tended to issue passports only to loyal supporters

21. Humphrey, *Human Rights and the United Nations: A Great Adventure* (Dobbs Ferry, N.Y.: Transnational, 1983), pp. 261–62.

22. *New York Times,* September 29, 1973; Hannum, pp. 24–51, presents a reasoned refutation of the broad interpretation of the Covenant's permissible restrictions.

of the regime.[23] But it was the Soviet model that exerted the greatest sway. By the early 1950s, the Soviet approach to controlling international movement was emulated by most of the states of Eastern Europe and by China, Mongolia, and North Korea.

Eastern Europe was subject to special factors. Among these was a policy of promoting population growth that was, at least on the surface, reminiscent of classical mercantilist attitudes. The catastrophes of war, genocide, and human dislocation had severely depleted populations; in addition, the region had, in the 1950s and 1960s, experienced a sharp drop in birth rates. Regions like East Prussia, Silesia, Pomerania, and the Sudetenland had been depopulated through mass expulsions. The result was a chronic shortage of labor, plus grave concerns about the new regimes' ability to replace the (mainly German) expelled populations with ethnic Poles, Czechs, and so forth, in an effort to create demographic facts reinforcing the new borders.

Marxists were never enthusiastic supporters of Malthus; the gospel of limits to population growth was regarded as antiproletarian. This attitude was reinforced by the pervasive nationalism of the postwar world, which increased consciousness about the role of size in state power. The governments of Eastern Europe therefore adopted policies aimed at encouraging more births.

They also curtailed emigration. In the words of one Hungarian economist, it was "quite obvious that the socialist countries—like other countries—intend to prevent their professionals, trained at the expense of their society, from being used to enrich other countries." International travel would be encouraged only "if the individual and social interests are in harmony."[24] Any conflict between the wishes

23. United Nations, Economic and Social Council, Commission on Human Rights, Subcommission on Prevention of Discrimination and Protection of Minorities, Document de Séance No. 34, March 28, 1962, *Résumé des renseignements concernat l'Iran,* p. 3; Reginald Parker, "The Right to Go Abroad: To Have and to Hold a Passport," *Virginia Law Review* 40 (November 1954): 856.

24. Péter Vas-Zoltán, *The Brain Drain: An Anomaly of International Relations* (Leiden: A. W. Sijthoff, and Budapest: Akadémia, 1976), p. 28.

of an individual and the interests of society was due to misconceived egotism on the part of the individual.

East European spokesmen further maintain that they are keeping would-be emigrants from suffering from insufficient linguistic and cultural preparation, from an absence of family and friends abroad, from being thrown headlong into social systems with inadequate welfare programs. Frequent references are made to those who have returned, frustrated and embittered, from attempts to settle in the West. In this view, the idea of letting an individual suffer the consequences of his own decision is inconceivable. Some observers maintain that the Soviet regime and its allies purposely induce a kind of social infantilism among the population at large. A Bulgarian representative endorsed this view, perhaps unintentionally, when he underlined the welfare benefits provided for the young by calling his country "a good nursery."[25]

Eastern European officials also stress the debt an individual owes the socialist state, which offers thorough care from birth, including subsidized education and training through to the highest levels. Since society makes a large investment in each person, especially during the early years, great hostility is shown those who make use of their training to seek greater personal gain elsewhere. Defenders of the system sincerely believe that every individual should repay society by remaining a working member of it. They justify the imposition of an "education tax" on emigrants as a logical effort by the state to recoup its investment. On the other hand, exit visas are often liberally granted to older citizens who have already done their part.

The postwar experience of Eastern Europe revealed, even more sharply than the Soviet case, some of the dilemmas that Marxist regimes face regarding emigration. Many of these states were more

25. Personal interview with a diplomatic representative of Bulgaria, May 2, 1984. This section is based on, among other sources, a series of personal interviews with diplomatic representatives of Hungary, Romania, Bulgaria, and Yugoslavia during May, 1984.

economically advanced, historically more open, and more closely linked to the rest of Europe than the Soviet Union had been. It was easier, and more natural, for their citizens to contemplate crossing a border in response to economic or political pressures, especially in East Germany, bordered as it is by a state of the same culture and language.

The threat of manpower loss was therefore quite real, and it came at a time when these regimes could least afford it. The danger was particularly great with regard to skilled personnel. Marxist states typically place great stress on rapid modernization and development, and achieving those goals depends on the services of highly trained professionals. But few groups feel more threatened by Marxist governments than this one. From a position of privilege and high reward, they are reduced to salaried servants of the state. The Marxist commitment to egalitarianism undermines the incentive structure that professionals thrive on—and which is usually available in neighboring lands.

Thus, to prevent a brain drain, an open emigration policy might force a state to readjust its wage structure, at a cost to other economic priorities, not to mention ideology. This was the conclusion, for example, of Zsuzsa Ferge, a Hungarian sociologist who studied the economic impact of her own country's relatively liberal emigration policies: as Hungary began to compete with the Western labor market, it was forced to increase rewards to professionals.[26] Representatives of Romania and Bulgaria, on the other hand, argue that they cannot afford to match Western salaries, and that, without a restrictive emigration policy, they "would become like Africa."[27]

Eastern bloc nations do not explicitly forbid emigration, since

26. Information supplied by Wesley A. Fisher, Secretary, American Council of Learned Societies—Soviet Academy of Sciences Commission on the Humanities and Social Sciences, International Research and Exchanges Board, March 28, 1984. Ferge's work is apparently not available in English.

27. Personal interviews with diplomatic representatives of Romania, May 21, 1984, and Bulgaria, May 2, 1984.

this would conflict with international obligations and norms. Their regulations on foreign travel all implicitly recognize the right to leave, subject to the requirements of law; Hungary and East Germany spell it out. The reality begins to emerge in a look at the actual requirements for leaving. The applicant is required to obtain the permission of various bodies apart from the passport office, such as his place of work, his cooperative housing committee, the police, even members of his family. In some cases no time limit is set for the completion of administrative action, and usually no appeals are allowed. Permission can be denied on a number of grounds, including national security and "interests of the state." In addition, stringent limits may be placed on the export of currency or other property; stiff taxes and fees may also be imposed. Much is left to administrative discretion, which is guided by unpublished internal directives. Setting policy in private, authorities can modulate the trickle of emigration as they see fit. So, while anyone can apply, the odds against success are extremely high. Sanctions against attempts to leave without permission are severe, reflecting the official hostility toward deserters. Illegal departure for a capitalist state is usually defined as treason; among those invoking the death penalty are Albania and Romania, which recently executed a marine pilot after his second attempt to flee.[28]

The overall attitude of authorities toward travel abroad was illustrated by the treatment of Czechs who happened to be caught outside their country by the Soviet invasion in 1968. Those who delayed their return home were warned that staying abroad without permission was a criminal offense; an individual could obtain subsequent permission to emigrate (necessary for undertaking return visits) only after spending five years abroad and receiving a pardon from the president of Czechoslovakia for committing a criminal act. At the same time, residents who applied to join relatives abroad were

28. Toman, pp. 119–69; Amnesty International, *The Imprisonment of Persons Seeking to Leave a Country or to Return to Their Own Country* (London: Amnesty International, 1986), pp. 6, 14.

informed that "it is contrary to the State's interest to allow Czechoslovak citizens long-term private sojourns abroad, and that includes emigration." In addition, the authorities made it clear that they would not permit any emigration to join Czech citizens who were "residing abroad without the permission of the Czechoslovak authorities."[29]

Permission to emigrate is granted primarily to members of minority groups with a homeland or with other strong ties elsewhere. As noted, in some cases, governments have been eager for such groups to leave. As a result, emigration policies are often subject to conflicting impulses. The case of the Germans in Poland is a good example. After the initial push aimed at expelling Germans, a continuous flow of voluntary emigration reduced the number of ethnic Germans to only about 56,000 by 1956. However, there remained roughly another million citizens of "German descent," who, while partly Polonized, were still the target of petty discrimination. Polish authorities were torn between the desire to be rid of all Germans and countervailing economic, ideological, and demographic considerations. In 1970, as part of a normalization of relations with West Germany, Poland agreed to a broad definition of "Germans" in Poland and expedited their emigration. Even then, permission to leave was rarely granted to professionals, and factory managers were given the right to veto the departure of key workers.[30]

Likewise, Poland after 1967 sought to be rid of its Jews. This impulse grew out of an internal struggle within the Polish Communist Party. Even though only 30,000 Jews, most of them thoroughly assimilated, remained in the country, anti-Semitism was used as a convenient weapon by the Polish nationalist wing of the party.

29. Gerard Cohen Jonathan and Jean-Paul Jacque, "Obligations Assumed by the Signatories," in *Human Rights, International Law, and the Helsinki Accord*, ed. Thomas Buergenthal and Judith R. Hall (Montclair, N.J.: Allenheld, Osmun, 1977), p. 58.

30. C. C. Aronsfeld, "German Emigration from Poland," *Soviet Jewish Affairs* 3 (1972): 111–15.

The campaign culminated in a speech by party leader Wladyslaw Gomulka on March 19, 1968. Blaming Jews for recent unrest, he declared that those attached to Israel were "free" to emigrate. In practice, about 25,000 Jews were forced from the country by various means, without too many fine distinctions being drawn. All were portrayed as Zionists heading for Israel—an important fiction for the Polish government, which did not want the Jewish exodus to serve as a model for non-Jews.[31]

As it had in the 1930s, the Soviet Union also allowed the departure of certain national minorities after World War II. During the 1950s, there were small-scale repatriations of Germans, Poles, Japanese, and even Spanish from Soviet territory (the last group being a legacy of the Spanish Civil War).[32] Unlike the Poles, however, the Soviets through the end of the 1960s refused to extend the idea of repatriation to Jews. When asked about the subject in 1956, Nikita Khrushchev said: "I shall tell you the truth. We do not favor these trips." Later, in 1960, he denied that any Soviet Jews wanted to go to Israel.[33] The Soviets had, after all, been engaged in a policy of assimilating minorities for over a generation, and they were dealing with a Jewish population some seventy to eighty times as large as that of Poland. They also feared the precedent of group emigration in a country with so many restless nationalities.

In recent years, emigration has also been used in Eastern Europe as a safety valve to control dissent. After 1968 the Czechs exiled a

31. Josef Banas, *The Scapegoats: The Exodus of the Remnants of Polish Jewry,* trans. Tadeusz Szafar (London: Weidenfeld and Nicolson, 1979), esp. pp. 50, 54, 138–39, and 172–73.

32. George Ginsburgs, "Emigration and Immigration," in *Encyclopedia of Soviet Law,* ed. F. J. M. Feldbrugge (Dobbs Ferry, N.Y.: Oceana, 1973), pp. 245–46.

33. *Réalités* 136 (May 1957): 67; *Pravda,* July 9, 1960, both quoted in William Korey, *The Soviet Cage: Anti-Semitism in Russia* (New York: Viking, 1973), pp. 192–94. At the time there were 9236 invitations pending from Israelis to their relatives in the Soviet Union; see Korey, p. 194, and Salo W. Baron, *The Russian Jew under Tsars and Soviets* (New York: Macmillan, 1976), p. 288.

number of prominent dissenters, including Zdenek Mlynar, a former member of the Czechoslovak Politburo. Others allowed to travel abroad were told they would be allowed to return home only if they refrained from open criticism of the regime. The German Democratic Republic expelled Wolf Biermann, a prominent poet and entertainer, then suggested emigration to those who protested his departure. The same fate befell six Romanian intellectuals who addressed to President Nicolae Ceausescu a letter demanding civil rights. In all such cases, however, the governments made it clear that "exit permits were available only to heretic intellectuals, not to ordinary people."[34]

Romania has, however, demonstrated its independence from the Soviet Union in this as in other matters by pursuing a somewhat more liberal line on exit visas, within very strict limits. Romanian authorities admit that they do not favor emigration, seeing in it no benefits for Romania, so they have imposed an intimidating array of procedural obstacles. Nonetheless, they have in recent years permitted an annual emigration of about 30,000 to 40,000, composed mostly of ethnic Germans and Jews. Travel for family reunification is also permitted, most frequently to the United States (which is today home to about 300,000 to 400,000 Romanian immigrants). There is, however, considerable pressure for additional emigration.

Hungary has loosened up even more. Citizens over the age of fifty-five are freely allowed to leave, and arrangements for family reunification are relatively liberal. As a result, a few thousand people emigrate legally each year—a number lower than Romania, but representing a higher proportion of those seeking to leave. Most retain their Hungarian citizenship and are free to return for visits. Rules are also generous for foreign travel, compared to other states in Eastern Europe. Hungarians are permitted one trip abroad each year, if financed by outside sources; they may purchase hard currency

---

34. Charles Fenyvesi, "The New Exiles," *The New Republic*, September 23, 1978, p. 24.

for foreign travel once every three years. Each year, some 500,000 of the population visit Western countries, with as many as 5000 of them using the opportunity to remain abroad illegally. The government has apparently come to terms with this outflow.

Why should Hungary be different? According to Hungarian officials, the country's central position in Europe, plus its relatively strong dependence on foreign trade, makes it desirable to have more communication with the outside world. Perhaps more to the point, Hungary enjoys greater prosperity than most Soviet bloc nations, and there are consequently fewer would-be emigrants. The government has over the last two decades put more stress on consumer goods and on closer ties with the West in order to cement domestic stability. As noted, it is willing to pay the cost of such openness in the form of higher wages to its own professionals.

For Eastern Europe as a whole, however, the example of Hungary is less representative than that of East Germany. Until 1952, the lines between the occupation zones in Germany could be easily crossed in most places. In that year, however, in response to growing manpower shortages, the Soviet Union instituted tight border controls around their zone. In 1956, as large numbers of "visitors" to West Germany defected, the authorities of the new East German state (established in 1955) practically eliminated all travel to the West. But the door remained open in Berlin, which continued to be administered jointly by the Four Powers. Furthermore, the Federal Republic (West Germany), intent on weakening the rival regime, encouraged the flow from east to west by offering generous resettlement assistance to all refugees from East Germany. West German radio and television, easily received in East Germany, harped on the superior standard of living in the West. Finally, the side-by-side proximity of the two systems in Berlin constituted a clear comparison, to the disadvantage of East Germany, that few East Germans could ignore.

The East Germans tried to contain the outflow as best they could; any East German headed to Berlin with a suitcase was likely to be stopped. Those actually caught trying to cross the border were subject to heavy penalties. But so long as free movement continued within Berlin, such measures were ineffective. Once a person was in the city, the Western sector was but a subway ride away. By August 1961, an estimated 3.5 million East Germans—about 20 percent of the population—had left. The impact on the economy, already ravaged by Soviet stripping of its occupation zone after World War II, was devastating. In 1960, only 61 percent of the population was of working age, compared to 70.5 percent in 1939.[35] The loss was disproportionately heavy among professionals—engineers, technicians, physicians, teachers, lawyers, skilled workers. One observer, Curtis Cate, described it not as a brain drain, but as a "cerebral hemorrhage."[36] Overall, the direct cost of the manpower losses has been estimated at $7 billion to $9 billion; Walter Ulbricht, the East German party leader, later claimed that West Germany owed him $17 billion in compensation, including reparations as well as manpower losses.[37]

As depicted in the Western press, this movement was in large part politically motivated. In this view, those fleeing East Germany were driven by the repression and regimentation of the Ulbricht government. Of course, some did leave because of persecution by the regime or opposition to it. But there was also a reverse flow from the West into the German Democratic Republic (GDR), prompted in part by political identification with Marxism. Between 1950 and 1964, about half a million people, or 36,000 a year, moved from West to East Germany.

The bulk of westward movement seems to have been driven by economic forces. Every new East German economic crisis swelled the

35. Jonathan Steele, *Socialism with a German Face: The State That Came in from the Cold* (London: Jonathan Cape, 1977), p. 120.

36. Curtis Cate, *The Ides of August* (New York: M. Evans, 1978), p. 129; see also John Dornberg, *The Other Germany* (Garden City, N.Y.: Doubleday, 1968), pp. 103–05.

37. Dornberg, pp. 17, 105.

outflow, while periods of stability sapped it. This presented severe problems for a regime bent on implementing radical change. Austerity programs and other policies causing widespread dislocation increased the flow and thus aggravated the conditions that had necessitated the harsh measures in the first place. A vicious cycle was set in motion: the onset of an economic crisis produced emigration, which in turn aggravated the economic crisis.

Everything came to a head at the end of the 1950s. In 1958, the GDR embarked on an ill-conceived seven-year plan calling for a big jump in industrial output and the collectivization of agriculture. Havoc resulted. Matters were made worse by a severe drought that devastated rural areas. The flow to West Berlin rose from 144,000 in 1959 to 199,000 in 1960 and 207,000 in the first seven months of 1961. Orderly planning became almost impossible. Entire towns and districts were without physicians, crops went unharvested, and fifteen-year-olds were put to work running streetcars. The economy was on the verge of collapse.

The Ulbricht government had long pressed the Russians for a peace treaty that would formally establish East German sovereignty and control over all of Berlin. Khrushchev had gone so far as to issue the West an ultimatum on Berlin in 1958, but he had been forced to back down. The Soviets renewed their threats about Berlin in 1961 but were unwilling to risk general war over the city. However, as the tension over Berlin grew, increasing the flood of refugees to the west, the East German government became desperate. On June 15, 1961, Ulbricht held a rare press conference at which he asserted that "the enticing of human beings away from the capital of the GDR belongs to the methods of the Cold War. Many espionage agencies—West German, American, English, French—which are based in West Berlin, are involved in *Menschenhandel* [slave trade]." Proposing an autonomous status for West Berlin, Ulbricht said that "no one has any intention of building a wall." But he made it clear that the outflow had to stop. "It goes without saying that the so-called refugee camps in West Berlin"—the transit camps at which refugees were processed en route from West Berlin to West Germany—"will be closed down."[38]

In the end, the East Germans felt they had little choice but to seal off West Berlin. Fritz Selbmann, a member of the East German State Planning Commission, later recounted: "We debated the wall for a long, long time. For years we hesitated, for years we repeatedly postponed the decision. Just a few weeks before August 13 we were all against it. At that time, when Walter Ulbricht said in a press conference, 'No one has any intention of building a wall,' it was true. No one did. But then as the refugee flow became worse and worse, we were simply forced by circumstances to do something."[39] Ulbricht went to Moscow on August 1 to obtain Soviet backing. According to an account of the meeting that later leaked out, initial Soviet hesitation was overcome by Soviet economic experts (especially Anastas Mikoyan) who asserted that the GDR was indeed losing its technical and industrial elite and that it faced the real possibility of complete economic breakdown and counterrevolution.[40]

The East Germans finally made their move on August 13. According to the decree of the GDR Council of Ministers, control such as "is usually introduced along the borders of every sovereign state" were put in place along the sector lines in Berlin in order "to put an end to the hostile activities of the revanchist and militarist forces of Western Germany and West Berlin." Henceforth, East German citizens would require special permission to cross these lines. On the same day barbed wire and other barriers were erected around the city. Two days later, police and army engineers began to construct a more permanent concrete wall.

Though justified as an "anti-Fascist protective wall," the barrier was taken inside East Germany as a confession of failure. Ulbricht himself, while still claiming that he had had no choice, later de-

38. Quoted in Cate, p. 61.
39. Quoted in Dornberg, pp. 105–06.
40. Cate, p. 143.

scribed it as his greatest propaganda defeat.[41] In any event, the wall did accomplish its purpose. With the flow blocked, the East German economy revived and, after two years, began an impressive advance. Precisely as calculated, when other options were foreclosed, people came to terms with the system.

Today, the GDR, like other East European states, provides in law for travel and emigration but has procedures sufficiently intimidating to deter most would-be applicants. The real policy, as elsewhere, is set out in unpublished directives and guidelines. Occasionally, though, the policy finds open expression, as in a 1972 edict forbidding able-bodied young people from traveling to any western country except under extraordinary circumstances.[42]

The major exception has been family reunification. From the erection of the wall until mid-1984, about 293,000 East Germans were allowed to join family members in West Germany. The movement has been accompanied by an unusual arrangement whereby the Federal Republic has "ransomed" defectors from the GDR. This setup began in absolute secrecy in 1963 as a means of allowing some political prisoners to leave in return for badly needed cash and material. During the 1960s the people released were mainly traditional opposition elements, but since then most of those let go have been imprisoned only for having tried to leave the country illegally. From the East German viewpoint, the payments are seen as compensation for the damage such individuals have inflicted on the socialist order, as well as reimbursement for the cost of their education.

This commerce has become so institutionalized that it is built into East German economic planning, and in more recent years it has been extended to payments to "expedite" family reunifications. Former Deputy Chancellor Erich Mende, who negotiated the original deal, now denounces the arrangement as "a traffic in human beings that is very close to a slave trade." At the same time, Mende ac-

41. Steele, p. 116.
42. William Solyom-Fekete, *Legal Restrictions on Foreign Travel by the German Democratic Republic* (Washington: Library of Congress, 1978), p. 11.

knowledges the value of the controlled exodus as a safety valve for East Germany: "We are removing so-called oppositional elements and normalizing the coercive Communist state. . . . We are sterilizing resistance to the Communists."[43]

While other East European regimes tend to regard the 1961 East German crisis as a cautionary tale, its lessons are not quite so clear-cut. The German situation was quite unique. East Germany was contiguous to another German state, one quite prosperous and attractive. West Germany campaigned continuously to encourage the traffic. Strong family ties extended across borders, and communications (especially radio and television) from the west could not be easily blocked. Finally, roughly a quarter of the refugees were not actually East German but refugees from the "eastern territories" who were simply relocating a second time.

Even for a state in the position of the GDR, not all emigration is injurious. The unchecked movement before 1961 had some positive consequences from the regime's viewpoint. It removed the more vociferous sources of opposition, such as anti-Russian nationalists. A process of ideological "natural selection" left the Communist Party with a more dedicated membership. In fact, East Germany's massive outflow may help to explain why it has not experienced the political ferment of Hungary, Poland, or Czechoslovakia. Even the crime rate dropped in the 1950s, probably in part because the criminally inclined were drawn to richer and easier targets in the West.

The uniqueness of the situation can be seen in the way West Germany's presence made itself felt on the GDR even *after* the wall was built. It encouraged the East Germans to give higher priority to consumer goods than other Soviet bloc nations do. Partly as a result, East Germany enjoys the highest living standard in Eastern Europe, with a per capita income that in 1974 surpassed Britain's. The country's affluence is so great relative to its allies that authorities within the Soviet Union limit the distribution of East German magazines, with their lavish displays of consumer riches.

43. *New York Times,* July 29, 1984.

Today, the vicious cycle has been broken. If the doors were opened, it seems certain that many fewer would leave. Since 1974, pensioners have been allowed to travel abroad fairly freely; only about half of one percent use the opportunity to move permanently.[44]

Nonetheless, for all its uniqueness, the East German experience made a deep impression on the rest of Eastern Europe. The near collapse of the German Democratic Republic seemed to prove the risks of uncontrolled international movement. It seemed to suggest that, when faced with the allures of the capitalist West, a state committed to egalitarianism could defend itself only by removing the temptation of emigration. Images of the East German "slave trade" appear frequently in any Eastern European discussion of the issue.[45] For those already predisposed to control as a way of life, the shadow cast by such an image is very powerful.

An American Variant

From the standpoint of international movement, the impact of the Cold War was not limited to the East. Even nations with traditionally open borders became more restrictive in both attitude and practice. Most notably, in the United States, the individual's right to have a passport, and thus to travel abroad, became a serious public issue for the first time. American passports, like most others, had originally been issued as a simple letter of identification and recommendation. After 1856, they were issued only by the secretary of state, and at his discretion. But since one could still travel during this period without a passport, the occasional refusal of the secretary to issue such a document was not a serious matter.

A 1918 statute, however, made it illegal to depart from or enter the United States without a valid passport. While the law was

44. Dornberg, p. 117.
45. This was confirmed in a number of personal interviews, with both diplomatic representatives of Eastern European states and emigrants from these countries (including Arkady Shevchenko, a former high-ranking Soviet diplomat).

allowed to lapse, similar laws in other countries made passports a practical necessity for international travel. As a result, the State Department's customary discretion over the issuing of passports suddenly gave it control over international travel by Americans. This power was confirmed by a 1926 law, still in force, that established a modern passport system. In 1941 it was again made illegal to leave or enter the country without a passport; the requirement became permanent with passage of the Immigration and Nationality Act in 1952.

Meanwhile, the State Department was asserting that its traditional control over passports gave it the right to prevent any travel abroad that was "not in the best interests of the United States." It began denying passports on the basis of individual political beliefs. In addition, the Internal Security Act of 1950 explicitly prohibited the issuance of passports to members of the Communist Party, and the State Department subsequently denied passports to those who refused to file an affidavit concerning party membership.

For more than a decade, then, departure from the United States was effectively regarded as a privilege rather than a right. Many passport applications and renewals were denied, often on obscure grounds and with little explanation. Since the State Department held that its actions were a function of the government's foreign policy powers, it maintained that its decisions were not reviewable by the courts. The head of the department's Passport Office became, for all practical purposes, the arbiter of foreign travel by American citizens. Among those refused passports were Paul Robeson, the singer and actor, and playwright Arthur Miller, who was not allowed to see one of his own plays in Brussels. Even Americans who worked for the United Nations were sometimes prevented from traveling abroad in the performance of their duties.

Such actions came under frequent court challenges, and in 1952, a U.S. district court ruled (in *Bauer* v. *Acheson*) that the State Department had acted improperly in revoking the passport of an American journalist working in Paris without hearing or notice. The decision established the principle that foreign travel was protected by the Constitution and could not therefore be restricted without due process of law. In *Kent* v. *Dulles* (1958), the Supreme Court ruled that the 1926 and 1952 laws did not provide due process. Further, it reaffirmed that the right of exit was part of the concept of liberty and thus deserved the protection of the Fifth Amendment.[46]

Finally, in *Aptheker* v. *Secretary of State* (1964), the Supreme Court ruled against the State Department's denial of a passport to Herbert Aptheker, the prominent Communist theoretician and historian, and further invalidated the section of the 1950 act that had prohibited the issuance of passports to Communists. This established that political belief alone was not sufficient grounds for limiting foreign travel. Along the same lines, a U.S. district court ruled in 1972 (*Woodward* v. *Rogers*) that, in the absence of an overriding and substantial national interest, requiring a loyalty oath in order to obtain a passport was unconstitutional.

These decisions would seem to invalidate any general government restrictions on the right of travel based on political considerations. However, the State Department continues to assert its right in individual cases to limit foreign travel within the limitations imposed by the courts. The latest version of the department's regulations, drafted in 1980, permits revocation of a passport if the secretary of state "determines that the national's activities abroad are causing or are likely to cause serious damage to the national security or the foreign policy of the United States." Defenders of this prerogative argue that it derives from the government's responsibility for national security, that revocation of passports is an appropriate means of protecting that security, and that due process is provided by both administrative and judicial appeal procedures.[47]

46. Goodwin-Gill, pp. 32–33; Paul Lansing, "Freedom to Travel: Is the Issuance of a Passport an Individual Right or a Government Prerogative?" *Denver Journal of International Law and Policy* 11 (Fall 1981): 29–30.

47. Evelyn Capassakis, "Passport Revocations or Denials on the Ground of National Security and Foreign Policy," *Fordham Law Review* 49 (May 1981): 1178–96. For an opposing view see Lansing, pp. 15–35, and Parker, pp. 853–73.

This position gained support from the recent case of Philip Agee, a former Central Intelligence Agency employee who incurred the ill will of the U.S. government by publicly identifying CIA activities and agents in a number of countries. Agee understandably preferred to conduct his campaign from abroad, in order to avoid constraint, and the State Department revoked his passport in order to curtail his travels. Agee filed suit, but in a 7–2 decision (*Haig* v. *Agee*) the Supreme Court in 1981 backed the State Department. The court ruled that congressional silence on the matter implied acquiescence in the department's claims of authority on national security grounds, and that therefore no specific statutory authority was needed. Since Agee was never actually indicted for a criminal offense, this decision confirmed the State Department's power to deny passports on grounds other than illegal conduct.

In addition, the Supreme Court, in *Zemel* v. *Rusk* (1965), has upheld the right of the State Department to restrict travel to certain areas. Subsequent decisions, however, removed any criminal penalties for doing so. In other words, until Congress makes travel in banned countries a crime, the State Department can invalidate passports for travel to those countries, but it cannot act against anyone who is admitted to those countries without his passport (this applied to some antiwar activists who visited North Vietnam). The State Department's authority was further expanded in 1984, when the Supreme Court, in *Regan* v. *Wald,* upheld a ban on travel to Cuba that the Reagan administration had imposed in 1982. The U.S. government justified the measure as part of its economic warfare against Cuba, and the court accepted this as a legitimate exercise of executive authority in foreign policy. Similar measures were invoked against Nicaragua in 1985.

Another dimension of U.S. practice on international movement is the traditionally restrictive attitude toward the entrance of visitors. While such restrictions date back to 1798,[48] the worst instances have

48. Parker, p. 854.

occurred since 1952, when passage of the Immigration and Nationality Act (the McCarran Act) authorized the exclusion of Communists, homosexuals, and other broad categories of "undesirables." Literal-minded implementation of the act has led to the exclusion of such dangerous radicals as NATO officials, Charlie Chaplin, and, more recently, a Canadian naturalist who had joked about shooting down American planes with his rifle.

In short, American courts turned back an attempt to impose unprecedented limits on the rights of American citizens to travel abroad. But the State Department still asserts the authority to prevent the departure of any citizen on national security grounds, and to limit travel to the United States. Thus, while the record of the United States is superior to that of many other states, it still falls short of the ideal of free international movement.

The Inglés Study

Following adoption of the Universal Declaration of Human Rights in 1948, the United Nations undertook a series of studies on the status of the rights it guaranteed. It is revealing that a study of compliance with the right to leave was completed only in 1963, was formally referred to member states only in 1973, and is only now being updated. The contrast to the shelf-yards of material turned out by the U.N. on other rights could not be more striking.

The initial proposal for such a study came in 1952, in the Subcommission on Prevention of Discrimination and Protection of Minorities, which contemplated a survey of measures to combat discrimination in both immigration and emigration. Countries with immigration policies that could be described as discriminatory, the United States among them, sought to eliminate immigration from the scope of the study, on the grounds that it was not a right in the same sense that emigration was. In 1954, the Commission on Human Rights directed that the study focus on article 13(2), that is, on emigration alone. In the same year, Judge José Inglés, a prominent Philippine jurist with a long and distinguished legal career who was then serving on the subcommission, was appointed to report on how such a study might be conducted. Members of the subcommission serve, at least in theory, as independent experts rather than government representatives.

The debate over immigration, together with East European opposition to any discussion of emigration, prolonged the gestation period of the study beyond what was normal even at the U.N. Inglés presented preliminary reports at the 1955 and 1959 sessions of the subcommission, but it was not until 1960 that the body finally approved a full-scale study. Inglés was appointed Special Rapporteur to carry out the study, and at last work proceeded at a normal pace.

Three years later, the study was completed and published. It is, by all accounts, a forthright and honest document. Inglés has been described by other participants as tough, judicious, and dedicated to seeing the project through, despite great obstacles. Rather than rely on staff assistance, Inglés drafted nearly the entire document himself, giving it a unity and directness unusual in such studies.

His fundamental conclusion: "As regards the right of a national to leave his own country, the situation is far less favorable and may be said to be retrogressive. . . . greater numbers of people are effectively confined behind their national boundaries today than in previous periods of history."[49] Inglés added that "whereas Governments once erected walls to keep foreigners from entering a country, today walls are built—both figuratively and literally—to keep nationals hemmed in."[50] In a passage that stirred an especially vociferous response, he referred to the "Chinese wall" built between East and West Berlin in 1961 as a warning "that an ancient and basic right of the human being is in jeopardy."[51]

Both during and after the study, critics on the subcommission, mainly from Soviet bloc states, insisted that since the study was part

49. Inglés, p. 58.
50. Ibid.
51. Ibid., p. 4.

of a series on discrimination, it should focus exclusively on the matter of equal treatment regarding the right to leave. Inglés resisted this pressure, arguing that "perhaps the most serious form of discrimination in respect of the right of everyone to leave his country occurs when all nationals, with the exception of the ruler or members of a small governing clique, are not allowed to go abroad for any purpose whatsoever."[52] He could not escape the fact, however, that he was largely dependent on information supplied by governments themselves, which were not always forthcoming.

Nonetheless, the subcommission staff prepared reports on ninety countries. Of these countries, twenty-four guaranteed the right to leave in the Constitution or in basic laws, and another twelve did so by judicial interpretation. Fifty had no explicit recognition of the right, and the remaining four furnished no information on this point. Inglés pointed out that the absence of legal recognition did not necessarily mean that the right was not respected—any more than the existence of such recognition meant that it was respected.[53]

Regarding permissible limits on the right, the study accepted most of those made on grounds of public order, health, and morals, categories that covered the denial of exit privileges to minors, paupers, fugitives from justice, persons with legal obligations, and habitual criminals. Many countries claimed that these were the sole grounds on which they denied the right to leave; the Soviet Union, for example, declared that it refused exit permits only to those facing criminal charges, serving sentences, or shirking military obligations.[54]

Inglés took the position that national security limits were warranted only if the individual committed a specific offense punishable

52. Ibid., p. 16; see also Sidney Liskofsky, "The Contribution of José D. Inglés," in Vasak and Liskofsky, p. 488.

53. Inglés, p. 5.

54. United Nations, Economic and Social Council, Commission on Human Rights, Subcommission on Prevention of Discrimination and Protection of Minorities, Conference Room Paper No. 85/Rev. 1, February 7, 1963, *Summary of Information Relating to the Union of Soviet Socialist Republics,* p. 5.

by law, rather than as a general preventive measure. Knowledge of classified material should serve as grounds for denial only if it presented a "clear and present danger." He rejected the claim of "interests of the state"—a concept not recognized in any international document—maintaining that it fostered a policy "which virtually confines the bulk of the population within their national boundaries."[55] Inglés's position, if accepted, would invalidate the claims not only of the Soviet bloc nations but also of the United States and other countries claiming the right to deny passports on grounds of national interest. Judging from the report, several nations followed the American lead on this point. Liberia, for example, withheld passports if a person's "activities abroad would be prejudicial to the interest of the country . . . [or] the orderly conduct of the State's foreign affairs." In Cameroun, documents were denied those "whose presence abroad . . . would prejudice Cameroun's good relations with a foreign state." In Jordan, "adherence to Communist doctrines" was grounds for barring exit from the country.[56]

Inglés pointed to those instances in which governments practiced ethnic discrimination in deciding who could leave. Blacks were restricted from leaving South-West Africa (a former German colony under South African mandate) and Jews prevented from departing Eastern Europe and Morocco.[57] In general, however, discrimination was becoming less an issue as many regimes exercised grand impartiality in barring the departure of all population groups.

55. Inglés, pp. 39–40, 42, 45, 59.

56. United Nations, Economic and Social Council, Commission on Human Rights, Subcommission on Prevention of Discrimination and Protection of Minorities, Conference Room Paper No. 72, December 21, 1962, *Summary of Information Relating to Liberia*, p. 3; Document de Séance no. 27, January 3, 1962, *Résumé des renseignements concernant le Cameroun*, p. 3; Conference Room Paper No. 70/Rev. 1, January 8, 1963, *Summary of Information Relating to Jordan*, p. 2. Like the United States, many if not most democracies allow the withholding of passports on national security or national interest grounds, even if such provisions are rarely invoked; see Hannum, pp. 90–151.

57. Inglés, pp. 16, 20–28.

Overall, Inglés stressed the need to get behind legal facades and look at actual practices, noting that "it is hardly ever possible to deduce solely from the perusal of legal texts the extent to which this right is enjoyed by the nationals of a country."[58] As an example, the study cited an unnamed country requiring seventeen different documents, including an invitation from abroad and proof of pre-payment, or guarantee, of all expenses. This procedure, it concluded, "has the effect of making the enjoyment of the right to leave a country dependent upon excessive documentation which is compounded by the fact that most of the documents can be obtained only from the Government concerned, and hence subject to the approval of the Government."[59]

Some countries, the study noted, did not require officials to give reasons for a denial. Many allowed for no appeal, with no judicial review nor any political or legislative recourse. Inglés also noted cases in which illegal departures incurred heavy sanctions—a clear indication that more was at stake than the violation of procedures.

Aside from the cases cited here, Inglés made few references to countries by name. But many of his strictures were clearly directed at Soviet bloc nations, and they reacted angrily to the report. The U.S. expert on the subcommission, Morris Abram, later noted that he was "shocked" by the East European reaction to the report. Publicly, the official Soviet position was that no one wanted to leave the Soviet Union. Privately, the Soviets hinted that the debate could have serious negative repercussions for the position of Soviet Jews.[60]

In a counteroffensive of sorts, the Polish expert on the subcommission, Wojciech Ketrzynski, tabled a "new principle," asserting that full enjoyment of the right to leave and return depended on

58. Ibid., p. 18; see also Ved P. Nanda, "The Right to Movement and Travel Abroad: Some Observations on the U.N. Deliberations," *Denver Journal of International Law and Policy* 109 (1971): 115–16.

59. Inglés, p. 50.

60. Personal interview with Morris Abram, May 4, 1984; interviews with two close observers of the meetings.

"the general well-being of each society as a whole." It was essential, he continued, to achieve "an equitable distribution of goods" so that the right to leave was not limited to a few. Furthermore, political tensions in the world had to be reduced in order to create "an atmosphere favourable to the free movement of persons from country to country."[61]

At the time, however, the Western position on the subcommission was strong (only three of its eleven members, including Inglés, were from Third-World countries), so that Soviet and Polish participants found themselves relatively isolated. Also, subcommission members could only criticize and suggest changes in the study; they could not rewrite it. The only votes taken came on referring the study to the Commission on Human Rights and on an accompanying set of proposed draft principles.

Nevertheless, the Soviet member, Boris Ivanov, displayed remarkable tactical ingenuity by providing a steady stream of objections. In the initial debate over the study, Ivanov disputed the subcommission's spending so much time on such a narrow problem. He criticized Inglés for dealing with issues aside from discrimination while ignoring other, mainly economic issues that were of critical importance. Ivanov maintained that the central concerns of the study were artificially created and, in any event, properly belonged to the sovereign jurisdiction of states. Dealing with such matters, he claimed, could encourage groups to engage in provocation. Ivanov also faulted Inglés for using such tendentious material as anti-Soviet propaganda furnished by Jewish organizations.[62]

At other sessions, Ivanov strongly attacked the study's reference to the Berlin wall, declaring that it "violated the directive of the

61. United Nations, Economic and Social Council, Commission on Human Rights, Subcommission on Prevention of Discrimination and Protection of Minorities, *Summary Record,* Fifteenth Session (E/CN.4/Sub.2/L.270, January 21, 1963) (New York, 1963).

62. Records on all the Subcommission sessions are from *Summary Record* (E/CN.4/Sub.2/SR.382, 384, 385, 394, 395, 396, and 397, January 15–26, 1963).

Commission on Human Rights that material used in the studies should be objective." On another occasion, he defended the wall, asserting that "when that border had been open, it had been used, relentlessly and systematically, by subversive forces to suck out the life-blood of the German Democratic Republic and plunder the workers in an attempt to shake the foundations of socialism in that country." And, touching the real core issue in the debate, Ivanov declared that the individual's right to leave must be weighed against national sovereignty and development policies.

Finally, the draft principles came up for a vote. They included a strong restatement of the right to leave and return, a call to eliminate financial requirements for exit, provisions for expeditious administrative treatment and for a right of appeal, and the elimination of sanctions against those trying to exercise that right.

Ivanov announced he would not support those principles that constituted interference in the internal affairs of sovereign states. "There were, of course, no difficulties about leaving the Soviet Union or returning to it," he declared, but added that it was wrong to ask new states to abolish laws protecting their economy and national security. In the final debate, Ivanov suggested that, since everyone agreed the matter needed further study, the pending resolution should simply be postponed until the following year.

Ivanov, sometimes joined by Poland's Ketrzynski, abstained on most of the provisions, especially those dealing with procedures rather than general principles. Both voted against the operative sections of the resolution referring the study and draft principles to the full Commission on Human Rights, and they abstained on the resolution as a whole.[63] But all the other members voted in favor, and thus the matter finally reached the commission—some fifteen years after the Universal Declaration of Human Rights had been proclaimed.

Like most U.N. activities of this kind, the debate over the

63. *Summary Record* (E/CN.4/Sub.2/SSR.396, January 25, 1963).

resolution attracted little attention. For example, the subcommission debate and the Inglés study did not receive a single mention in the *New York Times* during the debate, from 1961 to 1963. The West perhaps tended to consider the matter a lost cause. Moreover, the issue did not have the same kind of natural constituency enjoyed by many related issues, such as religious liberty or racial discrimination. When the 117 nongovernmental organizations with consultative status at the U.N. were asked for comments, only 15 responded. The only countries interested in the issue, it seemed, were those that were hard to leave; others appeared indifferent. This tendency increased over the following years as the preoccupations of the Third World came to dominate international forums—preoccupations that did not include free international movement.

Finally, during the 1960s the International Covenant on Civil and Political Rights, and other international agreements covering the right to leave, were being drafted. In the minds of many observers, this fulfilled the need for further action on the subject.

But if the genesis of the Inglés study—to date the main U.N. activity on international freedom of movement—received meager attention, its subsequent disposition was even more cloaked in obscurity. When the study was discussed in the Economic and Social Council in April 1963, the Soviet representative urged that it not be circulated. However, the Soviets were resoundingly outvoted on this question,[64] and the study was circulated for comments by member states. Most responded positively, suggesting only minor changes. But Poland suggested that the principles be rewritten with "less detailed" provisions and that they be presented in declaration or resolution form rather than as a formal convention. The Soviet Union argued that the study was "not urgently needed and is not a matter of top priority." The Soviets further faulted the study for not giving "due weight" to the claims of national sovereignty. They

64. United Nations, Economic and Social Council, *Summary Record,* Nineteenth Session (E/CN.4/SR.770, April 3, 1963) (New York, 1963).

called for further careful study to take "due account of the opinions expressed" by member states.[65]

As it happened, the Soviets worried for nought. There was no general clamor for completing the study. At the 1964 session of the Commission on Human Rights, consideration of the resolution was postponed to the following year "owing to lack of time." The same exercise was repeated at every annual session until 1969.[66] In that year, the commission, finally recognizing that the matter had been unduly delayed, assigned it priority status for the next session. But by then, not surprisingly, there was talk of updating the study, since most of the information in it was by now seven or eight years old. In late 1969 Inglés asked the Secretary General to circulate a request for information on any changes in governmental practices.[67] By late 1970, some twenty-nine countries had responded. Most reported no changes; a few had added legal guarantees through new constitutions or adherence to international agreements.[68]

Finally, in March 1971, Inglés was allowed to present his study to the Commission on Human Rights. But owing again to lack of time, the commission deferred consideration to the next session.[69]

65. United Nations, Economic and Social Council, *Note by the Secretary General* (E/CN.4/869, December 23, 1963) (New York, 1963).

66. The Commission on Human Rights meets annually every spring. All records of Commission sessions are found under United Nations, Economic and Social Council, Commission on Human Rights, *Report on the Twentieth Session* (E/CN.4/874, February 17–March 18, 1964) (New York, 1964), and similar citations for the 21st through 29th sessions, 1965–73.

67. Inglés, "The United Nations Study of Discrimination in Respect of the Right of Everyone to Leave Any Country, including His Own, and to Return to His Country," in Vasak and Liskofsky, p. 476.

68. United Nations, Economic and Social Council, *Note by the Secretary General* (E/CN.4/1042, with Annexes and Addenda, November 6, 1970) (New York, 1970). By 1985, Hannum was able to report that 75 countries (including a few that violate it in practice) had formal constitutional guarantees of the right to leave and/or return (pp. 219–22).

69. United Nations, Economic and Social Council, Commission on Human Rights, *Report on the Twenty-Seventh Session* (E/CN.4/1098–1138, February 26–March 26, 1971).

By this time, the lack of positive action by the United Nations had galvanized outside organizations to push the issue. In February 1971, fifteen organizations urged that the matter be given top priority. Following continued inaction in 1971 and 1972, the International Institute of Human Rights (directed by the renowned French statesman René Cassin), the Jacob Blaustein Institute for the Advancement of Human Rights, and the Uppsala University Faculty of Law organized a colloquium on the right to leave. Given the prominence of the participants and the timing of the event, the colloquium—held in Uppsala, Sweden, in June 1972—attracted some attention.

Inglés, in a paper read at the colloquium, said: "The situation with respect to the right of everyone to leave any country including his own, and to return to his country, is no less urgent today than when the report was completed in 1963. . . . the mass media have brought to our attention the sad plight of an increasing number of persons denied the right to leave the country of their birth or the country of their sojourn, as well as of numberless refugees prevented from returning to their respective countries."[70]

The organizer of the colloquium, Sidney Liskofsky, recalled that consideration of the issue by the commission had been postponed for a decade "for the transparently false reason of the lack of time." He suggested that it was now the responsibility of nongovernmental organizations to pick up where the United Nations had left off.[71] The colloquium issued an eloquent Declaration of the Right to Leave and to Return, calling the right "essential for the effective enjoyment of other human rights." It set forth a set of principles encompassing those proposed by Inglés and going beyond them on such matters as harassment and property rights of would-be emigrants.[72]

Whether because of the prodding or because further delay had simply become untenable, the Commission on Human Rights finally acted in March 1973. The United States introduced a strong reso-

70. Inglés, "The United Nations Study of Discrimination," p. 485.
71. Liskofsky, pp. 491–92.
72. Text of the Declaration in Vasak and Liskofsky, pp. xxi–xxvi.

lution backing the study, but, sensing a lack of support, substituted a milder resolution. Even that, however, gave way to a more diluted resolution offered by Ecuador, Ghana, India, and Pakistan. While this statement affirmed the importance of the right to leave, it merely drew the attention of member states to the draft principles. The resolution even failed to include the routine closing paragraph retaining the subject on the commission's agenda, an omission that was noted approvingly by the Soviet delegate as a confirmation that the right was not a fundamental one.[73] The resolution was adopted.

The Economic and Social Council took up the matter in May of the same year. Proponents of the right to leave succeeded in pushing through a resolution that restored the item to the agenda of the Commission on Human Rights. The critical paragraph of the resolution drew the attention of governments and international organizations to the draft principles and expressed the hope that they would take the right to leave into account when considering relevant regulations. This paragraph passed in a 12–5 vote, with 7 abstentions, reflecting some drop in support in the ten years since the subcommission voted on the Inglés study.[74]

It was a modest result, considering the long ordeal that led up to it. The arduous process reflected the reality of a world in which the right to leave and to return was coming under increasing assault in practice. Throughout the 1960s and 1970s, the atmosphere for protecting the right of personal self-determination had clearly deteriorated. This raised a disturbing possibility: Was the Inglés study, modest as it was, to mark the high point of international concern for free international movement in the modern era?

73. United Nations, Economic and Social Council, Commission on Human Rights, *Report on the Twenty-Ninth Session* (E/CN.4/SR. 1186–1242, February 26–April 6, 1973).

74. Only four nations—the Soviet Union, Hungary, Poland, and Mongolia—voted against the resolution as a whole. United Nations, Economic and Social Council, *Official Records,* Fifty-Fourth Session (January 8–10 and April 17–May 18, 1973) (New York, 1973).

5

Emigration and Expulsion in the Third World

Indeed, to open the door for unrestricted emigration would run counter to the vital interests of any developing society.

—Hussein A. Hassouna, Egyptian diplomat, 1973

The Integrative Revolution

Until recent times, most transnational movement occurred from the developed to the less developed world. Over the last century, however, the reverse has been true. As floods of migrants stream out of Asia, Africa, and, to some extent, Latin America, conflict over the right of personal self-determination has shifted to what, until recently, was the periphery of the international system.

The problems in these areas are not basically different, but the scale has grown enormously. If the consolidating monarchies of Europe produced refugees in thousands or tens of thousands, flows now are measured in millions. If restrictions on exit in the past affected only the relatively few ready to exploit such opportunities, they now weigh heavily on entire populations who have been made aware of the benefits of mobility.

These massive population flows reflect the intense pressures that beset much of the Third World. The process of nation-building that is taking place in many countries carries a built-in stress that seems to produce refugees as a matter of course. A second pattern is an effort to block the loss of highly skilled emigrants to the developed countries, in combating what is termed reverse transfer of technology or, more commonly, brain drain.

New nations are thus torn between a wish to be rid of those who don't fit in and a desire to make those with needed skills fit in. This explains much of the inconsistency and vacillation on both issues, just as medieval Spain alternated between converting and expelling Jews. The same states appear both as refugee-producers and as injured parties in the brain drain debate. Some have been known to bemoan the loss of badly needed professionals while deliberately creating the conditions that made them flee.

The brain drain has been a matter of special concern to Third-World nations because of intense pressures on these nations for rapid development combined with the relative scarcity of skilled personnel. But, as the next section will show, a closer look leads to some surprising conclusions about the relevance of emigration curbs for national development. The assumption of a direct and simple relationship is, it turns out, superficial.

As for refugee flows, they are commonly attributed simply to persecution.[1] But here, as well, there is more to it. When ruling elites embark on an effort to strengthen national unity, they tend to turn on groups whose language, ethnicity, religion, culture, political beliefs, or socioeconomic status do not fit in. This process is driven by political and ideological urges, by an "architectonic compulsion."[2]

1. G. J. L. Coles ("The Problem of Mass Expulsion" [background paper for Working Group of Experts on the Problem of Mass Expulsion, International Institute of Humanitarian Law, San Remo, Italy, April 16–18, 1983], p. 9), is one of many to comment on the astonishing lack of general studies on the causes of refugee flows, as opposed to the substantial literature on legal and humanitarian responses and descriptive case studies.

2. Aristide R. Zolberg, "State-Formation and Its Victims: Refugee Movements in Early Modern Europe," in *Beyond Progress and Development: Proceedings of the Symposium on Macro Political and Societal Change,* ed. N. J. Berting,

In fact, the act of purging the body politic may even damage the economy and society (though there may be short-term profit in the sequestered property of those expelled). In opposition to the common image, it is not a matter of simple narrow-mindedness (though prejudice underlies it), but a drive for conformity that is characteristic of certain phases of national consolidation. Marxists agree in attributing refugee flows to broad historical forces, which, in the contemporary Third World, they identify as injustice, exploitation, and economic weakness. They admit, however, that the "progressive restructuring" of a society may also produce refugees.[3]

For all its divisions, early modern Europe mostly consisted of homogeneous states. The great majority of Englishmen or Frenchmen shared a sense of being "English" or "French." They spoke the same language and belonged to the same culture. But when the idea of the nation-state was transposed to the developing world, there existed little sense of commonality on which to build. In its place was a dizzying diversity. Africa as a whole, for example, has an estimated 800 ethnic groups and 1000 distinct languages, and a typical African state might contain dozens of each. In drawing borders, colonial powers paid little attention to such divisions. Furthermore, colonial policies frequently accentuated existing differences by playing one group against another in classic divide-and-rule style. The introduction of new groups through population transfers, such as Asians in East Africa, also proved disruptive. In addition, colonialism deepened inequalities within societies, driving a sharp wedge between Westernized and traditional sectors.

W. Blockmans, and U. Rosenthal (Rotterdam: Faculty of Social Sciences, Erasmus University, 1983); see also Louise W. Holborn, *Refugees: A Problem of Our Time. The Work of the U.N. High Commissioner for Refugees, 1951–1972* (Metuchen, N.J.: Scarecrow, 1975), p. 829, on Africa, and references to the "integrative revolution" in Sadruddin Aga Khan, *Study on Human Rights and Massive Exoduses,* United Nations Economic and Social Council, Commission on Human Rights, (E/CN.4/1503, December 31, 1981) (New York, 1981), p. 37.

3. This was the phrase used by a Bulgarian representative on one of the U.N. bodies dealing with refugees (personal interview, May 2, 1984).

Finally, many of the coercive practices employed in forging national unity were bequeathed by the colonial powers. The Western nations may have imparted democratic ideals, but they also provided an example of authoritarian government in action. When, for example, Ghana in 1957 adopted a Deportation Act, it followed a model established by British colonial authorities. And when Uganda forced the Kabaka of Buganda—a tribal leader—from his throne in 1966, it was replaying his deportation by the British thirteen years earlier.

Further pressures have been created by the rush to modernize. As Third-World nations seek to make up a hundred years of development in ten, diversity often seems a block to efficiency. Ethnic conflicts and linguistic chaos complicate administration, disrupt effective planning, limit labor mobility, and otherwise inhibit progress. As an African jurist has written, "Most progressive Africans would have no hesitation in subordinating the concept of free association to that of national unity."[4]

National cohesion, though, is not the only cause of forced population movements; some regimes also use domestic groups as pawns in their international relations. Many Caribbean observers believe that the Duvaliers in Haiti used the threat of illegal emigration to the United States to coax more aid out of Washington. In 1971, India viewed the flow of refugees from East Pakistan (now Bangladesh) as a Pakistani ploy to avert Indian intervention. Both Thailand and Malaysia tend to regard the flood of refugees from Vietnam as an intentional effort to destabilize their countries.[5]

Overall, multinational or multireligious states have not been conspicuous successes in the post–World War II period, whether governed by democratic or authoritarian regimes. Cyprus, Pakistan,

4. S. K. B. Asante, "Nation Building and Human Rights in Emergent African Nations," *Cornell International Law Journal* 1–2 (1968): 94.

5. Myron Weiner, "International Emigration and the Third World" (paper delivered at the Harvard-Draeger Conference on Population Studies between Rich and Poor Countries, October 6–8, 1983), p. 9.

Ethiopia, and Lebanon have all been rent by civil wars, while India, Sri Lanka, Iran, Iraq, Sudan and other African states have had to contend with continuing instability. Not even Western states are immune to such conflicts: witness the cases of Ireland, Belgium, and Canada. The dilemma is that the push for national unity comes precisely at a time when ethnic and cultural identification is on the rise. No multinational state has been able to resolve this tension completely, and the temptation to use coercion is, in many cases, irresistible. And as often as not, that means promoting assimilation by forcing emigration and/or blocking it.

Certain groups are particularly vulnerable to homogenizing pressures, and these have contributed most of the Third-World refugees in recent years. First and foremost are ethnic or religious minorities that are traditional targets of hostility within particular societies. Examples include Baha'is in post–1979 Iran, Kurds in both Iran and Iraq, Tamils in Sri Lanka, Indians in Guatemala and Nicaragua, and tribal groups in Africa such as the Banyarwanda, expelled from Uganda in 1982. Resident aliens—who may have lived in a country for decades or even generations—often offer an inviting target, especially in Africa, where the expulsion of aliens has become common.

Ethnic groups associated with a national rival have an additional strike against them. Usually, these groups have close ties to neighboring or nearby states. Hindus were forced from East Pakistan in 1971, and more recently, ethnic Somalis from Ethiopia. In 1947, India and Pakistan exchanged minorities, as did Israel and the Arab world in 1948 and after, Rwanda and Burundi in the 1970s, and the Turkish and Greek sectors of Cyprus after 1974.

Changes of regimes or political strife can also make life difficult for minority groups. Thus, independence sent whites fleeing from Algeria, Angola, Mozambique, and Zimbabwe. The Hmong left Laos after the Communist victory there (they had cooperated with the American military). Political activists have been forced from

Pinochet's Chile, Somozista and Sandinista Nicaragua, and apartheid South Africa.

A regime bent on radical change may exert pressure on an entire social class. Much of Cuba's middle class left the island after Castro came to power, and Chinese merchants were squeezed from Vietnam (either for ethnic or political reasons or, more likely, a combination of the two). Sometimes the restructuring undertaken by a government forces more than just minorities to seek refuge. In both Cambodia under the Khmer Rouge and Afghanistan since 1979, the flow of refugees has constituted a significant portion of the total population. Most extreme was Equatorial Guinea in the late 1970s, when, under the infamous Macias regime, nearly one-half the population sought refuge outside the country.

The vast scale of modern refugee flows has given rise to what have been called *refugee-warrior communities*.[6] These communities depend on external aid to survive as a fighting group, typically in areas contiguous to their homeland, and the intrusion of geopolitical rivalries usually guarantees them a patron. They develop new exile leaders, adapted to the quasi-military style of life, who have a vested interest in the perpetuation of the conflict and are often opposed to a compromise settlement, since it would "liquidate" their struggle. The archetypical case is the Palestinians. Others include the Afghan resistance, the Khmers fighting the Vietnamese-backed regime in Cambodia, the Nicaraguan contras, and the Somalis on the border of Ethiopia. The presence of such groups adds yet another intractable dimension to the issue of free international movement in our time.

The Brain Drain Refrain
Just as many Third-World governments fear keeping the unwanted, they fear losing the wanted. However, the same pressures that propel

6. Astri Suhrke and Aristide R. Zolberg, "Social Conflict and Refugees in the Third World: The Cases of Ethiopia and Afghanistan" (paper presented at the annual meeting of the American Political Science Association, Washington, D.C., 1984), pp. 47–49.

the drive for unity often force a nation's more talented personnel to consider traveling abroad. The incentives for moving to more advanced lands are obvious. For skilled professionals, in particular, less developed countries lack the working conditions, infrastructure, and professional opportunities available in Europe and North America. Moreover, since many Third-World professionals have acquired their expertise in the West, they are comfortable with the lifestyle and familiar with career opportunities in that part of the world. Furthermore, developed nations give professionals preferential treatment in immigrant admissions.

The loss of skilled manpower first became a concern around 1960—not in the Third World but in Europe, which was losing professionals and scientists to the United States. (In fact, most European nations still lose a greater proportion of their students and professionals than do most developing countries.) Developing nations quickly picked up the theme, complaining that they were losing substantial numbers of their own skilled personnel. By one estimate, the United States, Britain, and Canada together enjoyed a "brain gain" in 1961 to 1972 worth $46 billion in educational costs saved by importing ready-made experts and technicians from the rest of the world.[7]

A 1968 report issued by the United Nations Institute for Training and Research (UNITAR) confirmed that there was, indeed, a sizable flow of skilled manpower from less developed to developed countries. It further found that the higher the level of skill—engineers, medical personnel, scientists—the greater the level of emigration. The study also determined that the flow was increasing and could be expected to continue increasing (except, perhaps, from South America).[8] Another landmark UNITAR study, directed by

7. Kathleen Newland, *International Migration: The Search for Work,* Worldwatch Paper 33 (Washington: Worldwatch Institute, 1979), p. 12.

8. *Outflow of Trained Personnel from Developing Countries,* Report of the Secretary General (New York: UNITAR, 1968), p. 5.

Gregory Henderson, was published in 1970. It noted that, from 1964 to 1969, Colombia lost 27 percent of its highly qualified professionals; Greece, from 1961 to 1965, lost 25 percent of its doctors, 27 percent of its scientists, and a full 35 percent of its engineers. Ten percent of all Indian doctors were working in Britain or the United States. According to a 1977 report for the United Nations Conference on Trade and Development (UNCTAD), Pakistan annually lost from 50 to 75 percent of its medical school graduates.[9] As of 1984, it is estimated that Third-World countries had lost between 400,000 and 500,000 professionals.[10]

But gross numbers do not convey the full story. Sudan lost only one percent of its labor force to emigration, but this included 70 percent of its medical graduates and such a large proportion of its top clerical personnel as to become "an obstacle to the efficient working of government."[11] In mid-1984, Jamaican Prime Minister Edward Seaga told the Governing Council of the United Nations Development Programme (UNDP) that from 1977 to 1980 alone, about 69 percent of his country's professional graduates moved to North America, representing a loss of about $194 million in educational costs. He concluded with evident frustration that such losses would continue, since "countries which have open societies cannot restrain this movement without violating essential human rights,

9. Gregory Henderson, *The Emigration of Highly Skilled Manpower from the Developing Countries,* UNITAR Research Reports 3 (New York: UNITAR, 1970), pp. 29, 130; S. M. Naseem, *Case Studies in Reverse Transfer of Technology (Brain Drain): A Survey of Problems and Policies in Pakistan,* United Nations, Conference on Trade and Development (TD/B/C.6/AC.4/3, December 20, 1977) (Geneva, 1978), p. 28.

10. United Nations, Conference on Trade and Development, *Proposals on Concrete Measures to Mitigate the Adverse Impact of Reverse Transfer of Technology on Developing Countries* (TD/B/AC.35/6, July 20, 1984). This report, from a meeting of governmental experts, gives a figure of over 400,000; a later UNCTAD report (TD/B/1018, September 17, 1984) estimates 500,000.

11. Newland, p. 11.

and at the same time cannot compete with the financial and other advantages offered by the industrialized countries."[12]

Despite this massive flow, the attention paid to the brain drain had faded by the early 1980s. A variety of factors was probably responsible—rhetorical overload, frustration over the lack of action, and the sheer intractability of the problem. International organizations had conducted one study after another—more than twenty by UNCTAD alone by 1984. Even then, there were calls for yet more data, a reflection of just how difficult it is to measure something as intangible as brains.

In addition, a small mountain of resolutions had been passed by the U.N. General Assembly, UNCTAD, and other international bodies. For the most part, these resolutions called on developed countries to encourage foreign students and professional workers to return to their native lands; advised less developed countries to provide more local education and more professional opportunities; and, of course, recommended further study. Some U.N. resolutions urged that international migration flows be more carefully organized and that government consent be sought for substantial flows, but without detailing what such organization or consent implied. They did not, however, call directly for restrictions on the right to leave. Clearly, it was difficult to devise countermeasures that were acceptable to all sides and consistent with basic human rights.

Sooner or later, however, the claims of national development were bound to impinge on freedom of movement. Henderson, in his 1970 UNITAR report, warned that "in a world of stark wealth-poverty, there are legitimate doubts as to whether complete freedom of movement is, in fact, compatible with the maximum development of developing countries."[13] Beginning in the 1960s, Third-World representatives began to express reservations to unrestricted emigra-

12. Edward Seaga, "Towards An International Fund for Manpower Resources" (address to the Governing Council of the United Nations Development Programme, June 12, 1984).

13. Henderson, p. 117.

tion on the grounds that such "political and civil" rights of the individual sometimes had to give way to the "economic and social" rights of society. Hussein A. Hassouna, an Egyptian diplomat, cogently summed up this position in a 1973 legal debate before the American Society of International Law over the right to leave:

> The right to leave a country is certainly an important right, but the importance attached to it is by no means universal. This reflects a basic difference of approach in which the Western countries emphasize political and civil rights, while the non-Western countries and all developing countries emphasize economic and social rights which, in their view, are essential for the exercise of political and civil rights. It follows from this basic difference of approach that whereas in Western opinion the right to leave should be absolute and unqualified, most developing countries see it subject to limitations and qualifications. Indeed, to open the door for unrestricted emigration would run counter to the vital interests of any developing society.[14]

In international forums generally, Third-World nations, preoccupied with the development imperative, have not given high priority to the right to leave. As an international civil servant from India put it, "We are not going to stop it, but we are not going to champion it either."[15]

Even such an advocate of free movement as Judge José Inglés acknowledged in his 1963 report that it was "understandable" that developing countries would act to prevent the loss of skilled manpower. Restrictions on exit, he noted, "might even be justified in certain cases," for example, when professionals accepted specialized

14. "Expulsion and Expatriation in International Law: The Right to Leave, to Stay, and to Return," remarks by Yash P. Ghai, Lung-chu Chen, Valerie Chalidze, Hussein A. Hassouna, and Sidney Liskofsky, *American Journal of International Law* 67 (November 1973): 136.

15. Personal interview with Rustum Lalkaka, Deputy Director, United Nations Interim Fund for Science and Technology for Development, April 9, 1984.

training at government expense in return for a specified period of service. Inglés added, however, that such restrictions could not be justified for industrialized countries, nor for preventing temporary departures in any part of the world. A more recent analysis of restrictions on movement allowed by the Covenant on Civil and Political Rights concludes that "vague assertions of 'brain drain' or other economic issues are insufficient," and that any limits must be "necessary to deal with a demonstrable socio-economic problem that threatens public order in a country." Such measures must also be proportional, temporary, nondiscriminatory, with adequate notice, and must not constitute a de facto general denial of the right to leave.[16]

Eastern bloc spokesmen have frequently encouraged Third-World nations to combat the brain drain with highly restrictive measures. Brain drain concerns appear to illustrate the justice of controlled emigration, helping to justify such policies in terms understandable to the Third World. The issue has, at times, brought the two blocs together in common cause against Western "exploitation." The Soviet Union and Eastern European nations have therefore incorporated the brain drain rhetoric into their own verbal arsenal. At times, their fervent enthusiasm for the issue has led them to make a case for direct controls that Third-World spokesmen seldom make for themselves.

A representative expression of these views is that of Péter Vas-Zoltán, a Hungarian economist, in a study published in Hungary. Vas-Zoltán directs attention to article 29(1) of the Universal Declaration of Human Rights, which holds that "Everyone has duties to the community in which alone the free and full development of his

16. José D. Inglés, *Study of Discrimination in Respect of the Right of Everyone to Leave Any Country, Including His Own, and to Return to His Country,* United Nations, Economic and Social Council, Commission on Human Rights, Subcommission on Prevention of Discrimination and Protection of Minorities (E/CN.4/Sub. 2/229/Rev. 1, 1963) (New York, 1963), pp. 44–45; Hurst Hannum, *The Right to Leave and Return in International Law and Practice* (Washington: The Procedural Aspects of International Law Institute, 1985), p. 43.

personality is possible." Following from this, he asserts that the community, or state, has the duty to provide professional training and that "the human capital created in this way becomes part of the nation's wealth in the broadest sense of the term." Consequently, the state has the implied right to prevent the loss of this capital, by "administrative" measures if necessary. [17]

Vas-Zoltán further argues that these measures are a necessary defense against the active recruitment of professionals by the West. He denies that socialist states are seriously threatened by such recruitment, and thus poses as a champion of Third-World interests. Since the American economy could not function without an influx of professionals trained at Third-World expense, he asserts, the U.S. government actively promotes the process; as evidence, he cites immigration laws favoring professionals (he neglects to mention that U.S. law, expressly designed to discourage brain drain, that requires foreign students to leave the U.S. for a period of time before applying for a more permanent visa). Such a situation, writes Vas-Zoltán, is symptomatic of the unequal power relations in the world system. [18] In sum:

> Any approach to Human Rights which attempts to justify brain drain is unacceptable because it relieves the individual of his moral duties by providing a formal and dogmatic interpretation of these rights; because it separates the principles of rights and duties; because it condones the continuous enrichment, without cost, of the prosperous, developed countries, at the expense of the less developed ones, which is essentially contrary to the greatest international economic and political task of humanity, namely, the effort to close the gap between the developed and the developing countries. [19]

17. Péter Vas-Zoltán, *The Brain Drain: An Anomaly of International Relations* (Leiden: A. W. Sijthoff, and Budapest: Akadémia, 1976), pp. 24, 25, 27.

18. Ibid., pp. 26, 67–69, 117–18.

19. Ibid., p. 29.

Some Third-World states have indeed tried to use direct measures to stem the flow of scarce professionals. In Mozambique, for example, the declared policy is to "discourage" emigration, and an applicant for an exit visa must justify his case; he is not allowed "just to emigrate." Given the need for skilled people, it is argued, the right to leave "must be implemented in accord with the situation in the country."[20] Other African states, less restrictive, may still use administrative measures to retain particular individuals, on grounds of their responsibility to serve the nation. The fact that many or most professionals work in the public sector gives governments more control in such cases.

A 1983 UNCTAD survey recorded five types of restrictive measures that states commonly used to plug their brain drains. The most direct—to which only a handful of countries would admit—was control of passports and exit permits. A few others required service bonding, or acceptance of obligations to work at home in return for subsidized study abroad. Some countries discouraged study or work abroad through tight controls on foreign exchange, travel taxes, or deposits for return passage. Others required that a given percentage of foreign earnings be remitted home (though the motive here was more often to earn foreign exchange than to curb emigration). Finally, some measures spelled out restrictions for professions where the manpower loss was most serious.[21]

Doctors and other medical personnel are frequently the target of specific measures. Haiti at one point flatly prohibited the departure of all doctors, dentists, nurses, and laboratory technicians. Thailand and Ethiopia also required periods of service for medical

20. Personal interview with Elias Jaime Zimba, Political Affairs Officer, Mozambique Mission to the United Nations, April 27, 1984.

21. United Nations, Conference on Trade and Development, *Consideration of Recommendations on Policies and Concrete Measures with a View to Mitigating the Adverse Consequences for the Developing Countries of the Reverse Transfer of Technology, including the Proposal for the Establishment of an International Labour Compensatory Facility* (TD/B/AC.35/2, June 17, 1983) (Geneva, 1983), pp. 9–12.

graduates, and other countries have sometimes stipulated that those applying to study medicine abroad must post bonds guaranteeing their return. A 1979 World Health Organization (WHO) study of the brain drain of medical personnel noted that "the countries concerned . . . claim that, in order to reconcile the rights of society with the rights of the individual, some personal freedoms may need to be restricted."[22]

In those cases where Third-World regimes have tried the restrictive approach, the results have rarely been positive. To be effective, such measures would require something like a police state. Partial measures only sharpen the urge to leave while there's still a chance; both India and Pakistan found this out when the passage of measures intended to keep doctors at home only pushed more to leave. The WHO study of physicians noted that penalties imposed on illegal departure had the unintended side effect of discouraging eventual return.[23]

Sri Lanka also tried the restrictive approach and found it wanting. In 1961 it adopted a Compulsory Public Service Act, which required all professional graduates to work for five years in public service. In 1971, a new passport law required professionals to send remittances from abroad, and, a year later, they were required to give a year's public service for each month of state-supported study abroad. In 1974, however, when a Cabinet committee concluded that "the heavy hand of the State" had not been effective in discouraging emigration, these measures were relaxed. Subsequently, the government shifted its attention to creating better employment opportunities at home, and Sri Lanka soon showed just how suc-

22. Alfonso Mejia, Helena Pizurki, and Erica Royston, *Physician and Nurse Migration: Analysis and Policy Implications* (Geneva: World Health Organization, 1979), pp. 183–85.
23. UNCTAD, *Consideration of Recommendations,* pp. 9–12; Mejia, Pizurki, and Royston, p. 472.

cessful affirmative programs could be in resolving the brain drain dilemma (such programs are further discussed below).[24]

The experience of Pakistan illustrates the problems that countries encounter in imposing even indirect restrictions. In January 1976, the government of Zolfikar Ali Bhutto proposed an ordinance that required thirteen categories of professionals to obtain "no objection certificates" from the relevant ministry before leaving the country; in addition, those professionals would be liable to a "capitation fee" of as much as 20 percent of all income earned abroad. A storm of protest ensued, forcing the government to withdraw the legislation a mere ten days later. Only public employees and doctors (already restricted since 1973) would have to obtain the certificates. Even this proved ineffective, as government employees could always resign their jobs, and large numbers of doctors managed to leave the country anyway.[25]

The 1983 UNCTAD study, after surveying emigration controls as a solution to brain drain in such cases as Pakistan and Sri Lanka, concluded that they were universally ineffective. Even Vas-Zoltán admits that "it has been proved in practice for decades now that brain drain cannot be stopped by administrative measures (e.g., by travel or visa restrictions)."[26] One reason for this is that most Third-World countries exercise only imperfect control over their borders. As Robert Myers put it in another leading study, "if an individual feels strongly that emigration is his best course, it is doubtful that passport control will stop him from migrating."[27] Moreover, the highly skilled are precisely those best positioned to evade controls, whether through favoritism, bribery, false documentation, expensive

24. United Nations, Conference on Trade and Development, *Case Studies in Reverse Transfer of Technology (Brain Drain): A Survey of Problems and Policies in Sri Lanka* (TD/B/C.6/AC.4/4, December 19, 1977) (Geneva, 1978), esp. pp. 11–17.

25. Naseem, pp. 19–20.

26. UNCTAD, *Consideration of Recommendations*; Vas-Zoltán, pp. 20–21.

27. Robert G. Myers, *Education and Emigration: Study Abroad and the Migration of Human Resources* (New York: David McKay, 1972), p. 334.

arrangements for physical evasion of border controls, or in the guise of legitimate temporary travel. Many are already located abroad as students; for example, as many as half of all professionals who choose residence in the United States have studied in American universities. Professionals also genuinely need to travel; a developing country that seals off its professionals from training and contacts abroad only handicaps itself.

Finally, many of the countries that lose professionals—Pakistan, for example—are simultaneously encouraging the outflow of unskilled and semi-skilled labor, which impinges on any anti-emigration policy. This interest constrains them from calling on the Western world to tighten its immigration laws, which would be one way of keeping brains at home. To the contrary, they often denounce the tight restrictions of Western immigration policy.

The brain drain must, indeed, be put in the perspective of overall migration from the Third World. Here again, a closer look challenges the common image. According to prevailing perceptions, migrants from the developing world come disproportionately from the poorest, most overpopulated lands and belong to the ranks of the urban unemployed and the rural poor. A growing body of evidence, however, suggests that this image is simply not accurate. For example, Jordanians working abroad have a higher level of education than the general population; emigrants from the Dominican Republic are generally better off than their fellow Dominicans and more likely to own land. In Saudi Arabia, almost half of all labor migrants are skilled. Even in the case of illegal Mexican immigrants in the United States—popularly portrayed as desperately poor—it now appears that most come from cities, are engaged in nonagricultural pursuits, and boast above-average levels of income and economic status.[28] Accord-

28. The evidence is summarized by Alejandro Portes, "International Labor Migration and National Development," in *U.S. Immigration and Refugee Policy,* ed. Mary M. Kritz (Lexington, Mass.: Lexington, 1983), p. 78. On Jordan and Saudi Arabia, see ibid.; on the Dominican Republic, see Sherri Grasmuck, "The Impact of Emigration on National Development: Three Sending Communities

ing to WHO, "The picture that emerges of the expatriate worker is a far cry from the "tired, poor, wretched" emigrant stereotype of the early part of this century. The economically motivated migrant is, rather, among the relatively skilled, educated, and, presumably, enterprising segment of the labor force."[29]

Perhaps this should not come as a revelation. Is it surprising that the urban, better-educated, and upwardly mobile sectors of the population are more aware of opportunities elsewhere and more motivated to exploit them? Or that members of traditional communities, relatively untouched by modernization, are the *least* likely to uproot themselves?

Should these nations be trying, therefore, to curtail outward movement? The answer to this question requires a closer look at the impact of emigration on Third-World nations. The overall demographic effect seems to be surprisingly slight. Only rarely has migration, permanent or temporary, caused a dramatic drop in total population. In the Caribbean, Puerto Rico and Surinam have each lost one-third of their population. The nations of North Africa have also suffered significant losses, ranging from 10.6 percent in Tunisia to 19.5 percent in Algeria. (These figures come from the mid-1970s.) North Yemen has lost 19 percent of its people, while Yugoslavia, Greece, Turkey, and Italy have all lost from 6 to 8 percent.[30]

But these are exceptions. The number of people lost to emigration each year amounts to only 2 or 3 percent of the Third World's annual population growth of 70 million to 80 million. Even in those countries where emigration is relatively high, the impact on the overall rate of population growth is meager. Thus, both Algeria and Morocco experienced above-average population growth even at the height of their labor emigrations; so did Mexico. Clearly, emigration is not a solution to excessive Third-World population growth.

---

in the Dominican Republic" (Occasional Paper no. 33, New York University, June, 1982), pp. 9–11.

29. Newland, p. 12.

30. Weiner, p. 4.

There is more controversy over the economic fallout from emigration. An influential school of developmental economists has challenged the benefits claimed for the international movement of labor. They maintain that the remittances sent home are not used productively, but are typically spent for consumer goods and, as a result, may have a distorting effect. The skills acquired abroad, they argue, are not easily applied at home, and are thus of little value. Exodus from agricultural areas may harm productivity and lead to the diversion of land to nonagricultural use. Finally, they stress, since it is the most productive and most needed who leave, emigration must harm a country's human resources.

In fact, many countries with high rates of emigration experience impressive economic growth at the same time. Of the eight countries with the highest levels of emigration during the 1960s, five had above-average rates of industrial growth; so did seven of the top nine emigration states in the 1970s. As for agricultural production, the same countries had at least average growth rates. To take one case, North Yemen is often cited as a country whose rural sector declined as a result of large-scale emigration; according to the World Bank, however, Yemen's agricultural production actually increased 3.7 percent annually during the 1970s.[31] In the Dominican Republic, to take a recent field study, the impact of emigration on agricultural production was mixed: while large-scale exodus did harm production in a small village, it had the opposite result in a larger rural town.[32]

In general, emigration seems to have much less impact, in either direction, than one would expect, but where effects are felt, they are more likely to be positive than not. In any event, most Third-World governments follow policies favorable to labor emigration, which would be difficult to explain if it were demonstratively harmful to their economies. One would have to assume that they are incapable of understanding, or at least acting in accord with, their own interests.

31. Ibid., pp. 12, 44–45.
32. Grasmuck, pp. 9–11.

But what about the brain drain? At first glance, the data on the costs of losing skilled personnel would seem to be conclusive. However, the statistics record only absolute numbers of professionals who have emigrated; they do not measure the actual harm done a nation's economy. As Henderson notes in his landmark study, "It is not possible to assess with confidence the loss (or profit) that the present migration of professionals inflicts on developing countries."[33]

As a result of numerous studies, however, we do know something about patterns of professional emigration and the motives of those who leave. And the data are very revealing. First, the incidence of the drain varies enormously from country to country. For instance, an extensive multination survey of the brain drain in the 1970s, conducted for UNITAR, found that the percentage of students abroad who plan to return home ranges from 98 percent for Ghanaians to only 30 percent for Egyptians. The bulk of professionals who migrate to the West are from a limited number of nations: India, the Philippines, Iran, Korea, Pakistan, Egypt, Greece, Turkey, Colombia, Argentina, and some Caribbean nations.[34] What most of these countries have in common is a large population base and an educational system that is relatively advanced, especially in relation to the professional opportunities available. In other words, the number of professionals being trained exceeds the immediate capacity to absorb them. This is probably typical of a midlevel phase of development: the fully developed states have adequate professional openings, while the least developed nations are not yet producing significant numbers of skilled professionals.

Many other countries, however, have scarcely been affected, among them Brazil, Venezuela, Mexico, and Saudi Arabia. Most African states have not experienced serious problems. In some cases where the problem was once onerous—for example, Benin—it has become less so in recent years. Some African states that do curb

33. Henderson, p. 116.

34. William A. Glaser, *The Brain Drain: Emigration and Return* (Oxford: Pergamon, 1978), pp. 24–28; see also Henderson, pp. 53–54.

emigration concede that the matter is not all that grave. An Ethiopian official reports that "the problem is not serious," and Mozambique has encountered "no real suffering" from the brain drain.[35]

Contrary to common belief, it is not the least developed countries that suffer most from the brain drain. And faster economic growth does not in itself seem to stem it. In fact, the least developed countries apparently have less trouble getting their professionals back; there is less competition for available openings at home, and adjusting to life in North America or Europe can be more difficult. As suggested, countries at a middle level of development have more trouble because of an imbalance between a higher number of professionals and the still-limited opportunities available. Pakistan loses a large proportion of its medical graduates, for example, simply because they cannot find work as physicians in their own country.[36]

Furthermore, it is important to take into account the political component of professional emigration. A surprisingly high percentage of "drainees" are actually members of minority groups who feel uncomfortable at home or who are politically at odds with the current regime. In some countries, intellectuals as a group are seen as suspect and are harassed. A former African cabinet minister serving as an expert on refugee affairs for a U.N. body has asserted that "the loss of skilled people in Africa is due more to political than economic factors," and many other African experts agree with him.[37]

Uganda is a case in point. Over the years, the expulsion or persecution of Asians, of certain tribal leaders and political figures, and of intellectuals generally, has deprived that country of a fair part of its professional elite. Similar treatment has forced Chinese out of

35. Personal interviews with Robert Sewade, First Secretary, Embassy of Benin to the United States, May 23, 1984, and Girma Haile-Giorgis, Ethiopian Mission to the United Nations, May 1, 1984; interview with Zimba.

36. Glaser, pp. 29–33.

37. Personal interview with Grace Ibingira, consultant to the U.N. Fund for Population Activities and former Ugandan Minister of Justice, April 27, 1984; also, interviews with African representatives from Gambia, Benin, Zambia, and Mozambique; Glaser, pp. 39–46.

Vietnam, Indonesia, and Malaysia. The outflow from Jamaica in the late 1970s, noted by Prime Minister Seaga in the speech cited above, was largely due to internal instability and economic crisis. The most intensive brain drain in the world has probably occurred in Haiti, which has lost as much as 75 percent of its skilled manpower since 1950—the result, almost entirely, of the disastrous policies of its government.

In the end, however, the decisive factors causing emigration appear to be working conditions and employment opportunities. More, even, than income levels, the ability to find satisfactory work in the area of one's training seems to influence the decision to stay or go.[38] In other words, *the principal motivation for emigration is the lack of suitable jobs*. As the Henderson report put it, "The chief general cause of brain drain appears to be the lack within developing nations of effective *demand* for professionals despite the presence of almost unlimited *need*. . . . In fact, though manpower shortages are often quite acute, the ability of most developing countries to absorb specific high-level skills is limited; often the actual numbers required are relatively small and a small rise in supply may quickly reverse a need recently acute."[39]

If this is the case, the attractions of the developed world are not the core of the problem, nor would restricting movement solve it. It is not even really a "drain," in that professionals who remained at home would contribute little more to development than those who left. Thus countries with the greatest outflows of professionals are not necessarily suffering more, since they are in no position to use the skills that are lost. This helps explain the oddity that Third-World nations facing the greatest brain drain threat have seldom responded by curbing emigration, and nations curbing emigration

38. Glaser, p. xxxix: "a crucial criterion is the balance between the education of professional persons and employment opportunities." See also pp. 33–36, 92, 115, 120–24, 125–28.

39. Henderson, pp. 39, 125.

have seldom faced a serious threat. There is little correlation in the Third World between serious brain drain experiences and attempts to limit freedom of movement, a fact that should make us suspicious about assumptions of a logical linkage between the two.

It is not surprising, then, that despite their expressions of concern most Third-World governments actually behave with indifference toward the whole matter. In the late 1960s, the U.N. Economic and Social Council asked member states to comment on proposals regarding brain drain; only nine developing nations bothered to reply. The U.S. State Department then surveyed U.S. embassies in seventy-six nations about students who failed to return from the United States, and only sixteen replied that the local government perceived a problem.[40] The level of interest actually demonstrated by Third-World states has not matched their level of rhetoric.

Furthermore, Third World leaders are no doubt aware that the traditional benefits of human movement do not lose their relevance in less developed societies. Developing nations obviously benefit when citizens are trained abroad, especially since someone else usually picks up the bill. Movement within a particular region can also be effective in diffusing skills and building cohesion, the Arab Middle East being a case in point. Finally, on a more mundane level, elites in Third-World countries do not want to give up the chance to study abroad.

Even without official controls, many powerful forces pull emigrants back home. As the WHO study on physician migration concludes: "When a country reaches the point where it can afford its expatriates [that is, where it can offer them suitable employment], most are likely to return of their own accord, given that ties with family, culture, and homeland are not easily broken." The study also suggests, with unassailable logic, that a country should either pro-

40. Ibid., p. 119.

duce no more physicians than it can employ, or should create jobs to employ those it produces.[41]

Examined up close, then, the brain drain would seem to offer little real conflict with the right of personal self-determination. Why, then, has the matter created such a stir? For one thing, the brain drain enables Third-World governments to take advantage of tensions between north and south. The "drained" countries are interested not so much in imposing restrictions on themselves as in gaining recognition for the responsibility of industrialized nations to assist the less developed. The brain drain is one index of the south's inability to compete with the north, a symbolic indictment of exploitation by the advanced world. Thus Third-World governments have proposed schemes whereby they would be compensated for the losses they incur.

The problems with such proposals are easy to imagine. In the first place, developed states question whether any real loss has occurred, using the same evidence discussed above. In addition, there is the old problem of calculating the value of brains. Should this be measured by the cost of a person's education, the cost of replacing services, the worth of future earnings, or some combination thereof? Finally, there is a tendency to resist the treatment of human beings as a commodity whose value is to be negotiated among states. In the end, the idea of compensation seems likely to go nowhere. Third-World governments would seem better advised to seek more positive solutions to their dilemma. In many cases, the elimination of political persecution, ethnic discrimination, and other forms of harassment would go far toward easing emigration pressures. Nations might also try to "indigenize" professional training by replacing Western educational styles with native approaches more closely tai-

41. Mejia, Pizurki, and Royston, pp. 415–16, 422. On the intention of most students to return to their homeland, even after extended employment abroad, see Glaser, pp. 14–19, 22–23.

lored to local needs and expectations. Other constructive proposals include:

    1. Programs for cooperative exchange of skills among developing states, as promoted by UNCTAD. When a Third-World state has a surplus in a particular occupational category, it might be advantageous to encourage an outflow to developing countries lacking such personnel in return for the same favor.

    2. The "Return of Talent" program of the Intergovernmental Committee on Migration, an international organization consisting largely of Western governments, which seeks placement of expatriates in their homelands or in neighboring countries. Where lack of knowledge of opportunities is a factor, such coordination can be an important catalyst.

    3. The Transfer of Knowledge Through Expatriate Nationals (TOKTEN) program, sponsored by the U.N. Development Programme, which has enabled 1000 expatriates to return to their native lands as visiting consultants. Though the program is not designed to bring about permanent return, it can offer many of the benefits of such a return.

    4. Jamaican Prime Minister Edward Seaga's proposal for an International Fund for Manpower Resources to finance the recruitment of skilled manpower in Third-World countries. Where skills are genuinely scarce and the major obstacle is funding of positions, rather than general infrastructure, such funding could be very effective in attracting expatriates or surplus personnel from other Third-World nations.

Positive measures, then, are the best answer to the threatened loss of skilled personnel in developing countries. In any event, the brain drain grievance should not serve as a weapon to attack the concept of free international movement. By identifying the "stealing of talents" with neocolonialism and the exploitation of the Third World by the First, the enemies of free movement are trying to delegitimize international movement completely. A key indication of this is that their arguments, presumably made on behalf of the Third

World, go beyond what the Third World claims for itself. One should regard such solicitude with skepticism.

Emigration and Expulsion in the Third World

Control of international movement is, of course, not uniform throughout the Third World. The incidence of refugee-creation and/ or denial of the right to leave is highest in Asia, lower in the Middle East, and lowest in Latin America. Africa, with a strong tradition of free movement, has experienced relatively few cases of denial of exit, but the creation of new nations has occasioned considerable displacement of the unassimilated. In all regions, however, two phenomena are striking: (1) the frequency with which the same states account for both expulsion and anti-emigration policies, and (2) the frequency with which these nations correspond to the radical, ideologized states in the area.

In Asia, with its strong tradition of government authority, emigration has generally been regarded more as a privilege than a right. Even where there is little interference in practice, the government in theory retains arbitrary discretion over permits to leave (as in, for example, Malaysia, the Philippines, Singapore, Thailand, and Pakistan). The only countries in which the right is written into law and subject to judicial review are Japan, Australia, and to some extent India.[42]

As Communist regimes were established or consolidated in

42. David Marshall, "The Far East," in *The Right to Leave and to Return,* ed. Karel Vasak and Sidney Liskofsky (New York: American Jewish Committee, 1976), pp. 345–411; and Niall MacDermot, "India, Sri Lanka, Pakistan, Bangladesh and Afghanistan," in ibid., pp. 413–30. The Vasak and Liskofsky volume is a collection of the papers given at the Uppsala symposium in 1973 and is a principal source for other states during this period as well. On India, see also M. P. Chandra Kantaraj Urs, "Right to Freedom of Movement outside One's Country," in International Commission of Jurists, Indian Commission of Jurists, and Mysore State Commission of Jurists, *International Year of Human Rights: Report and Conclusions of the Conference of Jurists on Right to Freedom of Movement* (Bangalore, India: 1968), pp. 25–51.

Asia, they uniformly eliminated free emigration. The same states also produced a large share of the continent's refugees. After 1949, a steady stream of Chinese flowed into Hong Kong. And in 1959 the Chinese takeover of Tibet led to the flight of the Dalai Lama and about 85,000 other Tibetans. Following the 1954 ceasefire in Indochina, which temporarily partitioned Vietnam, a large number of "preemptive" refugees, mainly Catholics, moved from the communist North to the capitalist South. And, of course, the 1975 consolidation of Communist regimes in Indochina provoked a large outflow over the succeeding years.

By the early 1970s, several other Asian states also restricted emigration, if not quite so tightly. It was very difficult to get a passport in revolutionary Burma. Permission to leave Indonesia or Taiwan could be denied for political reasons, and in 1972, getting out of Sri Lanka was described by one international human rights expert as "practically impossible."[43] Many of these same nations had also produced refugee flows, usually on an ethnic basis: from Burma, Hindus, Arakanese Muslims, Malays, and Karens; from Indonesia, Chinese, and, more recently, Papuans; and from Sri Lanka, Tamils. The Indian subcontinent also produced many refugees along ethnic-religious lines. As already noted, with the partition of India in 1947, an estimated 8.5 million Hindus and Sikhs fled from Pakistan, while some 6.5 Moslems left India;[44] and the creation of Bangladesh in 1971 sent about 10 million Bengalis and Hindus into India. As these cases indicate, most Asian refugee flows have been accompanied by a high degree of coercion.

By contrast, Middle Eastern governments, despite an authoritarian tradition, have generally placed few restrictions on movement. This may be due in part to the unifying influence of Islam, and more recently to a sense of common Arab nationality extending across borders. In more traditional patriarchal regimes, Saudi Arabia in

43. MacDermot, pp. 413–30.

44. Gunther Beijer, "The Political Refugee: 35 Years Later," *International Migration Review* 15 (Spring-Summer 1981): 29.

particular, women may not leave the country without consent of the closest male relative. By and large, however, movement is relatively free in the area.

The major exceptions are the radicalized regimes in Syria, South Yemen, Iraq after 1958, Libya after 1969, and Iran after 1979. Some of these states, like Iraq and Syria, constitutionally guarantee the right to leave but limit it sharply in practice. The same states account for many of the forced expulsions in the area. Iraq expelled Iranians in 1969, and Kurds in 1974 and after; Iran has vacillated between expelling troublesome minorities (for example, Arabs) and forcing them to stay (for example, Baha'is). In 1976, Libya expelled all Egyptians and Tunisians.

Some Middle Eastern states, including Egypt, Israel, Jordan, and Lebanon, reserve the right to block departure on security grounds, and they occasionally exercise this power.[45] Algeria, in 1973, suspended all emigration to France in reaction to racist incidents there involving Algerian workers, even though the Algerian economy had, to a degree, grown dependent on the export of labor.[46]

The largest body of refugees in the area is the Palestinians, estimated at 600,000 to 700,000 in 1948 and since increased to over 2 million, according to U.N. figures. Some of the original refugees (about 200,000) fled before the state of Israel was established; most of the rest fled before the advancing Israeli army in the 1948 war. There was one prominent instance of expulsion: 60,000 Arabs were expelled from the towns of Lydda and Ramle, which

45. Paul Weis, "The Middle East," in Vasak and Liskofsky, pp. 275–341. Restriction of departure for security reasons by Israel has been challenged by Amnesty International, on grounds that the procedure allows no chance for detainees to refute the charges against them. The Israeli government claims that it acts only on the basis of sufficient evidence of hostile activities. See Amnesty International, *The Imprisonment of Persons Seeking to Leave a Country or to Return to Their Own Country* (London: Amnesty International, 1986), pp. 11–12.

46. Stephen Adler, *International Migration and Dependence* (Westmead, England: Gower, 1981), pp. 72–89.

control access to the country's major airport.[47] Since 1967, Israel has also, on an individual basis, expelled several hundred activists in outlawed Palestinian organizations from territories occupied in the war of that year.

A like number of Jewish refugees came to Israel from Arab countries, mostly involuntarily. While Arab states sometimes barred Jews from leaving, this policy alternated with de facto coerced exit. Riots in Yemen in 1948 forced the entire Jewish community to flee. Governmental decrees and officially inspired pressure in Iraq had the same effect in 1950–51. About 14,000 Syrian Jews managed to escape an outbreak of persecution in 1947–49. In Libya the Jews fled (from sanctioned violence) in 1949, and Jews left Morocco and Tunisia in the following years. Egypt forced out most of its Jewish community in reaction to the 1956 Sinai war.[48]

Like the Middle East, Africa also enjoys a tradition of free movement. Many tribal groups lived a seminomadic existence, and precisely defined state borders were a nineteenth-century European import. On gaining independence, many African states guaranteed the right of emigration in their constitutions. However, this has sometimes been undermined by arbitrary rules.[49]

Tight restrictions on the right to leave have spread to only a few African countries: Somalia since the Mohamed Siad Barre take-over in 1969; Ethiopia since the deposing of Haile Selassie in 1974;

47. Few numbers are more controversial than the total of Palestinian refugees. The United Nations Relief and Works Agency for Palestinians in the Near East (UNRWA) had 2,093,545 refugees registered as of June 30, 1985. For summaries of the evidence on the creation of the Palestinian refugees see K. N. Radley, "The Palestinian Refugees: The Right to Return in International Law," *American Journal of International Law* 72 (1978): 566–614; Christopher Sykes, *Cross Roads to Israel: Palestine from Balfour to Bevin* (London: New English Library, 1967).

48. Joseph B. Schechtman, *On Wings of Eagles: The Plight, Exodus, and Homecoming of Oriental Jewry* (New York: Thomas Yaseloff, 1961).

49. For the general picture, see G. Lukongwa Binaisa, "English-Speaking Africa," pp. 431–37 in Vasak and Liskovsky; and Ousmane Goundiam, "Pays africains autre qu'anglophones," pp. 439–72 in Vasak and Liskofsky.

Mozambique and Angola since independence in 1975. Again, these states are the most heavily ideological in sub-Saharan Africa; in addition, most have had to fight wars. They also account for a good share of the continent's refugees. In Ethiopia, Eritreans and Somalis fled during a civil war. Angola and Mozambique both underwent significant "white flight" after independence. Many others have fled Angola in the course of protracted civil war, and Mozambique has experienced significant flight connected with ongoing conflict.

The clearest cases of direct expulsion occurred in Uganda, involving Asians in 1972 and various tribal groups since. In late 1982, for example, the youth wing of the Ugandan Peoples' Congress, with the support of local officials, drove about 80,000 members of the Banyarwanda tribe out of the country.[50] In Sudan, the Arab-dominated government's sporadic efforts to strengthen its control over the southern, black section of the country have caused many residents to flee.

From 1967 to 1972, successive waves of aliens were expelled in Ghana (Nigerians being the chief victims), Sierra Leone (Ghanaians), Equatorial Guinea (Nigerians), Niger (Dahomans), Uganda (Kenyans and others), and Zaire (various nationalities). In 1978, Gabon expelled Benin nationals in retaliation for Benin's condemnation of Gabon at an Organization for African Unity (OAU) meeting. In early 1983, Nigeria, beset by economic difficulties and growing panic over the presence of foreign workers, suddenly expelled about 2 million aliens, about half of them from Ghana. Again, in May 1985, it gave some 700,000 aliens a week to leave the country.[51]

Many other forced movements have had tribal origins. Some groups crossed borders to find refuge among their own kin; this occurred in Guinea-Bissau, Ghana, Burundi (where the Hutu fled from the Tutsi), and Rwanda (where the Tutsi fled from the Hutu).

50. Coles, pp. 32–33; Roger P. Winter, "Refugees in Uganda and Rwanda: The Banyarwanda Tragedy," *World Refugee Survey 1983* (New York and Washington: U.S. Committee for Refugees, 1983), pp. 28–31.

51. Coles, pp. 27–31, 33–36; *New York Times,* May 3, 1985.

In some cases, strife produced refugees by bringing tribal tensions to the surface, as in Zaire (then the Congo) after independence, Nigeria in the late 1960s, and war-torn Angola and Mozambique.

South Africa is a case apart. There, "pass" laws control the internal movement of blacks to a degree unparalleled almost anywhere else. Many blacks have been forcibly transferred within the country; many others have been pushed out. Regarding foreign travel, South African courts ruled in 1982 that access to a passport is a privilege rather than a right for both blacks and whites, and the Minister of Internal Affairs can revoke any passport without giving cause and with no appeal. Blacks are further inhibited by the requirement that those assigned to a "homeland" use the homeland passport. Most refuse to use such a document, since it implies recognition of the homeland concept, a central pillar of apartheid. Anyway, these documents are not recognized anywhere else in the world.

In Latin America, freedom of movement has a long tradition. As of 1973, all but two states in the region guaranteed the right to leave in their constitutions. In practice, a few countries introduced limitations that went beyond those permitted in the Universal Declaration of Human Rights, including exit permits and requirements that a married woman obtain her husband's consent.[52]

There are some exceptions. Cuba, whose policy has varied, will be discussed in the following section. Before the events of October 1983, the radical regime of Grenada made it difficult for political opponents to leave the country. Nicaragua, under the Sandinistas, has sometimes prevented opposition leaders from traveling abroad. It also requires government officials and doctors to receive special permission to leave. The Stroessner government of Paraguay has sometimes refused passports on political grounds. So did Haiti under the Duvaliers, who generally regarded emigration as a business,

52. Jesus Rodrigués y Rodrigués, "Amérique Latine," in Vasak and Liskofsky, pp. 207–29.

extracting up to $1,500 for an exit permit and taking a cut of remittances from abroad. The government also used emigration as a means of sterilizing the country against political opposition.[53]

The radicalized states in the hemisphere, as elsewhere, also account for a good proportion of the refugees. Apart from Cuba, there are now about 23,000 Nicaraguan refugees, according to the U.S. Committee on Refugees. Under the Somozas there had been about 100,000, most of whom returned to Nicaragua after the Sandinista victory.[54]

Other refugees in the hemisphere have included opponents of the Pinochet regime in Chile. Under a program organized by the Intergovernmental Committee on Migration, many in this category were allowed to leave the country peacefully. A number of Indians were forced out of Guatemala by the army's "pacification" program there, which was aimed at neutralizing areas on the Mexican border in which antigovernment guerrillas had been active. There were also refugees from war in El Salvador and from poverty in Haiti (though the United States regarded both as economic migrants rather than refugees, since recognition as refugees would tend to discredit American support for the El Salvador and Haitian governments, as well as increase refugee admissions to the United States). This judgment is disputed by many close observers, who regard the Salvadorans as primarily political refugees, and the Haitians as refugees from an oppressive system in which economics and politics are closely intertwined.[55]

Four countries in the Third World stand out in any discussion of emigration and expulsion, both because of the magnitude of their

53. Aaron Segal, "Haiti," in *Population Policies in the Caribbean,* ed. Segal (Lexington, Mass.: Lexington, 1975), pp. 197–205.

54. *World Refugee Survey 1984* (New York and Washington: U.S. Committee for Refugees, 1984), p. 39.

55. Leonel Gomez, "Feet People," in *Central America: Anatomy of a Conflict,* ed. Robert S. Leiken (New York: Pergamon, 1984), pp. 221–26; Segal, pp. 177–215.

problems and because of the way in which they illustrate the fine line between the two dimensions of control. These four cases—Vietnam, Afghanistan, Ethiopia, and Cuba—now merit closer examination.

Vietnam. After thirty-five years of nearly constant warfare, the socialist government of Vietnam emerged in 1975 with an ambitious agenda to reshape its devastated land. One consequence was about two million refugees over the next decade. The first wave consisted primarily of political opponents of the usual sort; after 1978, however, as relations with China worsened, mostly ethnic Chinese left. The regime denied it was expelling the Chinese, asserting instead that it was campaigning against unproductive urban elements that stood in the way of socialist transformation. In March 1978, the government abolished all "bourgeois trade" in Ho Chi Minh City (Saigon); of the 30,000 businesses it closed, 80 percent belonged to Chinese. The simultaneous introduction of a new currency wiped out the savings of most Chinese merchants. Many Chinese were dismissed from their jobs and threatened with transfer to remote "New Economic Zones." The flight began in earnest.

Further pressure was applied after the short China-Vietnam border war in February and March 1979. The complicity of the Vietnamese government was demonstrated by the involvement of local Public Security Bureaus, or political police, which drew up passenger lists, collected fees, and set departure dates. An entire boat industry sprang up to supply the flimsy 15- to 25-meter vessels on which refugees fled. Exit fees ranged from $1000 to $1300 in gold for each adult, plus $1800 to $3000 for a place in a boat. By one estimate, the Vietnamese government extracted $115 million from fleeing refugees in 1978 alone, a figure equal to the country's known official exchange holdings.[56] The U.S. Department of State

56. Guy Sacerdoti, "How Hanoi Cashes In," *Far East Economic Review,* June 15, 1979.

charged that "Vietnam has created elaborate but highly efficient machinery for virtually expelling what it considers its undesirable population."[57]

The response of the international community has been "one of the most successful humanitarian endeavors in history," says Roger Winter, director of the U.S. Committee for Refugees.[58] An international conference held in Geneva in mid-1979 established an Orderly Departure Program. Under it, Vietnam agreed to stop all "illegal" departures. An estimated 50–80 percent of attempted illegal exits were stopped, and by 1984, the numbers leaving under the Orderly Departure Program exceeded those leaving illegally. However, there was a waiting list of 400,000, and while Chinese had little problem obtaining approval to leave, ethnic Vietnamese were not so lucky; sometimes they posed as Chinese in order to get exit permits. Furthermore, despite repeated negotiations, Vietnam refused to allow "re-education camp" inmates to leave for the United States, apparently for fear of creating a political opposition in exile. This fear was also reflected in stern decrees against "fleeing abroad for counter-revolutionary purposes."[59] In addition, those applying for exit permits were reportedly harassed, and stiff penalties—including execution—were levied on those caught trying to leave illegally.

In another anomaly, since anyone who left illegally was granted asylum, there was a continuing incentive to flee; the existence of a hospitable admissions program in the United States (created partly as an anti-Communist reflex) itself exerted a pull. Chances of getting out legally were uncertain at best, while successful escape automat-

57. United States, Department of State, *Vietnam's Refugee Machine*, July 20, 1979. This document is a summary of available information circulated by U.S. representatives at the 1979 Geneva conference on Indochinese refugees.

58. Winter, Prepared Statement before the Subcommittee on Asian and Pacific Affairs, Committee on Foreign Affairs, U.S. House of Representatives, April 5, 1984.

59. Amnesty International, p. 17.

ically brought refugee status.[60] But then, any country that prohibits free departure makes those who escape into refugees.

Afghanistan. The events of 1978–79 imposed on Afghanistan—a tribal-feudal society still in the process of national integration—a full-blown twentieth-century social revolution. In the resulting chaos, the dynamics from two entirely different stages of development have combined to produce a massive refugee flow.

The initial revolution in Afghanistan, in April 1978, brought to power a radical government committed to fundamental change. But as power in the society was still dispersed in the hands of traditional local leaders, attempts to dictate social revolution from above led to the regime's isolation and weakening, forcing Soviet intervention in late 1979 to prevent its fall.

The flow of refugees had already begun before the Soviets moved, as a result of the fighting between government and local forces. The Soviet invasion at first slowed the stream of refugees, as an effort was made to conciliate traditional leaders. But as the Soviet army and the Afghan government relied increasingly on sheer firepower to quell resistance, the refugee flow grew to 3 or 4 million, roughly one-quarter of the population. (And that does not include those displaced internally.) The Afghan government (and, presumably, the Soviet Union) deny any deliberate policy of creating refugees; in the words of a government spokesman, the inhabitants of refugee camps in Pakistan are either nomads or people who have been misled by propaganda; they are said to be free to return, if only Pakistan would allow them to do so.[61] This does not square with most other accounts of the situation.

As in Vietnam, the nature of the war—heavy firepower used

60. Astri Suhrke, "Indochinese Refugees: The Law and Politics of First Asylum," *Annals of the American Academy of Political and Social Science* 467 (May 1983): 102.

61. Personal interview with Haider Refq, Chargé d'Affaires, Embassy of Afghanistan to the United States, May 16, 1984.

against mobile guerrila forces—has tended to displace a large part of the civilian population. Further disruption occurs as the Soviet/Afghan forces seek to combat the enemy by destroying its civilian base. Their reprisals against areas from which attacks had come seemed deliberately designed to terrorize, if not drive out, the general population. Refugees interviewed in 1980 reported a slogan frequently heard in official circles: "We need the soil of Afghanistan, not its people."[62]

Since about 1983, the government has sought to keep the population in place. Reliance on indiscriminate firepower has lessened, and so has the flow of refugees. The population is further rooted by an emigration policy that denies professionals permission to leave, indeed, that severely curtails all foreign travel. Bribery is often required to get a passport, and deposits or collateral are required as guarantee of return. All property is seized after a year's absence.[63]

Ethiopia. Like Afghanistan, Ethiopia was an isolated, traditional society, still in the process of national formation, upon which a social revolution was superimposed. Following the radical takeover in 1974, opposition to the new regime first developed among the Eritreans, an ethnic group occupying territory along the Red Sea. Their secessionist war produced a first wave of refugees, which may not have displeased the government in Addis Ababa. (In 1984, famine was being cited as justification for depopulating the same region by forcible population transfers.) Following a brief war with Somalia in 1978, many ethnic Somalis fled the Ogaden, an area of Ethiopia contested by the Somalis. Altogether, these disruptions produced the greatest concentration of refugees in the world, estimated at 5.5 to

62. Barnett R. Rubin, "Afghans, Beleaguered," *New York Times,* May 25, 1984.

63. *Country Reports on Human Rights Practices for 1983* (report submitted to the Committee on Foreign Affairs, U.S. House of Representatives, and the Committee on Foreign Relations, U.S. Senate, by the Department of State, February 1984) (Washington: U.S. Government Printing Office, 1984), pp. 1191–92.

6 million by 1980–81; about half that number were located outside the country.

All of this occurred while emigration was essentially forbidden to the population as a whole, and illegal departure was even punishable by death.[64] As noted, Ethiopia does not appear to be threatened by a brain drain; what brains it loses are largely those of political refugees. The country has also lost many military-age males following imposition of a universal draft.

Cuba. While Cuba does not face ethnic conflicts, it must contend with its proximity to a hostile superpower. With the United States a mere ninety miles away, disaffected Cubans are encouraged and attracted to a convenient alternate destination, where an émigré community has already been established. But, as in other Marxist states, those most likely to leave—skilled professionals—are also those most crucial to development. The regime cannot decide whether it is better off with or without such people, and its policies reflect this uncertainty.

Thus, after Fidel Castro came to power in 1959, about 100,000 political refugees left for the United States. Most of them were also professionals, including, by one account, half the doctors in Havana.[65] This flow was stopped by the Cuban government in 1962, during the Cuban missile crisis. In the years that followed, the Cuban economy, under pressures from U.S. sanctions, deteriorated badly, causing unrest among remaining members of the middle class. In 1965, Castro announced that they were free to leave. Consequently, "freedom flights" to the United States were arranged, and a steady flow left for Miami. Once again, however, the refugees included many better educated Cubans, and the government grew

64. According to an Ethiopian government representative, emigration and foreign travel are available to all Ethiopian citizens without limitations (personal interview with Haile-Giorgis). By all available evidence from other sources, this is simply not the case; see, for example, *Country Reports on Human Rights Practices for 1983*, pp. 126–27. On the death penalty see Hannum, pp. 59, 186.

65. Personal interview with Felipe R. Alvarez, First Secretary and Consul, Cuban Interests Section, Washington, D.C., May 24, 1984.

increasingly concerned about the loss of professional manpower. In May 1969, the regime stopped accepting new exit applications, and in 1971, Castro announced that the backlog of applications to leave had almost been cleared. The flights to the United States tapered off, and the last one left on April 6, 1973.

In addition to concern over the loss of needed skills, there are indications that the Cuban government was further convinced that a continuing exodus was undermining the legitimacy of the new order. The calculation was, in part, similar to that made a decade before in East Germany. As one close observer described official thinking: "With the airlift discontinued, many Cubans alienated from the government would have to make some sort of psychic adjustment to living in the reality of their country's present social system."[66]

When the Carter administration tried to normalize relations in the late 1970s, the two countries agreed to allow freed political prisoners to travel to the United States. But the talks broke down over Cuban involvement in Ethiopia, among other issues. Meanwhile, a new campaign in Cuba against "nonproductive" elements, combined with a general economic slowdown, created new pressures for emigration.

The stage was set in early 1980 for the Mariel boatlift. After 10,000 Cubans sought asylum in the Peruvian embassy, and after the U.S. government applauded their actions, Cuba called President Carter's bluff by opening the port of Mariel to anyone wishing to leave. This put an end to American political exploitation of the Cuban refugee issue, since the Carter administration, after initially welcoming the boatlift, was eventually forced to stop the flood of "illegal" entrants. Cuba also used the opportunity to unload some mental and social undesirables, though they constituted a very small portion of the total.

66. Barent Landstreet, "Cuba," in Segal, *Population Policies,* p. 141; interview with Alvarez.

Altogether, about 10 percent of the Cuban population has moved to the United States. Despite the Cuban government's mixed feelings about this flow, it provided some obvious benefits: the elimination of dissent, the reclaiming of property, the removal of barriers to radical change. Cuban policy should also be considered in the overall context of Caribbean emigration: since 1950, every country in the region except the Bahamas and the U.S. Virgin Islands has lost at least 5 percent of its population in net emigration.[67]

The position of the Cuban government is that it has always allowed everyone to leave, save for those subject to "the usual restrictions" required to protect the interests of the state. This stretches the matter a bit, and it is demonstrably not true for some periods. But the Cuban case does present some significant contrasts to Marxist regimes elsewhere. Consider, for example, how Cuba had dealt with the loss of professional manpower, which may have been more severe in per capita terms than for any other state, apart from Haiti. In the early years, Cuba's brain drain created severe problems; some factories were forced to lie idle for lack of technicians. But Cuba now sends doctors to thirty-two countries, and its technicians are active throughout the Third World. Whatever the limitations of the Cuban system, its accomplishments in professional education (though admittedly with some Soviet help) show what a nation can do to overcome the loss of skilled manpower, even under the worst conditions.

The remolding of Cuban society has, on the whole, produced considerable dislocation. But Cuba's experience shows that more than one pattern is possible in Marxist regimes.

As it happens, the most restrictive emigration policies in the Third World occur in Marxist countries. While restrictions and refugees often result from the general strains of development, the dra-

67. Segal, "Haiti," p. 17; see also John Scanlan and Gilburt Loescher, "U.S. Foreign Policy, 1959–80: Impact on Refugee Flow from Cuba," *Annals of the American Academy of Political and Social Science* 467 (May 1983): 127.

matic instances of coerced or denied emigration come where radical ideologies of state control are superimposed on developmental problems—especially in states suffering from problems of disunity at home or opposition from abroad.

Does Marxism in the Third World, or anywhere else, for that matter, necessitate restrictive emigration policies? Chapter 6 will deal with this question after completing the survey of contemporary control of movement. But, as this chapter reveals, development in itself does not necessitate the creation of refugees or the sealing of borders. Numerous cases show that development can take place successfully even with professional outflows, and without purging a population of minority or dissident elements.

The attitudes underlying the new serfdom in the Third World are not essentially different from those in Eastern Europe. In both cases, human beings are perceived as objects of state policy; accordingly, movement is viewed as a matter of convenience to the state. The doctrinaire regimes in Afghanistan and Ethiopia provide vivid illustrations. Their biggest problem, it would appear, is finding a population worthy of themselves.

6

The Contemporary Challenge to
Free Movement

{We} are being turned into an exploited and discriminated-against minority, into bondsmen of the twentieth century.

—*Veniamin Levich and Aleksandr Voronel, Soviet scientists*

Having now brought the picture up to date for most regions of the world, it is time to put all the pieces together. What is the scope of controls on international movement in the contemporary world? Clearly we have a problem of considerable magnitude; the countries that restrict free exit run into the dozens and include a significant part of the world's population.

In addition, at the end of 1984 there were over 10 million refugees around the world "in need of protection and assistance."[1] This does not include up to 3 million others who do not require assistance, usually because they have been resettled. Nor does it include as many as 7 million people displaced within their own countries, nor those who do not meet the strict U.N. definition of refugees (covering political but not economic causes). Many more

1. Figures from the U.S. Committee for Refugees, as reported in the *New York Times*, February 16, 1986.

181

simply go unrecorded. (One African refugee expert working for the U.N. estimates that up to 60 percent of all African refugees escape statistical measurement.[2])

A survey of current practice in emigration control and expulsion helps provide answers to our key questions. The Third World survey suggested that ideological and political motivations, more than economic considerations, are foremost in the urge to control international population flows; does this hold for other areas of the world? And is the link between denial of the right to leave and expulsion as marked elsewhere as in the Third World?

The thin line that so frequently seems to divide forced immobilization from forced exit suggests the usefulness of further case studies of fluctuations in coercive policies toward international movement. One such case is the Soviet attitude toward the emigration of certain minorities—Jews, Germans, and Armenians—since 1970. What calculations have shaped the dramatic variations in the outward flow permitted over the last decade and a half? More generally, are tight controls on international movement intrinsic to Marxism-Leninism, in the Soviet version or otherwise?

Finally, we must take note of a modest revival of interest in the issue of international movement in recent years. Increasingly, states are required to account for their policies on emigration and expulsion before various international forums, and to provide formal justification for their restrictions. Whether this will influence the content of the policies themselves remains to be seen, but the changing international climate provides an important backdrop to the discussion of policy options in the next and concluding chapter.

Control of Emigration Today

Contemporary control of emigration must be seen in the context of current levels of travel, both permanent and temporary, which are

2. Personal interview with Grace Ibingira, Consultant, U.N. Fund for Population Activities, April 27, 1984.

paradoxically very high by historical standards. The universality of movement can be glimpsed in the strange demographic patterns that have developed throughout the world. There are Turks in Sweden, Indonesians in Spain, Koreans in Paraguay, and Yugoslav Albanians in Mexico. Pakistanis travel to East Berlin in order to enter West Germany (that gate is still open to non-Germans), and Asians go to Bimini to be smuggled into the United States. Oil-rich states have attracted workers from throughout the developing world: There are Colombians in Venezuela and huge numbers from other Arab states and from Asia in Saudi Arabia, Kuwait, and other oil states of the Middle East. Nigeria was host to roughly 2 million people from neighboring lands (before they were expelled) and about one-quarter of the Ivory Coast's population consists of foreigners. And, in a variation on a theme, Vietnam has sent guest workers to Soviet bloc countries to help repay loans.

Efforts to stem this flow seem to have been fitful and of limited effectiveness. Many of these population movements are in theory temporary, but a natural settling process has taken place. That, in turn, has provoked reaction in the host countries. Middle East nations have turned away Arab laborers, who easily become assimilated, and begun to rely more on contract labor from Asian states. But the erection of such barriers has only produced an increase in illegal migration. In Africa and Latin America, in fact, this may be the dominant form of migration.

Despite appearances, however, this image of large-scale economic migration from underdeveloped and overpopulated nations is oversimplified, as chapter 5 demonstrated. So-called economic migrants are often responding as much to political repression as to material deprivation. Regarding the refugees from Ethiopia, for example, it is impossible to separate political pressures from famine, warfare, and other causes of their flight.

In fact, few countries are actually seeking to increase emigration for economic reasons. The U.N. Department of International Economic and Social Affairs periodically surveys national planners on their population policies, including immigration and emigration. The Fifth Population Inquiry, in 1982, elicited responses from 109 countries. Of these, only *five*—Mauritius, Rwanda, South Korea, the Philippines, and Thailand—stated that they were seeking to increase emigration. A few other countries, including Egypt, Malta, Tunisia, Bangladesh, and Senegal, reported that they were trying to maintain current levels of emigration (outside observers might add Mexico, Turkey, and Portugal to this list, among countries that did not respond to the survey). On the whole, however, few countries are striving to get rid of population for economic or demographic reasons.[3]

Some twenty-six of the responding governments reported that they were trying to *reduce* emigration. However, when these countries were asked about the impact of emigration on their socioeconomic development, only twelve responded that it had had a negative impact; thirteen said it was a positive factor. Thus many, if not most, of the twenty-six states seeking to reduce emigration were doing so for noneconomic reasons. Only the Philippines, Thailand, and Jamaica even mentioned brain drain concerns. Overall, for fully 80 of the 109 respondents, including 62 of 81 developing nations, emigration was not even significant enough to merit comment.

Furthermore, those states that do seek to change emigration levels do not always resort to coercive policies. Of the twenty-six governments that admit to actively discouraging emigration, only four (Mozambique, Iran, Nicaragua, and Syria) use direct restrictive measures. (See below.) On the other hand, many of the states that

3. Data on individual country responses were supplied by the Population Division of the Department of International Economic and Social Affairs, United Nations Secretariat; see also the summary published by the Population Division, *Report on the Fifth Population Inquiry among Governments: Monitoring of Government Perceptions and Policies on Demographic Trends and Levels in Relation to Development as of 1982* (ESA/P/WP/83, January 11, 1984) (New York, 1984); U.N. Department of International Economic and Social Affairs, *International Migration Policies and Programmes: A World Survey,* Population Studies, no. 80 (New York: United Nations, 1982).

do impose tight restrictions on emigration made no economic claims in the survey to justify such policies.

The limited relevance of economic motives becomes clear in the accompanying table, which identifies those nations that, according to the best available evidence, restrict the right to leave in a systematic way. (The omission of countries from the list does not necessarily mean they are free of sin, only that their sins are more sporadic.)[4]

The occasional restriction column includes those states that bar the exit of citizens often enough to form a pattern, but not so consistently as to constitute a predictable policy. The restrictions are usually directed at specific individuals and imposed on a case-by-case basis. The partial restriction column lists those states that feature systematic but partial curbs on emigration; in these cases, restrictions are generally directed at particular groups rather than individuals, but not at the population as a whole. And the tight restriction column includes states that, as a matter of policy, carefully control all exit. Although many may occasionally leave such states, legal exit is basically viewed as a privilege rather than a right.

A glance at this last category shows the most obvious common denominator to be not the level of economic development, nor the threatened loss of talent, but the nature of the regime. All twenty-one are ideologically doctrinaire one-party states, and, except for Burma, Iraq, and Somalia, define themselves as Marxist-Leninist.

4. The State Department appraisals are based on actual observation of practices within countries, and are therefore more useful than surveys that rely on announced policies and formal legislation. However, in some cases the observations are indirect (due to lack of a U.S. mission in the country), and there is sometimes a tendency to apply stricter standards to some states than others for political reasons. Allowing for this, however, the patterns that emerge accord by and large with other sources of information that were used to check the *Country Reports*.

The categories in this table overlap, to some extent, the suggestive spectrum of "exit rules" described by Myron Weiner, "International Migration and International Relations: Suggestions for Future Research" (talk prepared for Population Council Seminar, March 18, 1985).

Nations Restricting Free Emigration

	Occasional Restriction	Partial Restriction	Tight Restriction
AFRICA	Burundi	Cameroun	Angola
	Congo	Namibia	Ethiopia
	Ghana	Rwanda	Mozambique
	Kenya	South Africa	São Tomé and Príncipe
	Lesotho	Tanzania	Somalia
	Liberia	Togo	
	Malawi		
	Swaziland		
	Zaire		
	Zambia		
	Zimbabwe		
ASIA	Bangladesh	China	Afghanistan
	Indonesia		Burma
	Malaysia		Cambodia (Kampuchea)
	Nepal		Laos
	South Korea		Mongolia
			North Korea
			Vietnam
EUROPE	Yugoslavia	Hungary	Albania
		Poland	Bulgaria
			Czechoslovakia
			East Germany
			Romania
			U.S.S.R
MIDDLE EAST	Kuwait	Iran	Iraq
	Saudi Arabia	Libya	South Yemen
	Tunisia	Sudan	
		Syria	
WESTERN HEMISPHERE	Haiti Paraguay	Nicaragua	Cuba

Sources: U.S. Dept. of State, *Country Reports*, 1985; Charles Humana, *World Human Rights Guide* (London: Hutchinson, 1983); Hannum; Vasak and Liskofsky; Amnesty International; "The Atlas of Freedom: The Right to Emigrate," *Policy Review* no. 31 (Winter 1985): 48–49; correspondence with U.S. missions abroad; interviews with diplomatic representatives of selected countries, with staff members of international organizations, and with academic experts.

Most of the entries in the partially restrictive column are also authoritarian, and many are strongly doctrinaire. But the dominant pattern here is non-Marxist developing states, and it is here that economic motivations exert whatever influence they have. Countries like Sudan, Tanzania, Togo, Syria, and Iran seem to act on the basis of more clearly economic motives, including the feared loss of skilled personnel. In these cases, more than elsewhere, the perceived necessities of nation-building translate into somewhat coercive exit policies. It should be noted, however, that some of these countries engage in political controls as well. For example, Rwanda maintains that it is trying to increase emigration on economic grounds, but it often denies passports on security grounds to the politically suspect. South Africa (and, by extension, Namibia) also systematically curtails travel on political grounds. The government of Nicaragua has, on a variety of pretexts, blocked the departure from the country of opposition political leaders.

The category of occasional restriction usually involves the pattern of blocking opposition figures from foreign travel. This behavior is most typical, perhaps, of the more traditional type of autocratic government—Indonesia, Pakistan, the Philippines, South Korea, Taiwan, Saudi Arabia, Zaire, Haiti, and Paraguay. In such regimes, it is not surprising that the focus of concern is sources of potential opposition rather than general ideological or socioeconomic considerations.

On the whole, then, restrictions are more political than economic. They are instruments of control, related to conceptions that give priority to social organization and discipline. Even in the Third World, the most restrictive states are not necessarily those most threatened by such forces as brain drain, but those that have been most heavily influenced by the collectivist model (with the most explosive cases, perhaps, being those that combine both elements).

Expulsions, too, seem rooted largely in political rather than economic factors. Again, only a handful of states explicitly promote emigration on economic grounds. Of these, only one, Rwanda, produced a significant number of refugees, and they were the result more of ethnic hostility than economic calculation. Among other states that produced refugees, some (Iran, Haiti, Nicaragua, and Mozambique) actually claimed to be *discouraging* emigration.

The degree to which the creation of refugees is the result of a deliberate political decision can be debated. But such a motive seems clear in Vietnam and Cambodia, and it is arguably an element in Afghanistan and Ethiopia. Several other countries have also expelled or forced out smaller groups of refugees in recent years, among them Laos, Mongolia (deportation of ethnic Chinese in 1983), Burma (minority groups at various times), Nicaragua (the Miskito Indians), Rwanda, Iraq (Iranians and Kurds), South Yemen (tribal groups fleeing to North Yemen), Uganda (a new wave in 1984), Cyprus, Sri Lanka (Tamils), Indonesia, Sudan, and Iran. As noted, some Eastern European states have also expelled dissidents. In other cases, refugees result from hostilities rather than deliberate policy, but their flight may still be convenient to the government. Examples include Guatemala, El Salvador, the Philippines (Moslems in the south), Lebanon, and a host of civil wars in Africa (Angola, Mozambique, Chad, Zaire, Western Sahara).

From all of this, it is clear that probably more than half of the world's refugees were forced out at least partly because their governments wanted them to leave, or were content to see them leave, or put other priorities ahead of making their return possible.

Furthermore, as the number of refugees has multiplied, international hospitality has diminished. The progress achieved in the 1950s and 1960s has faded. Little repatriation or local settlement is currently taking place, and doors everywhere are slamming shut. Waves of boat people are once again leaving Indochina, but, whereas the world previously opened its arms to them, now East Asian states, anxious to keep the refugees out, are adopting actively hostile attitudes. In Europe, traditionally receptive states are tightening their policies on asylum and rejecting even cases that are clearly political in nature. The French at one point even started requiring passports of British day-trippers to Channel ports for fear of illegal immigrants. In some places refugees are interned or forbidden language courses lest they blend in too well.[5]

The United States, for its part, regards almost all Salvadoran refugees as economic migrants and routinely returns them home. The same is true of Haitian refugees. More generally, U.S. refugee assistance has shifted its focus from resettlement to assistance in place; expenditures for the former fell by 75 percent between 1980 and 1983.

As a result of such policies, de facto stateless refugees have, as in the 1930s, reappeared on the scene. There have been repeated cases of refugees "in orbit," shunted from one port of entry to another before being allowed even temporary refuge. Others have been held in detention for two years or longer. The Biharis, a Moslem but non-Bengali group in Bangladesh, have remained in a state of limbo since the secession of that country from Pakistan, not being wanted by either government. Many of the Banyarwanda who have fled from Uganda are not recognized as citizens by either Uganda or Rwanda. The Thais have officially closed their border with Cambodia, keeping most refugees penned up in the border area and unable to receive official refugee status in Thailand.

This situation creates pressure for forced repatriation, in violation of international legal principles and basic humanitarian principles. The Thais have attempted to return Cambodians by force. U.S. actions with Salvadorans and Haitians are highly questionable. Hong Kong routinely returns refugees to mainland China. Many African states have pressed their neighbors to repatriate refugees who fled for political reasons; both South Africa and Zimbabwe, for example, have tried to secure the return of dissidents from Botswana. Swaziland did repatriate some refugees to Mozambique in 1980, and Zambia has forcibly repatriated refugees to several countries. Kenya

5. *Economist,* May 12, 1984; *Sunday Times,* April 29, 1984; personal interview with Leon M. Johnson, Director, Office of Asylum Affairs, Bureau of Human Rights, Department of State, May 15, 1984.

and Tanzania, in late 1983, exchanged one another's refugees in an agreement that elicited a strong protest from the U.N. High Commissioner for Refugees.

More than ever before, individuals around the world risk being kept from leaving, and being forced to leave; being kept from returning, and being forced to return. The area of individual choice narrows as states adopt coercive policies that both confine and exclude. As recent cases show, governments have become increasingly adept at balancing the conflicting impulses of the new serfdom.

Varieties of Coercion: Some Recent Cases
The survey of contemporary control of international movement has again underlined the fact that those states that limit free exit most severely also tend to be the major perpetrators of forced exit. For example, of the ten countries that have produced the most refugees in recent years, five (Afghanistan, Ethiopia, Angola, Vietnam, and Cambodia) were rated as being in the most restrictive category in curtailing emigration. In the effort to control and shape population, how do governments combine denial of exit with expulsion?

The answer depends in part on the nature of the society, its stage of development, degree of homogeneity, level of national integration, and standard of living. In choosing whether to confine or expunge, a coercive regime will ask: What will be the real impact on development, if any? Which option will best promote internal assimilation and control? More stable, advanced states may have greater confidence in their ability to cope with dissatisfaction than by resorting to the safety valve of forced emigration.

The nature of the target population is also important: Is it a few malcontents, an ethnic group, an entire class, or the whole population? Obviously, the smaller the target, the less the risk in letting it go—though control without exit is also easier. When ethnic differences are involved, regimes seem especially prone to turn to expulsion. The basic question here is: Will the individuals or groups involved be more of a threat from within, or from without?

Policies are also shaped by the level of pressures the state faces (or imagines it faces), including economic forces, self-imposed ideological constraints (such as the Marxist threat to professionals), and hostile external forces. When applicants for exit threaten to give aid and comfort to an enemy, governments are, not surprisingly, more reluctant to let them leave. On the other hand, letting at least some out may serve other foreign policy goals, such as a desire to improve relations or to send a signal.

Consider the case of the German Democratic Republic. The unique pressures on East Germany have already been noted: the proximity to a prosperous neighbor, access to the West German media, close family and cultural ties. After the erection of the Berlin wall in 1961, however, only about 1000 people a month were allowed to leave.

Suddenly, in early 1984, the gates were opened, and by mid-March more than 6000 had left for West Germany, including an unusually high proportion of young people and skilled workers. Many had received permission to emigrate within twenty-four hours of applying. Several theories were advanced to explain the sudden liberalization: pending negotiations for more economic credits from West Germany, plans for a visit there by party leader Erich Honecker, rising unemployment, and a desire to be rid of the disaffected, especially members of the growing "peace movement." It was even suggested that the exercise was designed to aggravate growing anti-refugee sentiment in West Germany, thereby discouraging emigrants in the future.[6]

By the end of March, though, the East German government suddenly changed course and began arresting applicants; by the first week of May the flow had returned to "normal." About 25,000 had made it out. An estimated 480,000 more applications were still

6. *Chicago Tribune,* May 1 and May 15, 1984; *Wall Street Journal,* May 16, 1984; Ronald D. Asmus, "A New Wave of East German Emigration," RAD Background Report/45, Radio Free Europe Research, March 28, 1984; *Süddeutsche Zeitung,* March 8, 1984.

pending. That may explain why the authorities made such an abrupt about-face. Or perhaps the intended signal to the West had been given. We may never know. One way or another, the policy appears to have been a carefully calculated one.

In Cuba, too, recent policy seems carefully planned, if somewhat inscrutable. Since Mariel, exit visas have been difficult to come by. Applicants must obtain statements of character from the workplace, show an invitation if leaving on a visit, and make a deposit or other proof of funding if the trip is to other than a socialist country. Prospective travelers may be required to consult government agencies; for example, writers or musicians often must gain clearance from the Ministry of Culture. Neighborhood Committees for the Defense of the Revolution can make travel difficult if an individual is politically suspect. In addition, all emigrants must leave household goods and most other property behind.[7]

In general, Cuba seems willing to allow its discontented to leave, especially if they pose a potential security threat. But only within limits. Efforts are made to deter skilled professionals from emigrating. One method is to make it clear that anyone leaving will not be allowed to return. In the words of one Cuban official, "We are not playing games."[8]

Assessing Cuban policy in the post-Mariel period is difficult, given the deadlock over Cuban admissions to the United States. In addition to the general hostility the Reagan administration has shown the Castro regime, Washington refused to process most immigrants from Cuba until Cuba agreed to take back the 2700 Mariel "excludables" (mostly criminals and mental patients). Even political prisoners released by Cuba for deportation to the United States were not accepted. This stalemate was finally broken in late 1984, when Cuba agreed to take back the excludables, and the United States

7. Patricia Weiss Fagen, *Immigration, Emigration and Asylum Policies in Cuba* (Washington: Refugee Policy Group, 1984).

8. Personal interview with Felipe R. Alvarez, First Secretary and Consul, Cuban Interests Section, Washington, D.C., May 24, 1984.

accordingly began to process the backlog of Cubans already cleared for departure. Cuba's motives for making this concession after years of refusal were not clear. Perhaps the authorities wanted to relieve pressures within Cuba; perhaps they hoped to improve relations with the United States or Cuba's image generally. In any event, Havana suspended the agreement a short time later when the United States began its anti-Castro Radio Marti broadcasts.

Iran's treatment of the Baha'is is governed by a very different set of calculations. Iranian Baha'is have historically served as scapegoats and targets of persecution, especially in times of ferment. But the fundamentalist Islamic regime that replaced the Shah has waged an exceptionally ferocious campaign to eradicate the Baha'i faith.[9] The Iranian government has targeted the 300,000 Baha'is in the country not only for their "heretical" views, but also for their imagined links to Iran's external enemies, imperialism and Zionism. In 1979 the authorities seized all communal Baha'i property and, by the end of 1981, had demolished virtually all Baha'i holy places, including the main Baha'i shrine, the House of the Bab, in Shiraz. The government twice executed all members of the high Baha'i governing body, the National Spiritual Assembly, and systematically killed or incarcerated many other leaders. Baha'is are barred from all educational institutions, from government employment, and from all religious observances. Massive pressure, including torture, has been used to force conversions to Islam.[10]

Adding a new twist to an old story, the Iranian government has also prevented Baha'is from departing the country. Since 1981, all border posts require a declaration of one's religion from those departing; those identifying themselves as Baha'is are prevented from

9. Letter from Gerald Knight, Alternate Representative for the Baha'i International Community to the United Nations, August 8, 1984; interview with Douglas Martin, Director of Information, International Baha'i Community, January 5, 1986; see also Department of State *Country Reports on Human Rights Practices for 1983*, pp. 1254–66.

10. Ibid.; see also the documentation in *The Baha'is in Iran* (New York: Baha'i International Community, 1982).

leaving. This measure is apparently intended to prevent the further spread of what is termed the "virus" of Baha'ism, and to intensify the pressure for recantation. Since very few have been willing to identify themselves as Moslems (thus abjuring their faith), only those able to cross the borders illegally (an estimated 40,000) have escaped further persecution.

In Ethiopia, the problems of control are perhaps greater than anywhere else. The country suffers from a continuing civil war with Eritrean and Somali separatists, from crushing famine, and from a general breakdown of order. The tremendous tide of refugees has resulted partly from the government's own policies. And, as much as the authorities would like to contain that flow, it lacks the physical means to do so. The government's impotence and frustration were apparent in its denunciation of the recent airlift of Ethiopian Jews from Sudanese refugee camps to Israel as "illegal trafficking" in Ethiopian citizens. The ruling Dergue accused Sudan and unnamed "foreign powers" of "forcing and enticing [Ethiopians] to illegally cross over into the Sudan."

At the same time, the Ethiopian government often gave priority to its military aims ahead of relief efforts (by, for instance, unloading military equipment ahead of food in the ports, and by using the excuse of famine to relocate population from rebel-held areas). And while the regime continues to oppose emigration generally, these actions have in fact increased the refugee flow. It seems clear from its own actions that the Dergue would like to see an outflow of population from areas it cannot control, and while it officially accepts the return of ethnic Somalis to the Ogaden, in southern Ethiopia, it will not go out of its way to bring them back. Given the confusion of the situation, it was not always clear which Ethiopians the government wanted to stay put, which it wished to relocate forcibly, and which it would just as soon never see again. Whichever, the Ethiopian regime clearly assumed the right to decide who belonged in which category, and to act accordingly.

The government of Bulgaria, which has sometimes in the past

encouraged ethnic Turks to leave, has lately taken a hard line toward their emigration, in tandem with increased pressures to assimilate. Turks have, for example, been told to adopt Slavic names. But the most interesting case of emigration trade-offs has occurred in the Soviet Union. Through the mid-1960s, only a small trickle of emigrants was allowed out of the Soviet Union. As in the past, these were mostly cases of repatriation or family reunification involving members of ethnic groups with international ties. Even then, the numbers were minimal, as Soviet policy clearly sought to encourage assimilation of all groups.

Soviet opposition to emigration, as reviewed in chapter 3, springs from a combination of historical Russian isolationism and the peculiar characteristics of Soviet Marxism. Shaping the policy are such central features as the supreme power of the state, the stress on collective interest, the ideology of mobilization, the sense of threat from a hostile world, the fear of external communication, and the traditional view, dating back to Catherine the Great, that foreign travel is a privilege of the elite. These tendencies were reinforced after 1945 by the heavy wounds inflicted by the war: a decimated population, declining birth rates, labor shortages, and ethnic ferment.

To allow unchecked movement would run counter to all the basic instincts of the Soviet system as it has evolved over the years. The emigration activists in the Soviet Union know this best, noting—in a booklet of instructions for would-be emigrants—that "the authorities regard emigration by its citizens as an act that is antisocial, unpatriotic and hostile, and even an act of treason against the country."[11]

Given these attitudes, the prospect of emigration by ethnic Russians does not even arise in the Soviet Union. Pentecostal Christians, for example, have been almost totally excluded from emigration

---

11. *How to Emigrate to Israel from the USSR: By a Jewish Activist in the Soviet Union Who Must Remain Anonymous* (New York: International Council of B'nai B'rith, 1982), p. 1.

despite strong efforts to leave. Ethnic minority groups are sometimes more dispensable, but there is still fear that letting them go will encourage others to demand the same right. Soviet officials dread a massive exodus; one has publicly conjectured that up to one-half of all Soviet Jews would leave if they could.[12]

The emigration of Jews, in particular, raises another issue. By the end of the 1930s, Jews had become the most educated group in the Soviet Union, and they were especially prominent in the scientific and technical elite. According to the 1970 census, in the Russian Republic, 344 Jews of every 1000 over the age of ten had higher education, while for Russians the figure was 43 of every 1000. Fully 68.2 percent of the Jewish workers were ranked as "specialists."[13]

Thus General N. Shchelokov, Minister of the Interior, said that "We cannot supply specialists with higher education to Israel. We need them ourselves."[14] Such an attitude, if generally applied, would make professional success a detriment to the full enjoyment of human rights. In the words of two Soviet Jewish scientists, Veniamin Levich and Aleksandr Voronel, the Soviet attitude threatened to turn scientists "into an exploited and discriminated-against minority, into bondsmen of the twentieth century."[15]

Soviet brain drain claims must be taken somewhat skeptically. The Soviet Union is much more developed economically than other nations that usually complain about losses of skilled personnel. Furthermore, Soviet professionals applying to leave are usually dismissed from their positions anyway, thus ending their usefulness. One specialist, informed that he could not leave because of his badly needed

12. Leonard Schroeter, *The Last Exodus* (Seattle and London: University of Washington Press, 1974), p. 5.

13. For an overview of this topic, see Igor Birman, "Jewish Emigration from the USSR: Some Observations," *Soviet Jewish Affairs* 9, no. 1 (1979): 46–63.

14. William Korey, *The Soviet Cage: Anti-Semitism in Russia* (New York: Viking, 1973), p. 197.

15. Ibid., p. 314.

skills, noted ruefully that "This high evaluation of my abilities did not prevent the administration from removing me from being in charge of the laboratory and forbidding me to teach."[16] Moreover, throughout the 1970s, the number of Jews in important professional positions was reduced. On the whole, while the loss of professionals may be a consideration in Soviet policy, it has clearly never been the central concern.

During the 1970s the Soviet Union suddenly allowed more than 250,000 Jews—about 10 percent of the country's Jewish population—to leave. During the 1960s, the total had been less than 10,000. Similar increases occurred in the emigration of Germans (from 9000 in the 1960s to 56,000 in the 1970s) and Armenians (from about 8000 to 20,000).[17]

Official Soviet explanation for the sudden liberalization are varied and inconsistent. On the most rudimentary level, spokesmen insist that no limits to emigration exist apart from those sanctioned by international conventions.[18] Deputy Interior Minister Boris T. Shumilin, the top Soviet official on emigration, claimed in 1972 that 95.5 percent of all visa applications had been granted. In 1976, he said that 98.4 percent had been granted; again in 1977, 98.4 percent; and in 1978, for the third year in a row, 98.4 percent—something of a minor statistical miracle.[19] In the official view, then,

---

16. Letter from Roman Rutman, February 21, 1972, quoted in ibid.

17. Figures taken from the numbers collated by Benjamin Pinkus, "The Emigration of National Minorities from the USSR in the Post-Stalin Period," *Soviet Jewish Affairs* 13, no. 1 (1983): 3–36.

18. Konstantin U. Chernenko, *Human Rights in Soviet Society* (New York: International, 1981), p. 62. According to Mr. Sveridov of the Soviet Embassy in Washington, the Soviet Union is a signatory of the International Covenant on Civil and Political Rights and observes its commitments under the Covenant, and that is all there is to say on the subject; any objective study would simply report this (telephone interview, May 18, 1984).

19. Actually Shumilin's arithmetic for 1978 was somewhat careless; according to the figures that he himself supplied, the acceptance rate was 98.7 percent, and not 98.4 percent. This may say something about the Soviet attitude toward data. Sources: "On the Departure of Soviet Citizens for Other Countries,"

the number of departures simply reflects the number of applicants.

In fact, however, would-be emigrants must fill out a "pre-application questionnaire," which is used to disqualify many of those seeking to leave. In general, the Soviet Union accepts only those applications based on family reunification. Colonel Obidin, the Soviet visa chief, was quoted in 1976 on this point (pp. 211–12); in 1977, he reaffirmed to the *New York Times* that there is no "social basis" for emigration from the Soviet Union, that "family reunion is the only basis for issuing exit permission."[20] Another way to juggle the figures is simply not to act on an application, in which case it does not count as a rejection. As the available evidence makes clear, there is forever a large backlog of applications.

To understand why the government suddenly decided in 1970 to approve more applications, it is important to grasp the differing attitudes toward emigration that exist inside the Kremlin. Arkady Shevchenko, the highest-ranking Soviet official to defect to the West, confirms what outside observers have suspected: that there is a lively debate within the Soviet government between those willing to see the disaffected leave and those fearing any relaxation in official control:

> One camp held that no emigration should be permitted at all. Its members predicted—correctly, as events proved—that to open the door for Jews would invite pressure from other ethnic groups, such as the Armenians and the Germans who had settled along the Volga in the eighteenth century but had been deported to Kazakhstan during World War II. Moreover, a policy favoring Jews would anger ordinary Russians, whose own freedom to travel was severely restricted.
>
> The opposing school held that the Soviet Union would be stronger if it cleaned house. Reflecting Russian anti-Semitism, this

---

Novosti, December 20, 1972; United Press report, Moscow, June 19, 1974; *New York Times,* January 21, 1977; *Digest of Soviet Press "Sputnik",* no. 10 (1977); *Novosti,* November 15, 1978.

20. *New York Times,* November 21, 1977.

second group tended to think of Soviet Jews as inherently hostile to the state. Why keep people who do not want to live in the U.S.S.R.? Good riddance to them.[21]

Shevchenko goes on to say that in the early 1970s, foreign policy considerations tipped the debate in favor of liberalization. Generally, Soviet leaders do not like to give the appearance of bowing to outside pressure. In this period, however, the government was anxious to obtain most-favored-nation status from the United States, and to do so it knew that the country needed a better image abroad. The entreaties of Communist party leaders in France, Italy, and elsewhere may also have had special impact. One major jump in exit numbers, in late 1971, came immediately on the heels of Kosygin and Brezhnev trips to the West, where they had been exposed to sharp questioning on the subject. Another big spurt, in 1977–79, came as a Helsinki review conference was meeting in Belgrade and the SALT II treaty was being concluded.

More basic than international considerations, though, was the Soviet policy toward nationalities. Under the slogan "national in form, socialist in content," the government has promoted the Sovietization, and sometimes "Russification," of the numerous nationalities within the Soviet Union. As a KGB official told a Jewish dissident in 1982, "Our goal is to assimilate you, and people like you. You don't let us do it—you are our obstacle."[22] While, on the whole, the policy has been very successful, it has flagged in areas where a nationality has no territory of its own, has a base outside the Soviet Union, and in some cases also has a high proportion of urban professionals.[23] Thus, in the past, the Soviet government has recognized a "right" of repatriation for Poles, Greeks, Koreans, and Spanish.

Today, Jews, Germans, and Armenians possess some or all of

21. Shevchenko, *Breaking with Moscow* (New York: Knopf, 1985), p. 260; personal interview with Shevchenko, May 23, 1984.

22. Martin Gilbert, *The Jews of Hope* (London: Macmillan, 1984), p. 218.

23. Victor Zaslavsky and Robert J. Brym, *Soviet-Jewish Emigration and Soviet Nationality Policy* (New York: St. Martin's, 1983), p. 104.

these attributes and the Soviet government seems willing to make special allowances for them. Although the Soviet Union does not officially regard emigration to Israel as repatriation, it does recognize Jews as a nationality, and it recognizes Israel as the homeland of the Jewish people.[24] The revival of Russian nationalism has intensified the urge, already present, to reduce the Jewish prominence in the technical elite and to Russify it. Between 1970 and 1978, admission of Jews to institutions of higher learning dropped by 40 percent.[25] This only fed the pressure for emigration.

By the mid-1970s, therefore, Soviet authorities became more conscious of the internal benefits of emigration; as Shevchenko notes, their approach included a strong element of good riddance. Zhores Medvedev, the prominent exiled dissident, argued in 1978 that "as emigration is controlled, irreversible (through the confiscation of passports), and selective, the state now manipulates emigration opportunities for its own convenience, often just to rid itself of dissidents, the old and the useless, the not too bright, and the unemployed."[26]

The 1970s emigration thus provided the Soviet Union a cover for pushing out numerous dissenters, Jewish and non-Jewish, who had never sought to emigrate. The most prominent case was Alexander Solzhenitsyn, who had bitterly opposed emigration. But there were many other less heralded cases. Typical was the experience of Konstantin Simis, a lawyer who, after authoring an exposé on the Soviet legal system, was "invited" to emigrate or face trial. Simis described how his application—which would normally have taken months to process—was handled:

24. Especially in speeches supporting the establishment of Israel in 1947 and 1948; see Mitchell Knisbacher, "Aliyah of Soviet Jews: Protection of the Right of Emigration under International Law," *Harvard International Law Journal* 14 (1973): 95–96.

25. Zvi Gitelman, "Moscow and the Soviet Jews: A Parting of the Ways," *Problems of Communism* 29 (Jan.–Feb. 1980): 31, citing Soviet sources; see also Birman.

26. Medvedev, *Soviet Science* (New York: Norton, 1978), p. 152.

Colonel Zotov was the deputy director of the Visa and Registration Department. . . . He welcomed me like a long-lost friend: "Konstantin Mikhailovich. Why didn't you come straight to me? You don't have many days for your preparations—I understand perfectly. Let's see now—you make a list of the things you need to do, write down the offices that handle them, and I promise to help you. Give me the list, and if there are any problems, do not hesitate to call me at any time and I'll get things sorted out."

Then it started. Every office I visited gave me the same answer: "Come back in two (sometimes three) weeks." Back I'd go to Colonel Zotov, who would call the office concerned, and everything would be sorted out in a matter of hours as if at the wave of a magic wand.[27]

After 1979, the flow was again reduced to a trickle. Apparently, matters seemed to be getting out of hand. A top KGB official indicated that "emigration sentiment is not limited to Jews, Germans, and Armenians."[28] Dissent was spreading, the flow of applicants continuing unabated. Foreign interest in and support for emigrants was growing. Brezhnev's position seemed to be weakening, while the influence of the KGB—then pushing new anti-corruption and law-and-order campaigns—was rising, and this translated into crackdowns on dissidents and the emigration movement by traditional methods.

Perhaps even more important, détente was collapsing. By the end of 1979, U.S.–Soviet relations had gone sour, and the chances for Senate ratification of SALT II looked dismal. Then came the Soviet invasion of Afghanistan. In the wake of vociferous Western condemnations, the Soviet government no longer had much to lose in world opinion by indulging its natural instinct to close its gates.

By 1983, emigration was back to pre-1970 levels, consisting

27. Konstantin M. Simis, *USSR: The Corrupt Society* (New York: Simon and Schuster, 1982), pp. 209–10.

28. S. Tsvigun, "O proiskakh imperialisticheskikh razvedok" ["On the intrigues of the imperialist secret services"], *Kommunist* 14, pp. 88–99, quoted by Zaslavsky and Brym, p. 139.

mainly of the spouses and unmarried children of previous emigrants. Soviet authorities claimed that all those wanting to leave had already done so; the Helsinki Commission, however, estimated that another 250,000–400,000 had applied. The number who had been officially refused—the refuseniks—had grown to at least 10,000. (Most of the rest, presumably, were not refused outright, simply not acted on.) Some have been refused for over ten years; the record-holder, according to the *Guinness Book of World Records,* first applied for a visa in 1966. Many refusals appear to be arbitrary, in what seems a deliberate policy to deter others from applying.[29]

On April 20, 1983, the Soviet Union sent an important signal in the form of a dispatch from Soviet journalist Victor Louis, who is often used as a conduit for messages to the West. In an article for the Israeli newspaper *Yediot Ahronot,* Louis wrote, "Whether it pleases people or not, the chapter of mass Jewish emigration from the Soviet Union has reached its end. In Moscow it is now said openly: 'The last train has left the station.'"[30]

The article maintained that Jews seeking visas for Israel were actually looking for an easy route to the United States or Australia. (Most recent emigrants, in fact, had not gone to Israel.) Louis claimed that pessimistic letters from émigrés in the United States had persuaded others to remain in the Soviet Union, and he quoted a Soviet newspaper that described emigration as "burial alive." The article predicted that there would soon emerge a movement to return, and that the slogan of Soviet Jews would change from "Let My People Go" to "Let My People Return." Based on this and other statements, a reversal in Soviet policy does not seem likely until there is a significant improvement in East-West relations.

Looking back over the 1970s, the role of nationality clearly emerges in the contours of Soviet emigration policy. The exodus of Jews, Germans, and Armenians all followed the same pattern: a sharp

29. Gilbert, pp. 78, 83, 119.

30. *Yediot Ahronot,* April 20, 1983 (translation mine).

increase in the early 1970s, a peak in the latter part of the decade (1976 for the Germans, 1979 for the Jews, 1980 for the Armenians). The ups and down within that pattern were probably due to fine tuning in accord with changing foreign policy considerations. From the Soviet perspective, the primary focus is clear: how could emigration be used to achieve specific domestic goals without encouraging the idea that departure exists as an option for all?

The government's task is greatly complicated by the conflicting signals it sends to nationalities regarding assimilation. On the one hand, the Soviet Union presses minorities to blend in; accordingly, it discourages emigration. At the same time, however, the regime sometimes makes assimilation difficult—which serves only to encourage people to leave. This is especially true in the case of the Jews. According to available indications, most Soviet Jews would assimilate if given the chance. Consider the bitter recollections of one recent emigrant:

> After the war I graduated from the university and for 25 years I built electric power stations, working sometimes sixteen hours a day—for the good of the state, as the saying goes. But when my son finished school at the top of his class he was not given a gold medal, which entitles one to enter university without writing entrance exams. And in the exams they deliberately failed him. I went to visit the head of the selection committee. I've never been in a synagogue, but his reception room reminded me of one. Only Jews were there. I talked to some of them and went home. I knew it in advance but simply did not wish to face the fact. My son's failure was not accidental; state instructions were behind it. The state paid me this way for all my service. In several days we decided to emigrate. It was risky, because we had only a year for preparations, otherwise my son would be drafted. But we succeeded. I have wasted my life working for them. At least my son won't.[31]

As this account indicates, Soviet authorities might best be able

31. Zaslavsky and Brym, pp. 109–10.

to control pressures for emigration by ensuring full equality of opportunity. However, recent Soviet experience is not encouraging on this point. In the late 1970s, a new phrase was heard in party circles—"the Polish experiment"—a reference to Gomulka's expulsion of Polish Jews in 1968–69.[32] In a survey of recent Jewish emigrants, more than 35 percent felt that "their departure was more the result of the authorities' desire to get rid of Jews and dissidents than of any spontaneous decision of their own."[33]

This suggests that emigration pressure might not be quite the threat that Soviet authorities seem to feel it is, and that it could be reduced by simple measures such as opening more doors of opportunity within the Soviet Union. In fact, it is hard to conceive of a genuine collective Soviet interest that is credibly served by maintaining a sealed border. Unless an exodus reached truly massive dimensions—a highly unlikely possibility—a liberal policy would not seem to endanger Soviet security or economic development. The Soviets are surely past the point where they need fear an anti-Soviet community in exile, or a serious drain to their intellectual resources. The closer one looks, the more it appears that hostility to emigration is linked not to a concrete interest but to ideological reflexes, obsessive habits of tight control, and the traditional Russian suspicion of the outside world.

Many close observers feel that some recent emigrants would return if allowed to do so, and that fewer would leave than feared if the door were opened. The Soviets may, in any case, be fighting a losing battle in their effort to keep the country sealed. The growing power of international communications threatens to disrupt the regime's concerted control of information. And, despite the revival of mercantilist-like notions about population, it must soon become clear that restrictions on migration are not necessarily beneficial—and can be harmful—to a country's economic development.

32. Ibid., p. 40; interviews with recent Soviet emigrants.
33. Ibid., p. 70.

Is the new serfdom in fact a necessary consequence of Marxism? Or of socialism? The question deserves a closer look.

Socialism and Controlled Movement

In most places, the border between the German Democratic Republic and the Federal Republic of Germany is marked by parallel metal trellis fences with contact mines between them; until recently, some sections were equipped with SM-70 automatic shooting devices (these were dismantled as an apparent "humanitarian gesture"). Immediately to the east of the fence is an antivehicle ditch, then a tracking strip to detect footprints or other tracks, then a relief road to provide guards easy access, and finally another fence outfitted with electric and acoustic warning devices. Observation towers are usually located within sight of one other; where observation is difficult, attack dogs help out. Border guards have standing orders to shoot to kill anyone within fifty yards of the metal trellis fence. It has been called, with reason, "the most inhumane border on earth."[34]

For many, this barrier has come to embody the socialist world's insistence on curtailing movement. But many governments that describe themselves as socialist—Algeria, Senegal, Madagascar, to name a few—feature none or few of these controls. Even many regimes that call themselves Marxist do not fit the mold. Benin and the Congo, for example, have fairly liberal exit policies. China and Cuba are somewhat looser, at least relative to prevailing stereotypes. Hungary has allowed considerable openness without suffering any apparent threat to its domestic peace.

Most interesting is Yugoslavia. Just as it has diverged sharply from the rest of Eastern Europe in its political and economic structure, so has the country departed from regional norms when it comes to emigration policy. From the early 1950s on, the Yugoslavs adopted a more relaxed attitude toward travel abroad. Between 1953 and

34. CDU/CSU Group in the German Bundestag, *White Paper on the Human Rights Situation in Germany and of the Germans in Eastern Europe* (Bonn, 1977), pp. 27–30.

1961, the government tolerated, if not encouraged, the departure of about 300,000 people, many of them Turks or members of other minority groups (the figure, an official one, may be low).[35] Beginning in 1964, the country experienced a massive migration of Yugoslavs who left to work abroad, mainly in Western Europe. The outflow, partly organized by the government in order to reduce unemployment, reached a peak of one million people in the early 1970s.

In explaining what distinguishes Yugoslavia from other East European states, official spokesmen note the changes made in the domestic system after the break with Stalin. The introduction of "socialist self-management," they say, fundamentally changed perceptions about the role of the state. The decentralization of planning meant, among other things, that the state could not guarantee full employment.[36] Labor migration thus became an important means of mitigating unemployment; workers abroad also sent back remittances and, on returning home, brought new skills with them. While such movement had forced Hungary to raise the wages of professionals and reduce equality, it apparently made no great impact on the wage structure in Yugoslavia, given the fact that there was a labor surplus anyway, and that salaries in the decentralized system were set by individual enterprises already competing for skilled personnel.

Some problems did develop, however. As with labor migration elsewhere, it was not primarily the unemployed and unskilled but the relatively skilled who left. In addition, a disproportionate number of Croatians departed, creating concern over possible changes in the country's ethnic balance. The military feared the loss of draft-age men. From an ideological standpoint, too, the flow was criticized: "The whole rationale of socialist self-management seemed called into question, if not positively mocked, by such an explicit and sincere acknowledgement of the superiority of other systems. Two decades

35. John F. Besemeres, *Socialist Population Policies* (White Plains, N.Y.: M. E. Sharpe, 1980), p. 175.

36. Personal interview with Yugoslav diplomatic representative, April 30, 1984; *Yugoslav Survey*, 1983, p. 3.

of socialist education and upbringing were being abandoned to an onslaught of hostile ideological and political influences."[37]

These were precisely the fears and concerns that had led other Eastern European states to close their borders. Apart from imposing restriction on military-age males, however, the Yugoslavs resisted adopting coercive policies. Rather, the government stopped organizing the exodus and introduced incentives to attract workers back. In the end, though, the recession in Europe that began in 1973 was a more effective brake. By the end of 1982, only about 590,000 Yugoslav workers remained abroad. But the government still affirmed everyone's right to a passport, and denials were generally based upon universally recognized grounds. A small number of dissidents were denied the right to travel on security grounds. Otherwise, half the population possessed passports, and the door was open. Clearly, free movement is not incompatible with a planned economy.

What is it, then, about the Soviet model that makes it seem so essential to cloister an entire population? There are many authoritarian governments that, for all their brutality and heavy-handedness, do not circumscribe the right to leave. But in the Soviet Union and the countries that emulate it, the act of leaving carries special significance. It seems a renunciation of national allegiance or, even more important, an indictment of the entire political and economic system. This mentality is captured perfectly in the treatment of East Germans who visit the West German mission in East Berlin to discuss emigration. Upon leaving the mission, they may be arrested for violating article 220 of the criminal code, passing damaging information to foreigners. The logic of the authorities is that any East German, in explaining why he wants to emigrate, will inevitably say something negative about his country.[38]

37. Besemeres, pp. 39, 177, 192, 216–17.
38. Frederick Kempe, "East and West Germany Do a Minuet on the Wall," *Wall Street Journal,* May 16, 1984; see the cases reported in Amnesty International, *The Imprisonment of Persons Seeking to Leave a Country or to Return to Their Own Country* (London: Amnesty International, 1986), pp. 9–10.

Those who choose to leave also threaten regimes that aspire after total internal control. Such control is not a characteristic of all socialist or centrally planned economies. Nor is it an intrinsic attribute of states that choose Marxism as their guiding ideology, or those ruled by a single party. But when governments seek to control all aspects of a society's activities, as in Soviet-style countries, the denial of free movement may indeed be imperative.

In fact, the variation in emigration policies among socialist countries seems related more to emulation of the Soviet model than to anything else. Those nations that feature the strongest Soviet presence or the most orthodox Soviet-style systems also generally have the tightest borders. (On making new allies, the Soviet Union is usually quick to share its expertise in training border guards.) In North Korea—one of the most stalwart of Communist regimes— the right to travel is "perhaps the most restricted in the world," according to Freedom House.[39] Even tourism to other Communist nations is strictly prohibited. Albania, a Stalinist if not pro-Soviet system, and Mongolia are not much different.

But what these nations are copying from the Soviet Union may be as much *Russian*—that is, centuries-old traditions and attitudes— as it is *Communist*—that is, a necessary part of Soviet ideology. In some ways, the Soviet leadership has simply extended pre-Soviet practices on controlled mobility, combining a quasi-medieval Tsarist view of human movement with twentieth-century means of enforcement. This suggests that the spread of controlled movement might be, to some degree, a historical accident, in that it is not essential to socialist or even to authoritarian systems. It is unclear if controlled movement is essential even to the Soviet system. Many experts believe that, as elsewhere, most disaffected Soviet citizens would stay in their own country even if given the chance to leave. Valery Chalidze, an émigré and incisive critic of the Soviet system, argues that "it is

39. Raymond D. Gastil, *Freedom in the World: Political Rights and Civil Liberties, 1984–1985* (Westport, Conn., and London: Greenwood, 1985), p. 340.

hardly likely that in the USSR one could recruit enough malcontents ready to leave the country to begin a mass exodus capable of doing demographic damage to the USSR."[40] One should not underestimate the strength of family and cultural ties, the much-noted love of Mother Russia, the system's generous social benefits, and the sheer force of inertia—not to mention the shortage of immigration opportunities.

Even Nikita Khrushchev developed doubts about the wisdom of prohibiting emigration. In fact, his memoirs conclude with a passage on what he called "this disgraceful heritage of the closed border which lies like a chain on the consciousness of the Soviet state":

> Why should we build a good life for a people and then keep our border bolted with seven locks? . . . I think it's time to show the world that our people are free; they work willingly; and they are building Socialism because of their convictions, not because they have no choice. . . .
>
> We've got to stop designing our border policy for the sake of keeping the dregs and scum inside our country. We must start thinking about the people who don't deserve to be called scum— people who might undergo a temporary vacillation in their own convictions, or who might want to try out the capitalist hell, some aspects of which might still appear attractive to our less stable elements. We can't keep fencing these people in. We've got to give them a chance to find out for themselves what the world is like.
>
> If we don't change our position in this regard, I'm afraid we will discredit the Marxist-Leninist ideals on which our Soviet way of life is based.[41]

Until a bolder Soviet regime accepts this challenge, it will remain unclear whether controlled emigration is essential to the So-

40. Valery Chalidze, *To Defend These Rights: Human Rights and the Soviet Union* (New York: Random House, 1974), p. 104.

41. *Khrushchev Remembers,* ed. Strobe Talbott (Boston: Little, Brown, 1970), pp. 522, 525.

viet system. In any case, adherents of the Khrushchev approach may take heart from some encouraging recent signs. Among socialist nations, China and Hungary have liberalized their practices significantly; Poland too, despite setbacks under martial law, has made progress. Restrictions on foreign travel have also been loosened in Sri Lanka, Algeria, the Congo, Burkina Faso, Indonesia, Singapore, the Seychelles, Turkey, and Cyprus. Entry visas are slowly being eliminated among friendly states, and regional agreements for free movement have been concluded in Francophone Africa, among other areas.

And then there is the recent experience of Guyana. In October 1983, the government announced that public employees would no longer be allowed to spend their leaves outside the country. But massive resignations followed, and the order was rescinded a week later. If such determination were to spread, the world would have fewer barriers.

Reviving the Issue: Arenas of Accountability

In 1982 the United Nations Department of International Economic and Social Affairs published a survey of international migration trends.[42] The survey described recent population movements, region by region, and briefly catalogued the government policies that had shaped these movements. Shortly after, a curious "Corrigendum" was attached to the survey, deleting all passages on emigration from Eastern Europe. Accuracy was not at issue, only the fact that the survey had referred to the area in the first place. To judge from the "corrected" version, there had simply been no emigration from Eastern Europe.

The change, made in response to pressures from the states involved, shows the lengths to which certain governments will go to keep the issue off the agenda of international bodies.

42. United Nations, *International Migration Policies*.

This is nothing new, of course, but the efforts of late have grown more insistent, reflecting a rebirth of interest in the right to leave and remain. By the mid-1970s, Western governments were finally beginning to press freedom of emigration as an important component of human rights. Some arenas of accountability were established, imperfect but potentially embarrassing to practitioners of the new serfdom. As a result, there emerged a new sensitivity to discussions of emigration policy.

The Final Act of the Conference on Security and Cooperation in Europe (the Helsinki Conference), signed in 1975, marked the first time that human rights were formally recognized as a fundamental principle governing relations among states, and thus as a legitimate topic in government-to-government discourse.[43] Among other things, Helsinki committed the United States, Canada, and all European states (except for perpetually isolated Albania) to facilitate "freer movement and contacts, individually and collectively, whether privately or officially." The participating states also committed themselves to easing foreign travel for family visits or for "personal or professional reasons" and to dealing "in a positive and humanitarian spirit" with applications for family reunification or marriage to a foreigner. Additional provisions called for lower exit fees, simplified processing of applications, and reconsideration of initial refusals.

Some observers worried that the focus on specific classifications of emigration, particularly family reunification, would suggest that the right existed only in these cases. Indeed, not long after the conference, the head of the Soviet visa office, Colonel Vladimir Obidin, stated that "We are now putting a stop to all arbitrary emigration. In accordance with the decisions of the agreement at Helsinki we shall let people go only where it is for reunification of

43. William Korey, *Human Rights and the Helsinki Accord,* Headline Series no. 264 (New York: Foreign Policy Association, 1983), p. 17.

families."[44] But the Helsinki Agreement also obligates all signatories to observe the Universal Declaration of Human Rights and, if they have ratified it, the International Covenant on Civil and Political Rights; both documents specifically recognize a general right to leave. And, by setting emigration in the context of overall relations among the signatories, Helsinki established it as a legitimate item of international discourse.

The Soviets indirectly acknowledged this development by the vehemence of their objections to it. They accepted "Basket III," the human rights section of the accords, only as a trade-off for achieving their own goals in the agreement, which were to legitimize the post–World War II order in Eastern Europe and to secure greater access to Western technology. As M. Lvov, a Moscow commentator, put it, they saw the Western drive on human rights as an effort "to probe the ideological stability of the socialist system and open up broader possibilities for the infiltration of bourgeois ideology into the socialist countries."[45] More specifically, Péter Vas-Zoltán, the Hungarian brain drain specialist, asserted that arguments on "the free flow of people and ideas" belonged to "the more subtle methods of subversive propaganda aimed at winning over the public opinion of the intelligentsia in the socialist countries."[46]

The Soviets and Eastern Europeans had reason to fear the "free movement" issue. The review conferences that monitored compliance with Helsinki (Belgrade in 1977–78, Madrid in 1980–83) subjected Soviet bloc practices to unusually searching and prolonged inquiry. Helsinki monitoring groups sprang up in Eastern Europe. And,

44. From a statement made to a group of petitioners, translated and quoted by Michael Sherbourne, "Soviet Jewry Background Report on the 1975 Helsinki Agreement" (unpublished memo, London, December, 1976); account of the meeting in Gilbert, pp. 93–94.

45. M. Lvov, "European Conference: Experience and Significance," *International Affairs* (Moscow) 4 (1976): 44.

46. Péter Vas-Zoltán, *The Brain Drain: An Anomaly of International Relations* (Leiden: A. W. Sijthoff, and Budapest: Akadémia Kiadó, 1976), p. 28.

spurred on by the accord, an estimated 100,000 East Germans applied for exit visas.

But the governments of the area were in no mood for tolerance. The monitoring groups were hounded out of existence, and only cosmetic changes were made in regulations relating to foreign travel. In the Soviet Union, for example, the fee for an exit visa to capitalist countries was lowered from 400 to 300 rubles, the application fee (40 rubles) was now collected only if the application was granted, the maximum waiting period for appeals was reduced from a year to six months, and the required character reference from an employer was changed to a certificate of employment. But other obstacles remained, including a 500-ruble fee to renounce Soviet citizenship, payable upon leaving. As the U.S. Helsinki Commission reported in 1977, there were "no profound adjustments" in Soviet procedures.[47] In Eastern Europe as a whole, the only real progress was resolution of some family cases. East Germany and Romania actually imposed new obstacles on foreign travel, in addition to expelling Helsinki activists. Romania's leading newspaper *Scinteia* captured the prevailing attitude when, on September 4, 1979, it described people wishing to emigrate as dehumanized "renegades" who were committing treason against the country.

The reports of the Helsinki Commission over succeeding years repeat a familiar refrain. In the Soviet Union, emigration increased until 1979 but declined rapidly thereafter. Growing numbers of petty obstacles were imposed, such as requiring a closer family re-

47. U.S. Congress, House of Representatives, Committee on International Relations, *Implementation of the Final Act of the Conference of Security and Cooperation in Europe: Findings and Recommendations Two Years after Helsinki,* report transmitted by the Commission on Security and Cooperation in Europe, September 23, 1977 (Washington: U.S. Government Printing Office, 1977), p. 65. Also of use are the semiannual reports by the U.S. Department of State, Bureau of Public Affairs, *Implementation of Helsinki Report* (Washington: U.S. Government Printing Office, various dates). See also Stephen H. Meeter, "The Relation of the Helsinki Final Act to the Emigration of Soviet Jews," *Boston College International and Comparative Law Journal* 1, no. 1 (1977): 135–47.

lationship or denying applications if a majority of family members was still in the Soviet Union. Those granted exit visas have sometimes been asked to pledge that, once abroad, they will not forward invitations to relatives left behind. In Bulgaria, Czechoslovakia, and East Germany, occasional progress was made on family reunification and visits, but the general picture was still bleak. (Czechoslovakia even required emigrants to repay the cost of their education.) A major exception was Hungary, where policies were significantly liberalized.

Until 1981, Poland allowed relatively more foreign travel, even though about 20 percent of Polish tourists abroad did not return. But with the imposition of martial law in December of that year, this travel was restricted. As so often happens, while the Polish government was restricting emigration, it was simultaneously pressing detainees, mostly Solidarity activists, to leave the country for good.

In Romania there was considerable harassment of would-be emigrants. In late 1981, its government imposed an education tax on emigrants, ostensibly to recover the costs of their secondary and university education. This was later rescinded when the United States threatened to cancel Romania's most-favored-nation trade status.

Another, though less effective, arena of accountability is the U.N.-sponsored International Covenant on Civil and Political Rights. Promulgated in 1976, the Covenant had by 1985 been ratified by 85 countries, including most Eastern bloc states (though not, curiously, the United States). All signatories must submit periodic reports on their observance of the Covenant's provision to a Human Rights Committee representing signatory nations. Among the provisions is article 12(2): "Everyone shall be free to leave any country, including his own." Unfortunately, as noted in chapter 4, article 12(3) allows the right to be abridged on the broad grounds of national security, public order, and public health or morals.

In the first period of filings, beginning in 1977, most of the states that restrict emigration submitted perfunctory, legalistic reports that simply listed laws and decrees governing emigration and the issuance of passports. Some added that any restrictions in force were consistent with the exceptions permitted in the Covenant. Requests for additional information and statistics were often simply ignored. The Soviet representative, however, did have the following to say in response to some pointed questions regarding Soviet respect for the right to leave (as paraphrased in the official summary): "The emphasis by some members on cases of persons who wished to leave the USSR was not justified. All those wishing to leave the Soviet Union had left, with a few exceptions which were justified for the protection of State security, public order, property and family rights. There were no restrictions in respect of persons intending to leave the USSR. In fact, many people wanted to enter the USSR but encountered obstacles in the countries in which they lived."[48]

More forthright was the response from Romania at the 1979 session: "Romania did not encourage emigration because it has invested very heavily in the training, education and well-being of its citizens and . . . as a developing country, it needed all its human potentials."[49]

Some other countries were also forced to explain their policies. Chile, when pressed, responded that its denial of the right to return to those who had fled after the 1974 coup was temporary and directed mainly against those who had committed terrorist acts. Cyprus, in reply to similar questions regarding the right of Turkish Cypriots to return to areas controlled by the Greek Cypriot government, argued that the Turkish invasion force had for its part evicted Greek Cypriots and thus brought about a de facto population exchange. When the Senegalese representative was asked about the large deposit required of those traveling abroad, he responded that

48. United Nations, General Assembly, *Official Records: Thirty-Third Session, Report of the Human Rights Committee* (GAOR/A/33/40) (New York, 1978) (these summaries of the committee's deliberations will be cited hereafter as UNHRC Report, followed by year and document number).

49. UNHRC Report, 1979 (GAOR/A/34/40).

"Although the Act would appear to have the effect of limiting freedom of movement, it is justified, in particular, by the fact that it protects Senegalese workers, who often live in inhuman conditions abroad, and serves the interest of economic development." (Actually, though, Senegal is not a serious offender on this issue.)[50]

But the format of the country reports under the Covenant often allows very vague or questionable responses to go unchallenged. For example, Poland in 1980 claimed that only 0.6 percent of all exit visa applications were denied. Mongolia laconically maintained that all citizens had "the full right to travel abroad." Also, increasingly, countries simply ignored questions on article 12. Such was the response of Iraq in 1980, when asked to explain its travel restrictions "in cases defined by law," and of such countries as Tanzania, Kenya, Barbados, Rwanda, and Iran in succeeding years.[51]

In 1984, the Soviet Union submitted its second report, noting this time that travel abroad was permitted "for diplomatic or professional reasons"—implying that other reasons were unacceptable. On the topic of emigration, the Soviets asserted that they complied fully with Helsinki commitments on family reunification; as for other cases, they maintained there were "no objective reasons for emigrating," as there existed no unemployment or nationality problems in the Soviet Union. The Byelorussian delegate made the same claim: socialist transformations had removed all the social and economic reasons for emigrating. When asked about the declining numbers

50. On Chile and Turkey, see ibid. On Senegal, see United Nations, International Covenant on Civil and Political Rights, Human Rights Committee, Eighth Session, *Consideration of Reports Submitted by States Parties under Article 40 of the Covenant, Initial Reports of States Parties Due in 1979, Addendum 2, Senegal* (CCPR/C/6/Add.2, August 8, 1979) (New York, 1979). Revenue taxes on foreign travel, such as those imposed by the Philippines and Israel, are not considered an infringement of the right to leave if they do not seriously limit the number leaving. Hannum, however, questions the legitimacy of revenue taxes on the exercise of a basic right (p. 94).

51. UNHRC Reports, 1980, 1981, and 1983 (GAOR/A/35/40, GAOR/A/36/40, and GAOR/A/37/40).

of Jewish and other emigrants, both the Soviet and Byelorussian delegates claimed that this simply reflected a declining number of applicants.[52]

Some nations—barely more than a dozen—have also ratified the Optional Protocol to the Covenant, which empowers their citizens to submit individual complaints to the Human Rights Committee. These countries, however, are not generally the ones that have denied the right to leave. The only serious grievances submitted under the protocol came from Uruguayan citizens residing abroad, after the military regime in Montevideo refused to renew their passports. Several Uruguayans in exile appealed to the Human Rights Committee, which decided in their favor. The Committee ruled that, by denying a passport, Uruguay had violated the right to leave.[53] Only after a change of government, however, did Uruguayan policies in this matter change.

Concern over the broad exceptions contained in article 12(3) set in motion an effort to define those limits more precisely. In early 1984 the International Commission of Jurists, together with several other legal bodies, convened a conference of thirty-one distinguished experts on international law at Siracusa, Sicily, to consider the Covenant's limitation clauses. The experts came from a number of Western countries, as well as from Egypt, India, Hungary, Poland, the United Nations Center for Human Rights, and the International Labour Organization.

In line with recognized legal principles, the experts agreed that exceptions should not be interpreted so as to jeopardize the essence

52. United Nations, International Covenant on Civil and Political Rights, Human Rights Committee, Twenty-Third Session, *Summary Record of the 566th, 567th, 569th, and 571st Meetings* (CCPR/C/SR.566, 567, 569, 571) (Geneva, 1984). For a fuller analysis of the periodic reports under the Covenant, see Hannum, pp. 53–54, 215–18.

53. UNHRC, Communications 77/1980, 06/1981, 108/1981, R.13/57; *Report of the Human Rights Committee*, 1982 and 1983 (A/37/40, A/38/40). There is also a procedure for individual grievances in UNESCO, which has occasionally been relevant; see Hannum, p. 55.

of the rights in question; that the limits should be stipulated by law, with clear, widely disseminated rules; and that provision should be made for appeals and remedies. According to the jurists, "national security" should be invoked only to protect the survival of the nation, its territorial integrity, or its political independence against the threat of force, which should not be confused with the survival of the particular government that happens to be in power. It should never be used to justify systematic violation of human rights. The experts also urged a narrow reading of the "public order (*ordre public*)" clause, arguing that it should refer only to protecting basic social functions and not to the broader sense of "public policy" that the French phrase usually connotes. On the whole, the "Siracusa principles" would invalidate many, if not most, of the restrictions currently placed on foreign travel.[54]

Meanwhile, after a decade of silence, interest in the right to leave sputtered back to life in the U.N. Commission on Human Rights and its Sub-Commission on Prevention of Discrimination and Protection of Minorities. The commission had "noted" the 1963 Inglés report on the right to leave and return only in 1973, and little had transpired since then. The American Jewish Committee had tried to revive the issue in 1974 but was frustrated by the growing concern over brain drain, then near its peak, which prompted Third-World representatives to defer any additional discussion of the issue. In the following years, Soviet representatives led an effort to deny B'nai B'rith, another Jewish group, its consultative status before the commission; B'nai B'rith leaders felt that this was partly in retribution for the group's role in pressing the right-to-leave issue. (B'nai B'rith had been very active in providing material for the Inglés report and in publicizing Soviet denial of the right of

---

54. *The Siracusa Principles on the Limitation and Derogation Provisions in the International Covenant on Civil and Political Rights* (International Commission of Jurists, 1984). On the limited scope of these permissible exceptions see also Hannum, pp. 24–51, especially pp. 28–30, on national security.

Soviet Jews to emigrate.)[55] The Soviet campaign failed in a very narrow vote before the commission.

At the subcommission's 1981 session, Western representatives introduced a resolution asking the U.N. Secretary General to report on the follow-up to the Inglés study. In the words of the U.S. expert, the goal was to get "the thin edge of the wedge" into an issue that had been made more topical by the mass exodus of Soviet Jews.[56] The response of the Soviet expert, Vsevolod N. Sofinsky, was predictable. He contended that although he had no problems with the content of the resolution, there had been no previous discussion of it and besides, the lapse of time (since 1973) had been too great for the resolution to be considered an "ongoing" matter. Consequently, he would have to oppose it. Sofinsky's position attracted little support, however, and the resolution passed 16 to 1 with 3 abstentions.[57]

The Secretary General's report, dated August 6, 1982, put in print what everyone already knew—that there had been no follow-up since 1973, even though the commission had been instructed to review the status of the right to leave every three years.[58] This laid the foundation for a new resolution calling for yet another study. To this Sofinsky objected that such a study would only add to an already overburdened calendar and that he would therefore have to oppose it.

55. Personal interview with William Korey, Director of International Policy Research, B'nai B'rith, April 11, 1984.

56. Personal interview with John Carey, member of the Subcommission on Prevention of Discrimination and Protection of Minorities, April 11, 1984.

57. United Nations, Economic and Social Council, Commission on Human Rights, Subcommission on Prevention of Discrimination and Protection of Minorities, Thirty-Fourth Session, *Summary Record of the 929th Meeting* (E/CN.4/Sub.2/SR.929, September 9, 1981) (New York, 1981) (Subcommission proceedings will hereafter be cited as Subcommission, followed by session, meeting, date, and document number).

58. Subcommission, Thirty-Fifth Session, *Note by the Secretariat,* August 6, 1982 (E/CN.4/Sub.2/1982/27). The practice of three-year periodic reviews of human rights by the Commission was dropped when the Human Rights Committee, set up under the International Covenant on Civil and Political Rights, came into operation.

Supporters of a new study proposed as rapporteur C. L. C. Mubanga-Chipoya of Zambia—a move that helped win support from Third-World members. These members also pushed an amendment calling for consideration of the brain drain and of problems of entry to and employment in other countries. In this expanded form, the resolution was adopted by an 11 to 2 vote with 6 abstentions.[59]

The whole discussion had to be repeated the following year (1983), however, as the commission claimed the resolution was not in the proper format (a claim that John Carey, the U.S. expert on the subcommission, said "mystified" him[60]). The indefatigable Sofinsky argued that the subcommission was unjustified in repeating its action, or even in discussing the matter further; once again, however, the resolution was passed, this time by 18 to 2.[61]

In its final form, the resolution

> Requests Mr. Mubanga-Chipoya to prepare an analysis of current trends and developments in respect of the right of everyone to leave any country, including his own, and to return to his country, and the possibility of entering other countries, without discrimination, or hindrance, especially of the right to employment, taking into account the need to avoid the phenomenon of the brain drain from developing countries and the question of recompensing these countries for the loss incurred, and to study the extent of admissible restrictions in accordance with Art. 12, para. 3 of the Covenant on Civil and Political Rights.

The resolution had originally called on the rapporteur to present his findings to the subcommission in 1984, but with the delays this was changed to 1986 (for the report on the right to leave itself) and 1987 (other aspects of the study). As the General Assembly cancelled

59. Subcommission, Thirty-Fifth Session, 35th Meeting, September 8, 1982 (E/CN.4/Sub.2/1982/SR.35).

60. Personal interview with Carey.

61. Subcommission, Thirty-Sixth Session, 24th Meeting, August 31, 1983 (E/CN.4/Sub.2/1983/SR.24).

the 1986 subcommission meeting, even this schedule was set back one year further, with the initial report due only in 1987. This despite the fact that the Commission on Human Rights had in 1985 instructed the subcommission to take up the issue "as a matter of priority" and to submit as soon as possible a draft declaration on the right to leave and to return.[62]

However, by mid-1986 only 45 states, 3 U.N. specialized agencies, and seven nongovernmental organizations, had bothered to respond to the rapporteur's questionnaire distributed almost two years earlier. Furthermore, the answers that were submitted reflected the vagueness of the rapporteur's mandate. For example, the inclusion of concerns related to the brain drain presented an opportunity for rationalizing otherwise questionable limits on emigration. The rapporteur's 1985 progress report noted the common assertion "that a community has some legal claim on the skills and talents developed by members in that community"[63]—this, despite the growing body of evidence (outlined in chapter 5) that free movement does not necessarily conflict with a nation's economic well-being.

Like the Inglés study, the new report on the right to leave received meager attention, due to either the determined efforts of opponents or the relative passivity of presumed supporters. As hard as it is to imagine, the whole exercise seemed to be making even less impact than the earlier study had.

62. United Nations, Economic and Social Council, Commission on Human Rights, Forty-First Session, *Draft Report of the Commission* (E/CN.4/1985/L.11/Add.2, March 12, 1985), pp. 13–14.

63. Subcommission, Thirty-Eighth Session, Progress report prepared by Mr. Mubanga-Chipoya (E/CN.4/Sub.2/1985/9, July 10, 1985), p. 8.

7

Toward an Open World

> {*The aim of my foreign policy has been}* to go down to
> Victoria Station, get a railway ticket and go where the
> hell I liked without a passport or anything else.
>
> —*Ernest Bevin, British Foreign Secretary, 1946*

Emigration: An Index of Societal Health

If my analysis of the causes and motivations of contemporary emigration controls is correct, what are the appropriate responses? How
can the new serfdom most effectively be combated?

The issue of forced or denied emigration continues to suffer
from strikingly low visibility. A leading official of the Intergovernmental Committee on Migration, echoing a common view among
those active in the field, complains of "an appalling lack of serious-
ness" toward freedom of movement issues.[1] Of the human rights
that are most frequently violated, the right of personal self-determination seems to attract the least attention. Indeed, it might be
called the forgotten right.

This passivity has several sources. Many simply believe that
the prospects for change are dim. Others are deterred by the apparent
(though unsubstantiated) conflict between free movement and de-

1. Personal interview, Geneva, July 18, 1985.

velopment needs. In addition, those most directly affected are in the worst position to complain. Moreover, the issue is a highly sensitive one, evoking unusually hostile responses from vulnerable governments. Inglés has noted that his study, representing the United Nations' most concentrated effort on the right to leave, was "handled like a hot potato."[2]

Perhaps most important, *all* states find the implications of free movement somewhat disturbing. If some nations do not want to lose people, others do not want to gain them. Even those countries that have "gained brains" do not, contrary to the common accusation, go out of their way to rob poorer nations of their talent; the United States, as has been pointed out, even requires foreign students to leave the U.S. for an interval before requesting more permanent status. In an age of jealous sovereignty, a small, manageable flow suits both sides, allaying concerns over national identity and fears of alien intrusions.

Such attitudes, however, underestimate the forces that hold people in place and overestimate the flows likely to result in a world of open doors. Most people have no inclination to leave their native soil, no matter how onerous conditions become. Would-be emigrants must fight off the ties of family, the comfort of familiar surroundings, the rootedness in one's culture, the security of being among "one's own," and the power of plain inertia. Conversely, being uprooted carries daunting prospects: adjusting to alien ways, learning a new language, the absence of kith and kin, the sheer uncertainty of it all. For most people, deciding to leave requires a highly compelling set of circumstances, an unusually strong combination of push and pull. As we have seen, most of the mass migrations of modern history were not voluntary in the true sense of the word. Many migrants were forced or induced to leave; others fled desperate circumstances. To take the greatest "voluntary" movement of all, the Great Atlantic Migration included Irish fleeing starvation, Germans and Eastern

2. Personal correspondence with Inglés, February 16, 1985.

Europeans escaping brutal oppression, Italians pushed by abject poverty, and Russian Jews terrorized by pogroms.[3] Only rarely has a significant proportion of a country's population left without being expelled, and then only under extraordinary circumstances. Ireland is perhaps the most notable case. Outstanding recent examples include Cuba and East Germany, and, even in those cases, intense domestic pressures were not sufficient to force a mass exodus; it also took the proximity of a convenient alternative offering substantial hope of economic betterment. How many East Germans would have left had there been decent economic prospects at home and no German state next door?

Even at the height of the Atlantic migration, when millions headed for America to escape poverty and oppression, an estimated one-third of all immigrants eventually left, most to return to their countries of origin. The pull of home was simply too great. Among immigrants to South America, the percentages were even higher (53 percent for Argentina).[4] And, before the United States began limiting legal entrance from Mexico in 1968, making frequent crossings

3. The classic statement of the tremendous forces required to detach people from their native lands is in Oscar Handlin, *The Uprooted* (2d enl. ed., Boston: Little, Brown, 1973). Handlin reminds us that the essence of migration is alienation, that whoever left his village "began a long journey that his mind would forever mark as its most momentous experience," and that the move came only after tenacious effort to hang on to familiar ways and surroundings (esp. pp. 4, 26, 29–30, 35).

4. Frank Thistlethwaite, "Migration from Europe Overseas in the Nineteenth and Twentieth Centuries," *Rapports*, vol. 5 (Uppsala: International Committee of Historical Sciences, 1960), pp. 38, 39; W. F. Willcox, *International Migration*, vol. 2 (New York: National Bureau of Economic Research, 1931), p. 98, table 17. The U.S. estimate is based on figures from 1907 (the first year such statistics were kept) and afterward, projected backward. Simon Kuznets and Ernest Rubin, *Immigration and the Foreign Born* (New York: National Bureau of Economic Research, Occasional Paper no. 46, 1954), estimate that in the period from 1890 to 1910 about 40 percent of foreign-born U.S. residents returned to their countries of origin.

risky, an estimated eight of every nine Mexicans who came to work in the United States returned home.[5]

Fears of being inundated have no doubt been fed by perceptions of a globe that is rapidly shrinking. Transportation is easier and cheaper; information on global opportunities flows more quickly; traditional populations have been stirred by rising expectations. But even these factors have a double-edged significance. Improved transportation facilitates returns, and better communications convey a clearer picture not only of opportunities but of difficulties as well. Modernization creates expectations of a better life at home and abroad.

In short, respect for the right to leave hardly seems to threaten the havoc that both countries of origin and countries of destination seem to fear. Leaving aside labor migrations, which are usually temporary and (in theory) controllable, the pool of potential immigrants remains relatively limited.

For this smaller group, however, the right to leave can be vital. It is important in other ways as well. The right of personal self-determination is readily defensible, easily understood, and morally powerful. The reluctance of offending states to attack it in principle is proof of its strength. It is also a particularly comfortable issue for Western states in international human rights debates, since on few issues is the difference in performance as clear-cut and visible.

Furthermore, asserting the importance of the right should be less open to the common charge of interference in a country's internal affairs; by definition, questions of international movement involve more than one country. States have a legitimate interest in the forces that influence the flow of migrants into their territory, and cases of family reunification are a good example. Nations further have a stake

5. Robert Revelle, "Migration: A Positive Effect on Resources," in Select Commission on Immigration and Refugee Policy, *Staff Report, U.S. Immigration Policy and the National Interest* (Washington: U.S. Government Printing Office, 1981), pp. 193–94.

in preventing the use of expulsions and denied emigration as tools of foreign policy.

The conclusion is that constraint of free movement does not appear to serve any legitimate social or national interest. Stated another way, respect for free movement does not seem to threaten any legitimate collective interest. What the new serfdom does serve is the pursuit by governments of total control and perfect homogeneity. States that manipulate population flows should therefore be challenged to demonstrate that their systems can work without resorting to exit controls. Are sealed borders an inherent feature of Soviet-style governments, or was Khrushchev correct in concluding that free movement is compatible with Marxism-Leninism?

The extent of a country's respect for personal self-determination says something very basic about how it is governed. It is an index of a state's responsiveness to its citizens and, by extension, a measure of overall social health. If a political system is meeting essential needs, the pressure to leave will not pose a threat to those in power. On the other hand, steady emigration would spur a state to listen to its citizens and undertake the measures needed to diminish the flow.

This dynamic certainly operated at the height of the mercantilist period. In 1709, Prince Wilhelm of Nassau-Dillenberg, disturbed at the emigration fever sweeping his domain, dismissed corrupt officials, relaxed taxes, and increased aid to the poor.[6] Baron Turgot, the French statesman and economist, wrote in the late eighteenth century with regard to emigration to America that "the ease with which it will now be possible to take advantage of this situation, and thus to escape from the consequences of a bad government, will oblige the European Governments to be just and enlightened."[7]

6. John Duncan Brite, "The Attitude of European States toward Emigration to the American Colonies and the United States, 1607–1820" (Ph.D. diss., University of Chicago, 1937), p. 221.

7. Baron Anne-Robert-Jacques Turgot, *Oeuvres,* vol. 9 (Paris: Delance, 1810), p. 369, quoted by Albert O. Hirschman, "Exit, Voice, and the State," *World Politics* 31 (Winter 1978): 98.

In the modern era, too, reformers have recognized the contribution that open exit can make to social change. Roy Medvedev, the dissident Soviet historian who advocates democratization within a Marxist framework, writes:

> The right to choose one's place of residence within one's own country or abroad is now a generally accepted democratic liberty in most civilized countries of the world. Its introduction here would undoubtedly be a positive step and would have a healthy effect on the general political atmosphere within the country, not because certain "awkward" citizens would leave as a result, but because fear of a "brain drain" would force state and party bodies to take much more seriously all the democratic rights and freedoms that are formally proclaimed as belonging to all Soviet citizens.[8]

A former Soviet writer has characterized this positive impact of free exit in more vivid and personal terms:

> Now the writer in Russia, driven to extremes, doesn't soap the noose in grief; he feverishly tries to remember if he has among his kin even distant European relatives! And for this reason—oh, how difficult it has become for the Party administration to work with the writers! The administration, in true Soviet fashion, according to the principle of push comes to shove, just wants to put a bullet between the recalcitrant's eyes, but there's an order from above: "Don't, they'll scatter!"[9]

Other positive benefits of an open-exit policy have been touched upon: relief of pressures within the society, strengthening of inter-

8. Roy A. Medvedev, *On Socialist Democracy* (New York: Knopf, 1975), p. 216.

9. Anatoly Gladilin, *The Making and Unmaking of a Soviet Writer: My Story of the "Young Prose" of the Sixties and After,* trans. David Lapeza (Ann Arbor: Ardis, 1979), p. 512, quoted in Victor Zaslavsky and Robert J. Brym, *Soviet-Jewish Emigration and Soviet Nationality Policy* (New York: St. Martin's, 1983), pp. 142–43.

national ties and communication in an interdependent world, freeing of individual energies from conflicts with authority, and promotion of an atmosphere of individual dignity and mutual cooperation rather than passive acceptance of the unavoidable. All of this is clearly in the interest of the individual, but that does not mean that it is inimical to the interests of society as a whole.

Throughout, this study has extolled the value of personal self-determination as an individual right, as a guarantee of individual freedom from the dictates of the authorities. Generally, the right has been posed as a matter of conflict between individual and state. Often enough, it is precisely that. But need it be? A state that earns the loyalty and respect of its citizens through choice is, in the long run, far stronger than a state that relies on forced participation.

Some countries facing strong emigration pressure have demonstrated that there are alternatives to shackling the entire population. The cases of Ireland and East Germany offer an instructive contrast. As noted in chapter 2, no country in modern history has been more threatened with depopulation than Ireland. On the eve of the Great Famine, in 1841, the territory of the future Irish Republic had 6,529,000 inhabitants; by 1951, the number had dropped to 2,960,593. Massive outflows caused major drops of population throughout the second half of the nineteenth century and again following World War II. A book titled *The Vanishing Irish,* published in 1953, declared that "today Ireland is teetering perilously on the brink of near extinction."[10] Nineteenth-century emigration had apparently been beneficial, on the whole, to the country's economy; even so, the demographic threat faced by Ireland in the early 1950s was at least as drastic as that faced by East Germany in 1961.

But the Irish responded differently. In 1958, the government

10. *The Vanishing Irish,* ed. John A. O'Brien (New York: McGraw-Hill, 1953), p. 1.

adopted a national economic plan designed to stem emigration by improving opportunities within the country. Industrialization was promoted and incentives offered to attract foreign capital. By 1983, the standard of living had improved considerably; Ireland was now a member in good standing of the European Economic Community boasting per capita income of more than $5000 a year. Consequently, emigration dropped and population increased by about 20 percent, to 3,575,000.

The East Germans responded, as we have seen, in a totally different fashion.[11] Was the Irish response less effective, or are the Irish any worse off for not having adopted police-state methods? Perhaps the East Germans did not have the "Irish option": that is, they could not have used voluntaristic measures without changing the essential nature of their system—without compromising, say, their commitment to egalitarianism. But it remains an open question as to how much the Marxist-Leninist system is dependent on locking the gates. We have seen that other Marxist states have managed to survive with a more liberal approach. The East Germans did face a perhaps unique threat, but that does not establish that their response was the only viable one. When all is said and done, the approach they chose remains a telling comment on their system.

Those who have locked themselves into the logic of coercion seem, in the end, to be trapped by it. People respond to coercion by resisting it, which in turn only necessitates more coercion. Consider this recollection by a close observer of East Germany: "A young East German doctor told me: 'Now that the Wall has been built, I would walk across the border barefoot to get out of here.' Did that mean, I asked, that he would move to the West if the Wall came down? 'Of course not,' he replied, 'Then I would stay here.'"[12]

11. The East Germany–Ireland comparison is suggested and carried out by Hirschman, pp. 103–05. On the East German response see chapter 4.

12. John Dornberg, *The Other Germany* (Garden City, N.Y.: Doubleday, 1968), p. 96.

Free Emigration and U.S. Foreign Policy

It seems time, then, to challenge the international indifference commonly shown the right of personal movement. I believe that the United States should take the lead in focusing world attention on the issue. Guaranteeing the right to leave or to remain should become both a major objective and a major weapon of U.S. foreign policy.

Free emigration cuts to the heart of American concerns in the world. Throughout its history, the United States has defended the rights of the individual against the claims of the state. Few issues frame this concern so well as the right of free movement. More specifically, Americans have traditionally perceived their country as a haven for people subject to persecution in other lands. Mobility is built into the very essence of our nation. Moreover, a freer flow of people, goods, and ideas would increase pressure for changes within closed societies.

Many Americans have reacted with dismay to the steady debasement of international debate. The collectivist ethic, in its various guises, has been vigorously pushed in world forums. The United States needs clear, sharp issues that can help it reassert the importance of individual liberties. Few matters are as suited to this purpose as the right of personal self-determination.

In pressing this right, the United States should take emigration practices into account when assessing its relations with other countries. Concessions in such areas as trade and technology can be linked to liberalization of exit policies. And, through aid suspensions, economic sanctions, direct diplomatic pressure, and public exposure, we can burden countries that create refugees. Moreover, since most nations do not want to be faced with a sudden influx, it should be possible to organize a common front and ostracize offenders.

Above all, the United States should seek to use the court of world opinion. Morris Abram, the American expert on the U.N. panel that supervised the Inglés report, urges "constant use" of the issue as "a compelling moral indictment."[13] Indeed, our reticence to

13. Personal interview with Abram, May 4, 1984.

use the issue more often in international forums must be overcome. To take one possible approach, the United States has announced that U.N. voting records will be considered in the allocation of foreign aid; special attention could be paid to how a nation votes on freedom-of-movement issues.

Similarly, U.S. and international aid programs should evaluate the possible impact assistance could have on ethnic conflicts, economic dislocation, and other factors that commonly produce refugees. This would have far-reaching implications for U.S. foreign policy, since reducing sources of instability might at times conflict with broader geopolitical goals. Thus, aid to a hostile country like Ethiopia might seem better spent than aid to a friendly one like Haiti.

In addition, development aid must address legitimate complaints regarding the brain drain. It has been claimed that export-led growth produces greater pressures for migration, and that strategies based on internal market expansion would therefore reduce pressures for temporary labor migration.[14] More will be said in the next section about policies designed to discourage the creation of refugees.

The single most effective step the United States has ever taken against the new serfdom was the Jackson-Vanik amendment to the Trade Reform Act of 1974. This measure, perhaps the first American law directly based on the Universal Declaration of Human Rights, has been criticized (by Henry Kissinger, among others) on grounds that states will not alter their emigration policy in response to such direct and public pressure, and that quiet diplomacy is a far more effective approach. But the evidence is that Jackson-Vanik works, and works well.

In its key provisions, the Jackson-Vanik amendment withholds trade privileges (most-favored-nation trade status, credits, investment

14. Alejandro Portes, "International Labor Migration and National Development," in Mary M. Kritz, ed., *U.S. Immigration and Refugee Policy: Global and Domestic Issues* (Lexington, Mass.: Lexington, 1983), pp. 87–88.

guarantees) from those nations that block free emigration. The immediate reason for the amendment's passage was the Soviet Union's imposition of a diploma tax just as emigration from that country was opening up for the first time. But the legislation was founded on a revolutionary principle: that the concession most worth extracting from the Soviet Union was a loosening of emigration. The sponsors apparently believed that this, more than anything else, would serve as a concrete index of Soviet readiness to join the family of nations, and further, would have profound repercussions for the Soviet system.

As indicated by the diploma tax, the increased harassment of would-be emigrants, and a slowdown in the processing of applications, the Soviet Union was trying to reduce emigration during 1973 and 1974. But, while the Jackson-Vanik amendment was still being considered, Soviet officials signaled their willingness to come to terms with it, reaching informal agreement with the administration and Congress on the specific barriers that would be removed and the number of visas that would be issued if the measure were enacted. However, just before final passage, the Senate added an amendment, proposed by Senator Adlai Stevenson, that severely limited the level of credit available. This, by all accounts, made it a bad bargain for the Soviets, and a few days later they angrily renounced the whole arrangement.[15]

Had the credits been made available, it is probable that the Soviets would have gone along. In any event, anger over Jackson-Vanik did not prevent Moscow from increasing emigration between 1975 and 1979, apparently in pursuit of foreign policy aims, including most-favored-nation status (now that the United States had specifically linked that issue to emigration). The subsequent crackdown on emigration after 1979 was tied not to Jackson-Vanik but to the overall collapse of détente and to domestic Soviet factors (as

15. See the compelling case made by William Korey, "Jackson-Vanik and Soviet Jewry," *Washington Quarterly* 7 (Winter 1984): 116–28.

described in chapter 6). In sum, while Jackson-Vanik has not yet impelled the Soviets to modify their emigration practices permanently, it came close on one occasion and may have helped induce a substantial temporary improvement on another.

As a nation badly in need of hard currency to acquire coveted Western technology, the Soviet Union has a clear and overwhelming economic interest in gaining access to the rich American market. Soviet representatives make clear their continuing interest in obtaining most-favored-nation status, should generally improved relations make that feasible again. The White House might privately convey to the Soviets specific steps that would qualify them for this status. These steps might include:

1. The release and emigration of all those imprisoned for trying to emigrate.

2. The emigration of all those whose visa applications have been refused for longer than a given period (say three years).

3. Decisions within three months on all new applications.

4. Elimination of the requirement of parental consent for those over eighteen years of age, and recognition of the right of repatriation whether or not any immediate family is living in the country of destination.

5. An end to all punitive steps against, and harassment of, would-be emigrants.

This set of measures would not establish full Soviet respect for the right to leave or return, but it might constitute enough "substantial performance" to merit most-favored-nation status under Jackson-Vanik. It would also make Soviet emigration policy a legitimate bargaining issue in bilateral relations.

While the ultimate impact of Jackson-Vanik on the Soviet Union remains unclear, it has clearly been effective elsewhere. Three Communist countries have been granted these trade privileges in return for showing "substantial performance" on free exit. The importance of most-favored-nation status for Hungary, which has the most liberal emigration policies in the Soviet bloc, has been noted. In 1979, China expressly liberalized its emigration regulations to qualify for most-favored-nation status; availability of destinations is now the major obstacle to movement out of China.

With Romania, the amendment has had less impact than it might because the administration generally recommends most-favored-nation status as a reward for the country's independent foreign policy rather than its minimally liberal emigration policy. Nonetheless, Romania retreated in 1982–83 from an education tax under threat of losing its status, and, given the regime's general attitude toward emigration, it seems doubtful that *any* Romanians would get out were it not for Jackson-Vanik. All in all, if used under the right conditions, Jackson-Vanik can effectively serve to loosen emigration practices in other nations.

U.S. Refugee Policy

The American response to refugees has advanced considerably since the 1930s, when no refugees were admitted other than those permitted by rigid national-origin quotas. Still, progress has been fitful. In response to the dislocations of World War II, some 400,000 refugees were admitted under the Displaced Persons Act of 1948. However, the public was largely indifferent to the refugee issue, and passage of the law required a massive campaign by private humanitarian and charitable organizations. Even then, the measure might not have passed had it not been for the onset of the Cold War, which created sympathy for East European refugees. About 200,000 more refugees were admitted under the Refugee Relief Act of 1953. But there was still no established procedure for emergency situations, and Hungarians who fled the 1956 Soviet invasion were admitted under a broad interpretation of the "parole" authority granted the Attorney General by the 1952 Immigration and Nationality Act. Similar provisions were later made for refugees from Cuba and Indochina.

In 1965, in the most important legislative change since the 1920s, the whole system of national quotas was scrapped. The overhaul of the Immigration and Nationality Act of that year included a preference category for refugees from Communism and the Middle East (an indication of willingness to help resolve the Arab-Israel conflict), making up 6 percent of the total quota. Then, three years later, the United States accepted the obligations of the 1951 Refugee Convention by ratifying the 1967 Protocol.

Finally, in 1980, spurred by the flows from Indochina and Mariel, Congress ended fifteen years of debate by passing a Refugee Act that, for the first time, established a clear and consistent policy. In the first place, the American definition of a refugee was brought into accord with the international one, dropping (at least in law) the preferential treatment of refugees from Communism. Furthermore, refugee admissions were separated from normal quotas, making it possible to respond to sudden crises without disrupting routine immigration. Finally, the President was given more authority (in consultation with Congress) to set the number of admissions each year, a change intended to make it easier for the government to act quickly and without extraneous political pressures.

In practice, though, admissions were still highly selective. During the first two years under the new law, only 393 refugees from non-Communist nations were admitted.[16] Congress's role became largely pro forma, and with the State Department taking the lead, short-term foreign policy considerations usually prevailed. This meant a strong reluctance to admit that those fleeing non-Communist lands had a "well-founded fear of being persecuted," as the law put it. "It will not come as a surprise," writes Aristide Zolberg, "that in the eyes of foreign policy decision-makers refugees are almost never produced by allies and friends."[17] Thus, in 1984, only 3 percent of all applicants from El Salvador, and one percent from Gua-

---

16. Deborah Anker, "The Development of U.S. Refugee Legislation," in *Immigration and Refugee Policy (In Defense of the Alien)*, vol. 6, ed. Lydio Tomasi (New York: Center for Migration Studies, 1984), pp. 159–66.

17. Zolberg, "International Migration and Foreign Policy: When Does a Marginal Issue Become Substantive?" in Tomasi, p. 218.

temala, were granted asylum. Even Salvadorans with bullet wounds and torture marks have been forcibly returned on grounds that they were victims of a "generalized climate of violence" rather than individual persecution.

The double standard is most apparent in the treatment of fleeing Haitians. Frequently seized on the high seas, they are routinely deported to their homeland as "economic migrants." Yet Haiti's brutal poverty is inextricably linked to the country's political system. One of the leading students of Haiti, Mats Lundahl, concludes simply: "The main obstacle to economic development in Haiti has always been its government."[18] In the last years of the Duvalier regime, per capita income was only about $140 a year (the lowest in the western hemisphere), while 3000 families in Port-au-Prince enjoyed incomes above $100,000. An estimated 83 percent of government funds (largely unaccounted for) was spent in the capital, though 90 percent of the population lives outside it. A system of political repression, government monopolies, and unequal education helped perpetuate the prevailing order, and it remains unclear that Duvalier's fall will bring any quick changes. In such circumstances, the distinction between "economic" and "political" refugees becomes meaningless. As Chuck Lane, a critic of U.S. refugee policy, pointedly asks: "Would you rather be, say, a Polish doctor or a Haitian cane-cutter? Whose desperation is greater? To ask the question is to answer it."[19]

Unfortunately, the response of the U.S. government to such criticism has not been a more generous attitude toward Haitians, but a crackdown on Poles and others who, in the past, could have at least counted on sympathy for refugees from Communism. From

18. Mats Lundahl, *Peasants and Poverty: A Study of Haiti* (London: Croom Helm, 1979), p. 645; see also Aaron Segal, "Haiti," in *Population Policies in the Caribbean,* ed. Segal (Lexington, Mass.: Lexington, 1975), pp. 197–205, and *Current Economic Position and Prospects of Haiti* (Washington: World Bank, December 22, 1978).

19. Chuck Lane, "Open the Door," *The New Republic* 192 (April 1, 1985): 21.

1981 to 1984, the Immigration and Naturalization Service (INS) rejected 77 percent of Polish applications for asylum, including some 7000 Solidarity activists who might well fear persecution if forcibly repatriated. Refugees from Nicaragua, a nation the U.S. regularly condemns as a Marxist tyranny, now fare only marginally better than asylum seekers from the rest of Central America; only about 17 percent of Nicaraguan applicants were admitted in 1984. And, as relations with China improved, acceptance of Chinese refugees declined to 7.2 percent.

U.S. attitudes toward Cuban refugees have changed, too. In the event of another massive outflow from Cuba, current INS planning calls for the interception of all "illegal aliens" at sea and their safe return to Cuba or a receptive third country: "Current Presidential policy presumes that no general resettlement program will be undertaken for excludable aliens, but would accommodate a small number of aliens qualifying under humanitarian release criteria."[20] The post-1980 policy thus achieves greater consistency only by cutting back on the one instance of generosity that had previously existed in U.S. policy.

The government's new approach has some commendable aspects. It has made the United States one of the few nations to distinguish refugees from regular immigrants, to give them priority outside normal admission quotas, and to admit them in significant numbers at all. But a strong case can be made on humanitarian grounds for reducing the role of short-term political considerations and, more specifically, for reassessing the current narrow application of refugee criteria. It is sobering to think that many who benefited in the past from American hospitality—for example, Irishmen and Jews in the nineteenth century—would not qualify for admission today.

This is not an argument for totally depoliticizing refugee policy;

20. *Mass Immigration Emergency Plan for Southern Florida,* INS *Operational Role* (U.S. Department of Justice: Immigration and Naturalization Service, January 1983).

some political aims are necessary and defensible. But broader political goals should take precedence over the short-term considerations that prevail today. In addition, given the backlog of about 150,000 applications for asylum, admissions procedure should be speeded up.

A comprehensive refugee policy would consider, and try to influence, the *sources* of refugee flows. The importance of this task is tacitly admitted when administration officials use the specter of large refugee movements to argue for increased aid to El Salvador. Taking refugee creation into account is a good idea; unfortunately, as this and other examples illustrate, it is now too often used to embarrass foes and avoid embarrassing friends.

U.S. foreign policy should approach the refugee problem with much broader American interests in mind. For instance, it should seek to use its influence to avert crises rather than simply respond to them. Since we so often have to deal with the aftermath, it would seem logical to make prevention a central goal of our efforts. The INS has an operational plan for reacting to another Mariel-type influx, but is avoidance of such a crisis a component in U.S. policy toward Cuba? If it isn't, it should be.

It might not even be so far-fetched to require refugee impact statements, along the lines of existing environmental ones, to accompany major new initiatives in trade, aid, and other areas of foreign policy when potential refugee problems exist. Such impact can be positive as well as negative; aid, in particular, could be an effective means of defusing explosive situations. The concerted action of donor states did induce Uganda, in 1982–83, to halt the expulsion of the Banyarwanda. One positive feature of the Reagan administration's Caribbean Basin plan was its call for "accelerated economic development to reduce motivations for illegal immigration."

As for providing refuge, only a broadly humanitarian policy is consonant with American traditions and ideals. Refuge should be offered to those fleeing intolerable conditions, even if they have not suffered persecution in the narrow sense of the word. Vincent Palmieri, former U.S. Coordinator for Refugee Affairs, has suggested

238

that the traditional categories of refugees and immigrants be supplemented by a third—immigrants "of special humanitarian concern."[21] Others have suggested that a status of temporary "safe haven" be created for Salvadoran refugees and others caught in similar situations. Short of making changes in existing legislation, devising new guidelines for implementation could greatly help.

Such improvements would probably gain widespread public support. Recent surveys indicate that the vast majority of Americans support admitting genuine refugee cases. According to one survey, 79 percent favored admitting Soviet Jews, and 66 percent would welcome Salvadorans fleeing generalized violence.[22] Thomas Jefferson's plea of 1801 still strikes a chord: "Shall we refuse . . . hospitality . . . to the unhappy fugitives from distress? . . . Shall oppressed humanity find no asylum on this globe?"

Immigration Policy

The right to leave a country voluntarily is an empty one if there is nowhere to go. Accordingly, those who would promote this right cannot avoid discussing immigration policies. The world has, unfortunately, come a long way from mercantilist days, when nations competed for immigrants. Throughout the twentieth century, tight restrictions have been placed on entry. Population pressures, intensified nationalism, and increased ease of movement have all contributed to fears of uncontrolled immigration. The industrialized nations of the world have adopted policies to defend themselves against influxes from the struggling reaches of the Third World. The Federation of American Immigration Reform, which favors reduced immigration, estimates that just to keep pace with population, the nations of Latin America must create more new jobs each year than the United States has ever succeeded in doing in a single year. Similarly, the International Labour Organization projects that the

21. Palmieri, Foreword to Kritz, p. xx.
22. *World Refugee Survey 1984* (New York and Washington: U.S. Committee for Refugees, 1984), p. 31.

work force of Third-World countries will grow by 600 to 700 million between 1980 and 2000, more than the current total of jobs in all industrialized countries combined.[23]

Given the fears of being drowned in the migratory tide, the 1965 modification of the U.S. Immigration and Nationality Act appears as something of a minor miracle. The refugee provisions were discussed above; in addition, the 1965 law created an American immigration policy that has been described as "the most humanitarian and the most sensible immigration policy in our nation's history."[24] The amendments abolished national-origins quotas, giving preference to family reunification and needed skills. In order to avoid the appearance of racial or geographic preference, no more than 20,000 people were to come from any one country. Refugees and immediate family were to fall outside the ceiling (which has been 270,000 since 1980).

Nonetheless, some Americans fear we are simply losing control. For one thing, in recent years the United States has admitted twice as many immigrants as the rest of the world combined. And illegal immigrants now total 4 to 6 million, according to most estimates, though a recent study by a panel of the National Academy of Sciences puts the number at 2 to 4 million.[25]

One result is widespread concern about population growth. The current net immigration (including illegals) of one million a year, together with today's fertility levels, would translate into a national population of more than 400 million by the year 2080.[26] However, if immigration were limited to legal entrants, the population total would level off at a much lower point. The U.S. Select Commission

23. Interview with Roger Conner, Executive Director, Federation for American Immigration Reform, May 17, 1984; James Fallows, "Immigration: How It's Affecting Us," *Atlantic Monthly* 252 (November 1983): 45.

24. Elliot Abrams and Franklin S. Abrams, "Immigration Policy—Who Gets In and Why?," *The Public Interest* 38, no. 3 (1975): 325.

25. *New York Times,* June 25, 1985.

26. Leon F. Bouvier, *The Impact of Immigration on U.S. Population Size* (Washington: Population Reference Bureau, 1981), pp. 2, 4.

on Immigration and Refugee Policy estimated in 1981 that, even with a modest increase in legal immigration, zero population growth could be achieved by 2050. More important, analysts point out that small fluctuations in the fertility rate have far more impact on population growth than immigration and thus should be the primary focus of any debate over population.[27]

More serious objections have been raised on economic grounds. Most visible is the taking of jobs by newcomers. The grievance is hardly new. In 1714 John Toland declared that "The vulgar, I confess, are seldom pleas'd in a country with the coming of Foreners. . . . from their grudging at more persons sharing the same trades or business with them." But Toland also understood that immigrants don't just take jobs: "We deny not that there will thus be more taylors and shoomakers, but there will also be more suits and shoes made than before."[28]

The chief question, of course, is the balance between jobs taken and jobs created. One Canadian study, for instance, found that 5 percent of all adult immigrants started businesses within three years, which in themselves provided more than enough new jobs to compensate for the displacement of native Canadians.[29] This is hardly the last word on the matter, but it does caution against making sweeping judgments. On the whole, it seems that immigrants do well economically. As noted in chapter 5, migrants tend to be more resourceful than average, more highly motivated, more willing to run risks. Studies show that after a few years, immigrants generally

27. Ansley J. Coale, "Alternative Paths to a Stationary Population," in *Demographic and Social Aspects of Population Growth,* ed. Charles F. Westoff and Robert Parke, Jr., Commission on Population Growth and the American Future (Washington: U.S. Government Printing Office, 1972), pp. 569–603, cited by Michael S. Teitelbaum, "Right versus Right: Immigration and Refugee Policy in the United States," *Foreign Affairs* 59 (Fall 1980): 42; Select Commission on Immigration and Refugee Policy, pp. 100–03.

28. Quoted by Julian Simon, "Don't Fear Job Loss," *New York Times,* August 2, 1984.

29. Ibid.

earn more money than native-born Americans of the same ethnic and educational background. Mexican immigrants surpass the income level of native Hispanics in about 15 years, and black immigrants take about 11 years to overtake native-born blacks. Second-generation West Indian blacks eventually earn more than native-born whites. None of this is disputed by those who favor tighter restriction. In fact, they argue that this is precisely the problem, that the success of immigrants blocks the upward mobility of unskilled Americans.[30]

While there are surprisingly few dependable studies of the economic impact of immigrants, one of them—a 1982 survey by the Rand Corporation—concluded that, at current levels of immigration, "most analysts agree that immigrants will have little effect on the overall national economy." In 1964, the Urban Institute found that immigrants in southern California, rather than causing increased unemployment among other minorities, provided industries with more manpower, thus enabling them to produce higher profits and lower prices. During the 1970s, when southern California took in more immigrants than any other part of the country, it also led the nation in the creation of new jobs and enjoyed an above-average increase in per capita income. Summarizing several recent studies of illegal immigration, *Business Week* concluded that "on balance, the nation benefits more from the increased economic growth and lower inflation stemming from illegal immigration than it loses in jobs, lower wages and welfare costs."[31]

So much for the overall economic impact of immigration. What about the effect on welfare costs? Earlier studies tended to show that most immigrants (especially illegals) paid more in taxes than they

30. Various studies are cited by Whelan, "Principles of U.S. Immigration Policy," p. 475, and by Fallows, p. 55; interview with Conner.

31. W. Bute, K. F. McCarthy, R. A. Morrison, and M. E. Vaiana, *Demographic Challenges in America's Future* (Rand Corporation, May, 1982), p. 26; Thomas Muller, *The Fourth Wave: California's Newest Immigrants* (Washington: Urban Institute Press, 1984); "Illegal Immigrants: The U.S. May Gain More Than It Loses," *Business Week* (May 14, 1984): 126.

received in benefits, so that they were not a drain on the welfare system. However, some of the more recent research—like that of the Urban Institute—shows increased immigrant use of services, which indicates that the restrictionists might have an argument. A balanced summary concludes that immigrants do make substantial use of public services, but that legal immigrants tend to pay for themselves within a few years.[32]

Immigration has a more serious effect on the wages and working conditions of low-income groups. Evidence clearly indicates that a large inflow of unskilled labor depresses wages, especially when the immigrants are illegal and thus vulnerable to exploitation. Unskilled immigrants can usually find jobs, but in the process they help create a large pool of compliant, poorly paid labor. This, in turn, removes incentives for employers to improve working conditions; it also inhibits mechanization and productivity. When the Mexican bracero program was ended in the early 1960s, cutting the flow of cheap migrant labor, farm wages in affected areas rose by as much as five times; at the same time, productivity increased so rapidly that, within a few years, the total amount of wages paid out had declined. Experts argue that the current dependence on illegal alien labor has so detracted from efficiency as to make American agriculture less competitive with foreign producers.[33] Overall, Michael Teitelbaum, a leading immigration scholar, asserts that "There is no longer economic justification for large numbers of relatively unskilled and ill-educated immigrant workers and their dependents."[34]

When legal immigration from the western hemisphere was for the first time subjected to strict limits in 1968, illegal immigration predictably soared. The U.S.–Mexico border is notoriously porous, and there is suspicion on both sides of the immigration debate that

32. Teitelbaum, pp. 39–40.
33. Philip L. Martin, "Labor-Intensive Agriculture," *Scientific American* 249 (October 1983): 54, 57, 59; interview with Conner.
34. Teitelbaum, p. 35; see summary on pp. 35–39; also *Business Week*.

certain economic interests want it that way. Alejandro Portes, a critic of those seeking further to restrict immigration, cites earlier cases of mass deportations to argue that the border could be sealed if a serious effort were made, but that the border patrol's "already scant manpower is deployed in ways which minimize interference with agribusiness in the border region."[35] Roger Conner, spokesman for the restrictionist lobby, believes that a "small group of interested parties" has been able to prevent effective patrolling of the border even though both Congress and the public want the flow stopped.[36]

Clearly, more could be done to curb illegal immigration. For instance, in 1984 the task of improving technical methods for controlling the border was still entrusted to one man working with an annual appropriation of $400,000 (unchanged since 1975). The Baltimore police department had a larger budget than that of the border patrol, and twice as many police officers were assigned to the 209-acre U.S. Capitol ground in Washington as the number of guards assigned to the almost 2000-mile border with Mexico.[37] In 1985 the INS force was expanded by 1000 agents, the largest increase in its history, but full control of the border remains elusive. While sealing the border is probably an unrealistic goal, improved physical control is surely possible. Some border patrol personnel believe that the border could be made effectively secure at a cost well within the country's financial capability.

Control would certainly improve if the incentives for illegal entry were reduced. One way of achieving that would be to expand legal quotas for temporary workers. But the weight of experience counsels against such an approach. As in the past, it would depress wages, worsen working conditions, and decrease productivity. Preferring docile foreign laborers, employers would be less inclined to

35. Portes, p. 50.

36. Interview with Conner.

37. Interview with Gary Messina, Plans and Analysis Office, Immigration and Naturalization Service, May 23, 1984; Teitelbaum, p. 55; James H. Scheuer, "Let's Firm Up the Borders," *New York Times,* June 14, 1985.

tap the U.S. labor market.[38] It would be far preferable to bring in all those we want as full-fledged permanent immigrants. Enjoying full rights and privileges, such immigrants would stand a better chance of assimilating into American society. Limits could be set according to specific labor needs, thereby decreasing the danger of flooding.

Whatever cutbacks are made in illegal immigration should be done in consultation with Mexico. When the Simpson-Mazzoli bill first passed the U.S. Senate with provisions against hiring illegal aliens, the Mexican Senate reacted with a strong-worded resolution expressing "alarm and concern."[39] Clearly Mexican immigration must be a bilateral issue.

One thing is certain: the problem of illegal immigration cannot be solved simply by closing the border. The flow is an expression of human needs and aspirations. However daunting, the underlying problems on the Mexican side must be addressed. That means braking population growth, creating new jobs, increasing the purchase of Mexican goods, and instituting training programs for Mexican returnees (much as the French have done for Algerians ready to return home). Any effort to control illegal immigration without addressing its source will be futile.

On the American side, too, the problem must be dealt with at its source. As in Europe, immigration flows will diminish only when jobs are no longer available. This requires not only controls over the hiring of illegal aliens but also the restructuring of some occupations and industries (such as the mechanization of agriculture). Only then can the United States hope to reduce the unskilled immigration (mainly illegal) that can hurt lower-wage groups and delay

38. For a summary of the case against temporary-worker programs, see Peter A. Sehey, "Supply-Side Immigration Theory: Analysis of the Simpson/Mazzoli Bill," in Tomasi, pp. 65–66; see also F. Ray Marshall, *Illegal Immigration: the Problems, the Solutions,* FAIR Immigration Paper 3 (Federation for American Immigration Reform, Washington, August 1982), pp. 15–17; and Teitelbaum, "International Migration and Foreign Policy," in Tomasi, p. 221.

39. Teitelbaum, "International Migration," p. 222.

modernization, and which is almost entirely a response to economic opportunities. Where there is a genuine need for unskilled or semi-skilled workers that cannot be met on the domestic labor market, that need should be met by legal immigration. This may require increasing quotas; by one estimate, the country will need another 10 million workers by 2000.[40]

U.S. immigration policy should, first and foremost, show greater receptivity toward those coming on political and social grounds. These are the traditional immigrants, seekers of a new life who are fully committed to making the leap into a new society. Temporary emigration, especially that based primarily on economic motives, should be discouraged. This distinction, though not always easy to make in practice, could be better implemented if the selection process were modulated according to the situation in countries of origin. Primarily, this means providing higher quotas from particular countries where there are extraordinary pressures to emigrate, in place of the rigid country limits currently in force.

In defense of a liberal immigration policy, it should be recalled that:

1. The proportion of foreign-born in the overall U.S. population is at its lowest level since 1850, when such figures were first kept; the United States now ranks only ninth among all Western nations.

2. The flow of immigrants in relation to total population is now only 0.2 percent a year, compared with one percent at the turn of the century.

3. The assimilative power of American society has been demonstrated time and again. The battles over bilingualism have been fought before, among Germans, Chinese, native Americans, and others, and judging by past experience, the question is not whether Hispanic immigrants will learn English, but whether their children will remember any Spanish. Bilingual education programs

40. Bute et al.

are usually temporary, serving as a two- or three-year bridge to total English-language studies.

4. The United States still has the lowest population density of any industrialized nation, apart from Australia and Canada.

5. Emigration from the United States is growing; according to a new study, it has reached a level of 100,000 to 150,000 a year. (It will be recalled that the official immigration quota, excluding refugees and some nonquota categories, is only 270,000.)[41] Some estimates of emigration to Mexico (basically returnees) range much higher.

Carefully planned immigration could fill important economic needs; it could also help offset the aging of the national population. The Select Commission on Immigration and Refugee Policy reached this conclusion: "To the question: 'Is immigration in the U.S. national interest?', the Select Commission gives a strong but qualified yes. A strong yes because we believe there are many benefits which immigrants bring to U.S. society; a qualified yes because we believe there are limits on the ability of this country to absorb large numbers of immigrants effectively."[42]

The main recommendation of the Select Commission was to close the back door to undocumented/illegal migration and open the front door a little more to legal entry. In closing the back door, the Select Commission argued that no industry should depend indefinitely on alien labor. This position, if enacted into law, might mean sanctions on employers who hire illegal immigrants. It might also mean active measures to help modernize low-paying industries, especially agriculture. Among the more intriguing ideas is that of Philip Martin, author of an important study of migrant labor, who suggested "H-2 trusts" that would levy a tax on the earnings of

41. Robert Warren and Ellen Percy Kraly, *The Elusive Exodus: Emigration from the United States* (Washington: Population Reference Bureau, 1985).

42. Select Commission on Immigration and Refugee Policy, *Final Report, U.S. Immigration Policy and the National Interest* (Washington: U.S. Government Printing Office, 1981), p. 5.

alien farm workers and use the proceeds to finance the introduction of labor-saving production techniques.[43]

The Select Commission was very cautious about increasing the quota for legal immigrants, a reflection of the national mood following the sudden influxes of 1980. The task force recommended admitting 500,000 a year, including refugees. This is very modest, considering that in recent years the number admitted has ranged from 400,000 to 800,000. The initial recommendation of the commission staff was 750,000. Certainly if illegal immigration were substantially reduced, it would be possible to show much greater generosity.

One way or another, more hospitality should be extended to those lacking family connections here. As the law is now administered, up to 80 percent of all available slots go to relatives, creating dim prospects for other applicants, no matter how qualified they might be. The stress on family ties also translates into discrimination against ethnic groups with no previous migratory history here. Lowering the preference for relatives beyond the immediate family would create more room for others. Of course, more liberal quotas overall would mean room for both.

In addition, the 20,000 limit for each country should be modified or eliminated altogether. In practice, it discriminates against individuals who happen to come from the wrong country; for example, a German doctor can get a visa in about nine months, while a Filipino doctor must wait more than fifteen years. It would seem fairer to place all applicants on an equal footing. However admirable the original aim of the country limits (ensuring diversity), the stress on family ties means that there is little room for other categories in some countries under this low ceiling.[44]

In any event, it is essential to increase the limit for Mexico. Currently, there is a tremendous backlog of applications from Mexico

43. Martin, pp. 58–59.
44. Lane, p. 21; Whelan, "Principles of U.S. Immigration Policy," pp. 458–59, 469–71.

in nonpreference categories—those with no family connections or preferred skills—which have very slim prospects under the current system. This clearly increases pressure for illegal immigration. Only by solving this problem can the United States hope to stem the flow across the Rio Grande.

Since the Select Commission presented its report in 1981, a continuing effort has been made to enact its recommendations. The main vehicle for this, the Simpson-Mazzoli bill, was narrowly defeated in 1984. The legislation underwent many changes, but its basic components included sanctions on employers who knowingly hired illegal aliens and the legalization of illegal aliens who had resided here for a set period of time. The bill became bogged down over a series of controversial amendments—a measure to prevent discrimination against legal aliens and Hispanics, a proposal for a migrant workers' program, and a provision for federal welfare payments to states to provide for newly legalized aliens.

Obviously, many interests preferred the status quo to the Simpson-Mazzoli approach. Most adamant were agricultural employers, who could have become subject to heavy fines. Hispanics feared that despite any antidiscrimination provisions that the measure might contain, employers would simply refuse to hire anyone of Hispanic background. The Reagan administration was lukewarm as a result of the bill's projected costs, the prospects of an expanded bureaucracy, and the administration's close ties to California agribusiness. Nonetheless, leaving aside the temporary workers' program and some questionable changes in asylum procedures, the Simpson-Mazzoli bill offered a promising start. By confronting illegal immigration head-on, it would at least have cleared the path for other desirable changes in immigration law, including greater legal immigration.

Whatever its imperfections, current American immigration policy should not discourage activism on the international freedom-of-movement front. Moral logic does not require totally open borders as a precondition for opposing Draconian emigration policies, especially those that seek to keep whole nations in detention. But immigration policy becomes a genuine embarrassment when a country cannot even offer refuge to the comparative few who manage to escape a shackled society. The United States has, in recent years, found itself in this situation. From 1980 to 1984, it refused to process refugees from Cuba, including even political prisoners whose release the United States had negotiated. A small number of Romanians, cleared to leave by their own government, have had to wait long periods for U.S. entry visas; in the meantime they sit in limbo, since applying to leave cost them their jobs and social benefits (in 1985 agreement was reached to delay issuance of the Romanian documents until the U.S. entry visas were available). In mid-1984, Vietnam announced that, due to the backlog caused by U.S. immigration quotas, it had stopped issuing exit permits. The numbers involved in such cases were small, but the slowness of American procedures enabled these governments to deflect criticism of their own restrictions.

When it comes to immigration policy, the United States, like Caesar's wife, should be above suspicion. The changes in immigration policy suggested here could help bring that about. One immediate result would be to enhance America's ability to defend freedom of movement worldwide.

International Responses

International machinery already exists for exposing and condemning the contemporary assault on the right to leave or remain; the real challenge is to put that machinery to work. Unfortunately, at the United Nations, voting bloc solidarity has, in recent years, become a supreme virtue. Consequently, members of certain blocs have become virtually immune to criticism. The result is a breathtaking double standard in human rights discussions. Mass murder passes unnoted in countries like Cambodia, East Pakistan, Uganda, and Equatorial Guinea, while lengthy debates ensue on the equality of fringe benefits for Korean workers in Japan. Surprisingly, the Commission on Human Rights issued a report in February 1985 condemning the "gross violations of human rights" by Soviet troops in

Afghanistan, its first serious criticism of the Soviet Union by name in recent decades. It is too early to conclude that the double standard is on the decline, but such a development gives reason for hope.

Promoting the right to leave must be part of a general effort to establish fair and impartial standards at the United Nations; in the process, it might even be possible to upgrade the organization's level of discourse. A logical starting point would be the Mubanga-Chipoya study conducted for the Sub-Commission on Prevention of Discrimination and Protection of Minorities. This time, members could push for effective follow-through, including wider publicity for the study, better periodic reporting under such measures as the International Covenant on Civil and Political Rights, and commissioning of further reports on problematic practices mentioned in the study. Though legal formulations in themselves are only a first step, adoption of the draft declaration that is to accompany the study could certainly help push the issue into the spotlight. Furthermore, the Commission on Human Rights, among other U.N. bodies, could be encouraged to put specific countries guilty of gross violations on the spot. The number of grievances heard on this issue has, up to now, been minimal. And if the United States could bring itself to ratify the civil rights covenant, it could participate in strengthening that accord's reporting procedures.

Even these steps, sadly, would not add up to very much. It is still relevant to cite the remarks of Antonio Cassese, a leading international jurist, who, more than a decade ago, concluded that the prospects for protecting the right to leave through international procedures were gloomy: "They might serve to *focus the attention* on certain aspects of that right or on some specific situations involving its violation, but they are not in a position to *settle problems* raised by its being infringed by a number of States."[45]

The prospects are brighter on refugees. The crises caused by

45. Cassese, "On the Universal Level," in *The Right to Leave and to Return,* ed. Karel Vasak and Sidney Liskofsky (New York: American Jewish Committee, 1976), pp. 516, 518.

refugees have galvanized some host countries into action. More and more nations are agreeing to a broader, more realistic definition of refugee status, as reflected in the new standard adopted by the Organization of African Unity. The High Commissioner for Refugees, aided by private humanitarian organizations, continues to perform essential relief work, though, due to political sensitivities, his focus remains on dealing with the aftermath of refugee flows rather than trying to head them off.

But, in other forums, nations are beginning to deal with the causes of massive refugee flows, and not simply with their consequences. The great outpourings of the late 1970s, from Indochina, Ethiopia, and Afghanistan, triggered two important U.N. initiatives. Under Canadian prodding, the Commission on Human Rights commissioned a study of "human rights and mass exoduses"; the report, whose recommendations are discussed below, was prepared by Sadruddin Aga Khan, the former High Commissioner for Refugees, and was presented at the end of 1981. However, its controversial appendix, which discussed actual cases, was dropped from the report, indicating once again some of the underlying political limitations of international bodies.[46]

In another move, this one led by West Germany, the General Assembly in 1982 established a Group of Governmental Experts on International Co-operation to Avert New Flows of Refugees. Its mandate: to examine the causes of refugee flows and to suggest ways that other nations could help avert them. The group brought together experts from twenty-five nations, including most of the major source and host countries (Afghanistan and Pakistan; Ethiopia, Somalia, and Sudan; Vietnam and Thailand).

The group worked by consensus. No current cases were to be discussed, only ways to avoid creating new ones. In early sessions,

46. Aga Khan, *Study on Human Rights and Massive Exoduses,* United Nations, Economic and Social Council, Commission on Human Rights (E/CN.4/ 1503, December 31, 1981) (New York, 1981).

the American representative tried to focus on human rights, the Soviet delegate on the economic causes of dislocation.[47]

The early returns from the new group are not promising. As is customary in such bodies, the language used is exceedingly general. The interim report, for example, identified the sources of refugee flows as "oppressive and racist regimes, as well as aggression, colonialism, *apartheid,* alien domination, foreign intervention and occupation."[48] Since no individual cases are cited, each state is free to believe that such reprehensible conditions exist only elsewhere. In some cases, members of the group have simply asserted that new refugee flows could be averted if nations respected human rights, which is roughly equivalent to combating street crime by citing the laws on robbery.

Nevertheless, some worthwhile ideas circulated during the group's discussion, and some workable proposals were submitted. Even if such bodies succeeded only in making international condemnation more certain, their work would be worthwhile. In addition, sentiment has grown in favor of using U.N. economic leverage against refugee-producing nations, principally by withholding U.N. economic assistance. The sums involved are small, but such action could have clear publicity value. In one case, the U.N. Development Programme put a prior lien on a $10 million grant it had earmarked for Vietnam, directing the funds to refugee compensation instead.[49]

Aga Khan's report included a number of other proposals, all quite sensible. Among them: relating aid programs to the causes of mass exoduses, establishing more objective means for counting ref-

47. Personal interview with a U.S. governmental observer (the sessions of the New Flows groups are closed).

48. United Nations, General Assembly, Group of Governmental Experts on International Co-operation to Avert New Flows of Refugees, *Substantive Consideration of the Programme of Work,* Third Session, March 26–April 6, 1984.

49. Interview with Luke Lee, Director, Office of Planning and Programs, Office of the U.S. Coordinator for Refugee Affairs, May 17, 1984; see also Lee, "The UN Group of Governmental Experts on International Co-operation to Avert New Flows of Refugees," *American Journal of International Law* 78 (1984): 483.

ugees, setting up an early-warning system to identify potential trouble spots, and appointing a special representative who, with an observer corps, could intervene in such cases.

All that is lacking is the political will. Identifying causes and culprits is not the real problem; organizing effective countermeasures is. One promising model of international cooperation is the Geneva Conference on Indochinese Refugees held in 1979. It enabled interested states to apply combined pressure, with some useful results. Perhaps similar multilateral or bilateral forums could be held on an ad hoc basis.

One useful step would be to clarify international law on expulsion. Expulsion of citizens is clearly illegal by any reasonable interpretation of existing principles and documents, yet there exists no explicit statement prohibiting the practice. Some experts have proposed a draft convention that would codify existing principles. Perhaps most important, it would cover indirect as well as direct coercion, plus the failure of governments to protect citizens from persecution or harassment.[50] A clear and comprehensive statement of law is also needed for the mass expulsion of aliens, especially those who have resided in a country for a long time.[51] The current drafting of a U.N. convention for protecting migrant workers serves a useful, though limited, purpose.

On both emigration and refugee issues, regional organizations might be better positioned to act than international ones. Regional organizations bring together states that have closer relations among themselves, an immediate interest in one another's policies on movement, and, at least potentially, a greater inclination to cooperate. The European Convention on Human Rights, in particular, has

50. Luke Lee, "Mass Expulsion" (paper presented at the annual meeting of the American Society of International Law, Washington, D.C., April 14, 1984); Working Group on Mass Expulsion, *Report* (San Remo, Italy: International Institute of Humanitarian Law, 1983).

51. G. J. L. Coles, "The Problem of Mass Expulsion" (background paper for Working Group of Experts on the Problem of Mass Expulsion, International Institute of Humanitarian Law, San Remo, Italy, April 16–18, 1983), p. 84.

proved effective in handling disputes on freedom-of-movement issues. But here, as in other cases, human rights receive the greatest protection where it is needed the least.

Finally, nongovernmental organizations can help publicize abuses, mobilize world opinion, and press governments to take action. In recent years, for example, Amnesty International has expanded its efforts on behalf of persons imprisoned for trying to exercise their right to leave any country or to return to their own. Such organizations could be especially useful in supplying objective data to U.N. and other official bodies. The 1973 Uppsala conference on the right to leave showed just how valuable contributions from nongovernmental organizations can be.

Toward a More Open World

In a Lombard manumission ceremony of the ninth century, the slave about to be freed was taken to a crossroad. There he was released with the declaration that he now had "license and power to walk from the crossroads and live where he may wish."[52] Thus, eleven centuries ago, this simple ceremony recognized the organic connection between choice of location and human freedom.

We are still fighting, in a larger sense, for the right of everyone to walk from the crossroads. The ideal of an open world appears at first to be quite unrealistic and, to some, even undesirable. I have attempted to show both the continuing relevance of the ideal and its broader significance. Perhaps the strongest argument on its behalf has been the obstinate insistence by men and women, from all stations and all periods, that they are entitled to walk from the crossroads in the direction they choose, whatever barriers the authorities place in their way.

In the search for an open world, there are a number of models to build on. The ancient Mediterranean world is one. So is the British

52. W. L. Westermann, "Between Slavery and Freedom," *American Historical Review* 50 (January 1945): 223.

Commonwealth (at least until immigration into Britain was restricted in recent years). The period preceding World War I came as close as we have yet been to a world of free international movement. American history, too, offers a model of sorts. The continental scope of free internal movement has been central to the country's growth and prosperity, not to mention its political ideals and traditions. It is hard to imagine what the nation would have become had movement been subject to barriers erected by individual states.

At first glance, our present world appears to be far from such models. The free movement of the pre–World War I days is but a memory. The seemingly irreversible model of totalitarian systems, which has proved so effective in controlling population flows, is now practiced by about two dozen regimes around the world. Their practices are often imitated by nontotalitarian governments. Even the United States has reacted against the principle of unbounded travel. In most instances, the results have been dubious. Did we profit from closing the door to Communist Asia for two decades? Did we gain from having no contact with North Vietnam in the critical decade before 1965?[53] The imposition of foreign travel restrictions on U.S. citizens betrays a nervousness about an open world that does us little credit.

In the developing world, some nations have adopted a neo-mercantilist attitude in their imposition of controls on movement. Even worse, they have demonstrated an aptitude for expulsions and purges that imitate earlier Western models of nation-building at their worst. But the full picture is not so gloomy. Many forces are working in the opposite direction. Growing interdependence makes free movement more important than ever. Given the developing network of ties across national borders, it is becoming increasingly artificial to try to limit one dimension of international contact while allowing others to flourish. As national borders lose more and more of their sanctity, states that restrict movement are fighting a rearguard action.

53. Abba P. Schwartz, *The Open Society* (Oxford: Clarendon, 1978), p. 98.

For most of us, the prospect of a shrinking globe raises no alarm.[54] Even such a seemingly negative development as the brain drain has created benefits by finding an outlet for talent that might otherwise go to waste. We need to establish that nations need not be built by regimentation, that it is possible to achieve integration without either forced conformity or dislocation. Fortunately, Third-World countries are showing a growing appreciation of the fact that they have more to gain than lose by keeping their doors open. Consider, for example, the success of the culturally Chinese countries of Southeast Asia—Singapore, Hong Kong, and Taiwan—against the progress of closed China itself.

For every problem supposedly solved by restriction of international movement, there are solutions—often more effective—that respond in a positive rather than a negative way, that deal with the sources rather than the symptoms.

The right of personal self-determination seems to represent the ultimate conflict between state and individual. But my basic argument is that this can be transcended when a state reads its interests in a long-range way. In fact, the degree of compulsion in a state's policy on international movement serves as an index of the degree to which it is pursuing the aim of control itself, rather than authentic collective aims.

Despite the encroachment of the new serfdom, the ideal of an open world continues to beckon. The goal of Ernest Bevin, the British Foreign Secretary, is as relevant today as when he described it in 1946: "A diplomat asked me in London one day what the aim of my foreign policy was and I said, 'To go down to Victoria Station, get a railway ticket and go where the hell I liked without a passport or anything else.' I stick to that."[55]

In other words, the aim of unrestricted movement stands as a

54. The general argument for free movement is developed by Roger Nett, "The Civil Right We Are Not Ready For: The Right of Free Movement of People on the Face of the Earth," *Ethics* 81 (1971), esp. pp. 219–20, 225–26.

55. Quoted by Schwartz, p. 97.

kind of shorthand for the world in which we want to live. It is a pertinent and revealing standard by which to measure ourselves and others. There can hardly be a better test of a society's fundamental respect for human dignity—or its belief in itself.

Index